Thomas W. Taylor, Canadanian Presbyterian Church

The Public Statutes Relating to the Presbyterian Church in Canada

with acts and resolutions of the General Assembly, and by-laws for the government of the colleges and schemes of the church. Second Edition

Thomas W. Taylor, Canadanian Presbyterian Church

The Public Statutes Relating to the Presbyterian Church in Canada
with acts and resolutions of the General Assembly, and by-laws for the government of the colleges and schemes of the church. Second Edition

ISBN/EAN: 9783337192723

Printed in Europe, USA, Canada, Australia, Japan

Cover: Foto ©Lupo / pixelio.de

More available books at **www.hansebooks.com**

THE
PUBLIC STATUTES

RELATING TO THE

PRESBYTERIAN CHURCH

IN CANADA:

WITH

ACTS AND RESOLUTIONS OF THE GENERAL ASSEMBLY,
AND BY-LAWS FOR THE GOVERNMENT

OF THE

COLLEGES AND SCHEMES OF THE CHURCH.

BY

THE HON. THOMAS WARDLAW TAYLOR,

CHIEF JUSTICE OF THE COURT OF QUEEN'S BENCH, MANITOBA.

SECOND EDITION.

WINNIPEG:
HART & COMPANY, LIMITED.
1897.

PRINTED AND BOUND
BY
THE STOVEL COMPANY,
WINNIPEG.

PREFACE.

To many who take an active part in the work of the Church the public statutes are not accessible. Even the by-laws or regulations for the management of the colleges and schemes of the Church and the resolutions of the General Assembly bearing upon these, scattered as they are through the minutes of different years, cannot readily be referred to. The consequence is, that when at meetings of the Assembly and other Church Courts, questions arise in the proper disposition of which reference should be made to these statutes, by-laws and resolutions, members are in doubt and difficulty how to deal with them, and what course to pursue. To provide a remedy for this state of things as far as possible, the first edition of this little work was published.

During the years which have passed since then there has been not a little public legislation which affects various interests of the Church. The powers of some of the colleges as to conferring degrees in divinity, and the holding of property have been extended. The board of management of the Church and Manse Building Fund has been incorporated. New departments of Church work have been organized, and many of the by-laws and resolutions of the Assembly regulating the management of previously existing schemes have been varied and amended.

In the present edition all the public Acts of the Dominion and of the different Provinces which affect, the Presbyterian Church in Canada as a body, the colleges, or any of the incorporated schemes of the Church, have been collected.

The Acts as to the holding of congregational property by trustees, in the various Provinces in which such Acts are in force, are also set out. In New Brunswick there is no such general Act, and none has been found among the Acts of Prince Edward Island.

The law in the different Provinces upon such subjects as the solemnization of marriage and registration returns, so far as it is important for ministers of the Church, is given, corrected down to the present time.

The by-laws and regulations which govern the management of the colleges and schemes of the Church, as they are now in force, are all given in full.

The minutes of the General Assembly since 1875, have been carefully examined, and all the resolutions of Assembly appearing to be important and at present in force, have been collected. In this part of the work there may be some omissions, but an honest attempt has been made to give everything that seems of general interest and value.

In an appendix will be found three Acts, of older date, perhaps not now of importance, but possessing an historical interest.

Thanks for assistance are due to Rev. Dr. Bell, Rev. Dr. Patterson, Rev. Principal Macrae, D. D., Rev. Professor Gordon, D. D., Rev. Professor Scrimger, D.D., Rev. Dr. Campbell, (Montreal), Rev. Dr. Warden, Rev. R. P. Mackay, Rev. S. J. Taylor, Rev. Mr. Burns, and James Croil, Esq. Grateful mention should also be made of Mr. J. P. Robertson, Librarian of the Legislative Assembly of Manitoba, for affording access to the statutes of the various Provinces, to be found only in the Legislative library.

Should this little work prove in any degree an aid to those who are doing the work of the Church, the labour spent upon it will be amply repaid.

Chessels Croft, May, 1897.

TABLE OF CONTENTS.

PART I.—THE CHURCH.—Basis of Union, 1 ; Acts at Union of Presbyterian Church in Canada, Ontario, 4 ; Quebec, 10 ; New Brunswick, 18, 21, 24, 25 ; Prince Edward Island, 27 ; Nova Scotia, 30, 33 ; Manitoba, 36 ; Acts of General Assembly, 39.

PART II.—THE COLLEGES.—Queen's College, Charter 46 ; Acts 56, 59, 64 ; By-laws, 65 ; Knox College, Acts, 81, 84, 86, 88 ; By-laws, 89 ; Presbyterian College, Halifax, Acts 94, 98, 100 ; Morrin College, Acts 102, 106 ; Presbyterian College, Montreal, Acts 108, 111 ; By-laws, 112 ; College of Manitoba, Acts 117, 122, 123 ; By-laws, 125 ; Summer Session, 128 ; Resolutions of Assembly, as to Theological Professors, 132 ; as to Students, 134.

PART III—SCHEMES OF THE CHURCH.—Aged and Infirm Ministers' Fund, 136 ; Augmentation Fund, 139 ; Church and Manse Building Fund, 145 ; Foreign Missions, 150 ; French Evangelization, 163 ; Home Missions, 166 ; Temporalities' Board, 175 ; Widows' and Orphans' Fund, Presbyterian Church, in connection with Church of Scotland, 193 ; Widows' and Orphans' Fund, Maritime Provinces, 206 ; Widows' and Orphans' Fund, Western Division, 218.

PART IV—CONGREGATIONAL PROPERTY.—Ontario, 221 ; Quebec, 228 ; Nova Scotia, 230 ; Manitoba, 235 ; North-West Territories, 242 ; British Columbia, 244.

PART V—MISCELLANEOUS STATUTES.—Ontario, Marriage, 247 ; Registration of Marriages and Deaths, 249 ; Quebec, Acts of Civil Status, Births, Marriages, Burials, 250 ; Nova Scotia, Marriage and Registration Returns, 254 ; New Brunswick, Marriage, 255 ; Registration Births, Deaths and Marriages, 257 ; Prince Edward Island, Marriage and Registration Returns, 258 ; Manitoba, Marriage, 259 ; Registration Births, Marriages and Deaths, 261 ; North-West Territories, Marriage, 262 ; Registration Births, Marriages, and Deaths, 263 ; British Columbia, Marriage and Registration Returns, 264.

PART VI—RESOLUTIONS OF GENERAL ASSEMBLY.—Agents of the Church, 266; Calling and Settling of Ministers, 267; Church Life and Work, 268; College Endowment, 268; Estimates, 269; Foreign Missionaries, 269; Funds, 270; Judicial Committee, 270; Moderator. 271; Primary Jurisdiction over Students, 271; Printing Assembly Minutes, 273; Retired Ministers, 273; Roman Catholic Ordination, 273; Schemes of the Church, 273; Standing Committees, 274; Statistics, 274; Ordination of Students, 275; Systematic Beneficence, 275.

APPENDIX I.—Nisbet Academy, Act incorporating, 276.

APPENDIX II.--The Presbyterian Church of New Brunswick, Act incorporating, 278; Canada Presbyterian Church, Union Act, 283; Basis of Union, 286; Presbyterian Church of the Lower Provinces, Union Act, 288.

PART I.—THE CHURCH.

BASIS OF UNION.

Agreed upon and adopted by the Churches which form "The Presbyterian Church in Canada," and subscribed in the name and by the appointment of the Supreme Courts of the several Churches entering into union, by their respective Moderators, the 15th day of June, 1875. See Minutes 1875, p. 6.

The Presbyterian Church of Canada in connection with the Church of Scotland, the Canada Presbyterian Church, the Church of the Maritime Provinces in connection with the Church of Scotland and the Presbyterian Church of the Lower Provinces holding the same doctrine, government and discipline, believing that it would be for the glory of God and the advancement of the cause of Christ that they should thus unite and thus form one Presbyterian Church in the Dominion, independent of all other Churches in its jurisdiction, and under authority to Christ alone, the Head of His Church and Head over all things to the Church, agree to unite on the following Basis, to be subscribed by the Moderators of the respective Churches, in their name and on their behalf.

1. The Scriptures of the Old and New Testaments, being the Word of God, are the only infallible rule of faith and manners.

2. The Westminster Confession of Faith shall form the subordinate standard of the Church; the Larger and Shorter Catechisms shall be adopted by the Church, and appointed to be used for the instruction of the people:—it being distinctly understood that nothing contained in the aforesaid Confession or Catechisms, regarding the power and duty of the Civil Magistrate, shall be held to

sanction any principles or views inconsistent with full liberty of conscience in matters of religion. (*a*.)

3. The government and worship of this Church shall be in accordance with the recognised principles and practice of Presbyterian Churches, as laid down generally in the "Form of Presbyterian Church Government," and in "The Directory for the Public Worship of God."

Accompanying Resolutions.

Relations to other Churches.—1. This Church cherishes Christian affection towards the whole Church of God, and desires to hold fraternal intercourse with it in its several Branches, as opportunity offers.

2. This Church shall, under such terms and regulations as may from time to time be agreed on, receive ministers and probationers from other Churches, and especially from Churches holding the same doctrine, government, and discipline with itself.

Modes of Worship.—With regard to modes of worship, the practices presently followed by congregations shall be allowed, and further action therewith shall be left to the legislation of the united Church.

Funds for Widows and Orphans of Ministers.—Steps shall be taken at the first meeting of the General Assembly of the united Church, for the equitable establishment and administration of an efficient fund for the benefit of the widows and orphans of ministers.

Collegiate Institutions.—The aforesaid Churches shall enter into union with the theological and literary institutions which they now have; and application shall be made to Parliament for such legislation as shall bring

---

(*a*.) The General Assembly in 1889, with the approval of a majority of Presbyteries, adopted the following resolution:—"Subscription of the formula shall be so understood as to allow liberty of opinion in respect to the proposition, 'A man may not marry any of his wife's kindred nearer in blood than he may of his own.'" (West. Conf., Chap. xxiv., Section 4.) *See Minutes 1889, p. 58.*

Queen's University and College, Knox College, the Presbyterian College, Montreal, Morrin College, and the Theological Hall at Halifax, into relations to the united Church similar to those which they now hold to their respective Churches, and to preserve their corporate existence, government and functions, on terms and conditions like those under which they now exist; but the united Church shall not be required to elect trustees for an Arts Department in any of the colleges above named.

Legislation with regard to rights of Property.—Such legislation shall be sought as shall preserve undisturbed all rights of property now belonging to congregations and corporate bodies, and, at the same time, not interfere with freedom of action on the part of congregations in the same locality desirous of uniting, or on the part of corporate bodies which may find it to be expedient to discontinue, wholly or partially, their separate existence.

Home and Foreign Missions.—The united Church shall heartily take up and prosecute the home and foreign missionary and benevolent operations of the several Churches, according to their respective claims; and with regard to the practical work of the Church and the promotion of its schemes, whilst the General Assembly shall have the supervision and control of all the work of the Church, yet the united Church shall have due regard to such arrangements through Synods and local committees, as shall tend most effectually to unite in Christian love and sympathy the different sections of the Church, and at the same time to draw forth the resources and energies of the people in behalf of the work of Christ in the Dominion and throughout the world.

Government Grants to Denominational Colleges.—In the united Church the fullest forbearance shall be allowed as to any difference of opinion which may exist respecting the question of State grants to educational establishments of a denominational character.

STATUTES.

ONTARIO.—38 Vict., cap. 75.—An Act respecting the Union of certain Presbyterian Churches therein named. (*Assented to 21st December, 1874.*)

Whereas the Canada Presbyterian Church, the Presbyterian Church of Canada in connection with the Church of Scotland, the Church of the Maritime Provinces in connection with the Church of Scotland, and the Presbyterian Church of the Lower Provinces, have severally agreed to unite together and form one body or denomination of Christians, under the name of "The Presbyterian Church in Canada;" and the Moderators of the General Assembly of the Canada Presbyterian Church, and of the Synods of the Presbyterian Church of Canada in connection with the Church of Scotland, and the Church of the Maritime Provinces in connection with the Church of Scotland, and the Presbyterian Church of the Lower Provinces, respectively, by and with the consent of the General Assembly and Synods, have, by their petitions, stating such agreement to unite as aforesaid, prayed that for the furtherance of this their purpose, and to remove any obstructions to such union which may arise out of the present form and designation of the several trusts or Acts of incorporation by which the property of the said Churches, and of the colleges and congregations connected with the said Churches, or any of them respectively, are held and administered or otherwise, certain legislative provisions may be made in reference to the property of the said Churches, colleges and congregations, situate within the Province of Ontario, and other matters affecting the same in view of the said union; Therefore Her Majesty, &c., enacts as follows :—

1. As soon as the union takes place, all property, real or personal, within the Province of Ontario, now belonging to or held in trust for or to the use of any congregation in connection or communion with any of the said Churches, shall thenceforth be held, used and adminis-

tered for the benefit of the same congregation in connection or communion with the united body, under the name of "The Presbyterian Church in Canada."

2. Provided always that if any congregation in connection or communion with any of the said Churches, shall at a meeting of the said congregation regularly called according to the constitution of the said congregation, or the practice of the Church with which it is connected, and held within six months (*a*) after the said union takes place, decide by a majority of the votes of those who, by the constitution of the said congregation, or the practice of the said Church with which it is connected, are entitled to vote at such a meeting, determine not to enter into the said union, but to dissent therefrom, then and in such case the congregational property of the said congregation shall remain unaffected by this Act or by any of the provisions thereof; (*b*) but in the event of any congregation so dissenting as aforesaid at any future time resolving to enter into and adhere to the said united Church, then from the time of such resolution being come to, this Act and the provisions thereof shall apply to the property of such congregation.

3. Congregations may from time to time alter or vary any of the provisions contained in the trust deeds under which their property is held, or in their constitutions, which relate to the mode in which their affairs and property shall be managed or regulated, and to the persons who shall be entitled to take part in such management, or to vote at meetings of the congregation on questions affecting the affairs and property of the congregation or the management thereof; (*c*) but the sanction of the Presbytery under whose care such congregation is placed

---

(*a*) In the Province of Quebec, two years, 38 Vict., c. 62, s. 2.

(*b*) A few congregations did hold meetings pursuant to the provisions of this section, and determined not to enter into the union. In some instances litigation was the result of their action. See *Cowan* v. *Wright*, 23 Grant 616; *Hall* v. *Ritchie*, 23 Grant 630; *McPherson* v. *McKay*, 26 Grant 141; 4 Appeal Reports, 501; *McRae* v. *McLeod*, 26 Grant 255; *Deeks* v. *Davidson*, 26 Grant 488. As to the rights of property of religious organizations, and their members, and how far they are subject to the control of the Courts, see *Watson* v. *Jones*, 80 U. S. Supreme Court Rep. 679.

(*c*) As to the competency of a congregation to introduce new regulations, see *Att.-Gen.* v. *Murdoch*, 1 De Gex MacNaghten & Gordon Rep. 114.

shall be obtained before any such alteration or variation shall take effect.

4. The several clauses and provisions of the Act of the Legislature of Ontario passed in the 36th year of the reign of Her Majesty Queen Victoria, chaptered 135, and intituled " An Act respecting the property of religious institutions in the Province of Ontario," and amendments thereto, shall apply to the various congregations in Ontario in connection or communion with the Presbyterian Church in Canada: provided always, that before any of the powers of leasing, if for a period exceeding seven years, selling, exchanging or mortgaging be exercised by any congregation or by the trustees thereof, the sanction of the Presbytery within whose bounds such congregation is placed shall be obtained.

5. All other property, real or personal, belonging to or held in trust for the use of any of the said Churches or religious bodies, or for any college or educational or other institution, or for any trust in connection with any of the said Churches or religious bodies, either generally or for any special purpose or object, shall from the time the said contemplated union takes place, and thenceforth, belong to and be held in trust for and to the use in like manner of " The Presbyterian Church in Canada," or for or to the use in like manner of the said college, educational or other institution or trust in connection therewith.

6. But all such property, real or personal, as is affected by this Act, shall in all respects, save as aforesaid, be held and administered as nearly as may be in the same manner and subject to the same conditions as provided by the deeds of trust, Acts of incorporation, or other instruments or authority, under which the same is now held or administered.

7. As soon as the said union takes place, the corporation of Knox College shall stand in the same relation to the Presbyterian Church in Canada, in which it now stands to the Canada Presbyterian Church; and all the provisions of the Act of the late Province of

Canada, passed in the 22nd year of the reign of Her Majesty Queen Victoria, chaptered 69, and entitled "An Act to incorporate Knox College," shall continue to apply to said college and corporation; and all the rights, powers and authorities by said Act vested in the Synod of the then Presbyterian Church of Canada shall be vested in, apply to, and be exercised by the Supreme Court of the Presbyterian Church in Canada. And the corporation of Queen's College shall in like manner stand in the same relation to the Presbyterian Church in Canada, in which it now stands to the Presbyterian Church of Canada in connection with the Church of Scotland; and all the powers, rights and privileges hitherto exercised and enjoyed by the ministers and members of the Presbyterian Church of Canada in connection with the Church of Scotland, as corporators of the said college, and by the Synod of the said Presbyterian Church of Canada in connection with the Church of Scotland, in virtue of their relations respectively to Queen's College at Kingston, shall be exercised and enjoyed by the ministers and members of the Presbyterian Church in Canada, and by the Supreme Court of the said Presbyterian Church in Canada; provided always, that the said united Church shall not be required to elect trustees for any Arts department in Queen's College aforesaid. And the corporation of the Presbyerian College of Montreal shall in like manner stand in the same relation to the Presbyterian Church in Canada, as it now stands to the Canada Presbyterian Church; and the provisions of the Act of the late Province of Canada passed in the 28th year of the reign of Her said Majesty, chaptered 53, and entitled "An Act to incorporate the Presbyterian College of Montreal," shall continue to apply to said college and corporation; and all the rights, powers and authorities by said Act vested in the Synod of the Canada Presbyterian Church shall be vested in, apply to, and be exercised by the Supreme Court of the Presbyterian Church in Canada. And in like manner the corporation of Morrin College shall stand in the same relation to the Presbyterian Church in Canada, as it now stands to the Presbyterian Church of Canada in connection with the Church of Scotland; and all the provisions of the Act of the late Province of Canada, passed in the 24th year of the reign of Her said Majesty, chaptered 109, and entitled "An Act to incorporate Morrin College at Quebec," shall continue to apply to said College; and all the rights of the Synod of the Presbyterian Church of Canada in connection with the Church of Scotland shall be vested in the Supreme Court of the Presbyterian Church in Canada; and all the rights, powers and authorities vested by the said Act in the minister and congregation of St. Andrew's Church, Quebec, shall continue to be held and exercised by said minister and congregation in connection with the Presbyterian Church in Canada; provided, always, that the said united Church shall not be required to elect trustees for any Arts department in Morrin College aforesaid.

8. Whereas the ministers of the said Presbyterian Church of Canada in connection with the Church of Scotland are entitled to receive incomes from a fund called the Temporalities Fund, administered by a board incorporated by statute of the heretofore Province of Canada, and it is proposed to preserve to them intact, during their respective lives, their said incomes derivable from said fund; it is therefore enacted that the present members of the said board shall continue in office and manage the said fund on behalf of the said ministers now deriving revenue therefrom, and the income to said ministers shall be continued in full to them respectively during their lifetime and while Presbyterian ministers in good standing within the Dominion of Canada, whether in active service or retired, and whether in connection with the said Church or not; so soon as any part of the revenue accruing from said fund is not required to meet the payment of said incomes and other vested rights in the fund, and expenses therewith, the same shall pass to and be subject to the disposal of the said united Church; and any part of said fund that may remain to the good after the death of the last survivor of the said ministers, shall thereupon pass to and be subject to the disposal of the Supreme Court of said united

Church, for the purpose of a Home Mission Fund for aiding weak charges in the united Church ; and vacancies in the meantime occurring in said board shall not be filled up in the manner hitherto observed, but shall be filled up from among the members of the said united Church nominated by the beneficiaries of the said fund.

9. And whereas "The Canada Presbyterian Church" and "The Presbyterian Church of Canada in connection with the Church of Scotland," have each of them a fund for the benefit of widows and orphans of ministers pertaining to them respectively, and it is not deemed desirable that two such funds should long exist separately after the union, nor that there should be two separate organizations for the management thereof: it is therefore enacted that said two funds shall be kept separate, and the separate and distinct management and administration thereof continued by the boards respectively having the management and control thereof at the time of the union, so long only, and until the Supreme Court of said united Church shall have made provision for the amalgamation of said two funds and the management thereof, whereupon the said two separate organizations shall become extinct, and the said two funds shall pass to and vest in the trustees, body or persons indicated for the management thereof by the said Supreme Court ; and until such provision is made, vacancies occurring in either of said respective organizations shall not be filled up as hitherto, but shall be filled up by the remaining members of each of said organizations for their respective bodies.

10. As soon as the said union takes place, the Presbyterian Church in Canada, and any of the trusts in connection with the said Church, and any of the religious or charitable schemes of the said Church, may by the name thereof, or by trustees, from time to time take by gift, devise or bequest, any lands or tenements or interest therein, provided such gift, devise or bequest be made at least six months before the death of the person making the same ; but the said Church, and the said religious, or charitable schemes of the said Church, shall at no time take by gift,

devise or bequest, lands or tenements, or any interest therein, the annual value of which, together with that of all other lands and tenements theretofore acquired by like means, and then held by the said Church, or by the particular scheme in favour of which such gift, devise or bequest may be made, shall exceed in the whole $1,000 ; nor shall the said Church, or any of the religious, or charitable schemes of the said Church, at any time take by gift, devise or bequest, lands or tenements the annual value of which and of all the other real estate of the said Church, or of the particular scheme in favour of which the gift, devise or bequest is made, shall together exceed $5,000 ; and no lands or tenements acquired by gift, devise or bequest within the limits aforesaid, but not required for the actual use or occupation, shall be held for a longer period than seven years after the acquisition thereof, and within such period the same shall be absolutely disposed of, and the proceeds of such disposition shall be invested in public securities, municipal debentures or other approved securities, not including mortgages on land ; and any lands, tenements or interests therein required by this Act to be sold and disposed of, but which may not have been so disposed of, shall revert to the person from whom the same were acquired, his heirs, executors, administrators or assigns.

11. The union of the said four Churches shall be held to take place as soon as the Articles of the said union shall have been signed by the Moderators of the said respective Churches.

QUEBEC.—38 Vict. cap. 62.—An Act respecting the Union of certain Presbyterian Churches therein named. (*Assented to 23rd February, 1875*).

Whereas the Canada Presbyterian Church, the Presbyterian Church of Canada in connection with the Church of Scotland, the Church of the Maritime Provinces in connection with the Church of Scotland, and the Presbyterian Church of the Lower Provinces, have severally agreed to unite together and form one body or denomination of Christians under the name of "The Presbyterian Church in Canada;" and the Moderators of the General Assembly of the Canada Presbyterian Church, and of the Synods of the Presbyterian Church of Canada in connection with the Church of Scotland, and the Church of the Maritime Provinces in connection with the Church of Scotland, and the Presbyterian Church of the Lower Provinces, respectively, by and with the consent of the said General Assembly and Synods have by their petitions, stating such agreement to unite as aforesaid, prayed that for the furtherance of this their purpose, and to remove any obstructions to such union which may arise out of the present form and designation of the several trusts or Acts of incorporation, by which the property of the said Churches, and of the colleges and congregations connected with the said Churches or any of them respectively, are held and administered or otherwise, certain legislative provisions may be made in reference to the property of the said Churches, colleges and congregations situated within the Province of Quebec and other matters affecting the same in view of the said union : Therefore Her Majesty, &c., enacts as follows :—

1. As soon as the union takes place, all property, real or personal, within the Province of Quebec now belonging to or held in trust for, or to the use of any congregation in connection or communion with any of the said Churches, shall thenceforth be held, used and administered for the benefit of the same congregation in connection or communion with the united body, under the name of "The Presbyterian Church in Canada," or any other name the said Church may adopt.

2. Provided always, that if any congregation in connection or communion with any of the said Churches shall at a meeting of the said congregation regularly called according to the constitution of the said congregation or the practice of the Church with which it is connected, and held within two years after the said union takes place, decide, by a majority of the votes of those who, by the constitution of the said congregation or the prac-

tice of the Church with which it is connected, are entitled to vote at such a meeting, not to enter into the said union but to dissent therefrom, then and in such a case the congregational property of the said congregation shall remain unaffected by this Act or by any of the provisions thereof; but in the event of any congregation so dissenting at any future time resolving to enter into and adhere to the said united Church, then from the time of such resolution being come to, this Act and the provisions thereof shall apply to the property of such congregation.

3. Congregations may from time to time alter or vary any of the provisions contained in the trust deeds under which their property is held, or in their constitutions, which relate to the mode in which their affairs and property shall be managed or regulated, and to the persons who shall be entitled to take part in such management, or to vote at meetings of the congregation, on questions affecting the affairs and property of the congregation or the management thereof; but the sanction of the Presbytery under whose care such congregation is placed shall be obtained before any such alteration or variation shall take effect.

4. Whenever any congregation, society or mission, in communion or connection with said united Church, shall hereafter be desirous of acquiring any land, or real property of any description, whatsoever, for the site of any church, chapel, meeting-house, school, manse, glebe, burial ground or appurtenances thereto, the same may be acquired by trustees for any one or more of the said objects, which shall be designated in the deed of acquisition, and by any name assumed in said deed, sufficient to show the connection or communion of its members with said united Church, and the locality where such congregation, society or mission is to be established; and such deed shall not require to be registered at any prothonotary's office, but shall be subject to the ordinary laws of registration applicable to individuals, and such congregation, society or mission shall be entitled to ac-

quire, take and hold lands and real estate, for the purposes aforesaid, without license in mortmain.

5. For the relief of any of the said congregations, missions or societies in connection or communion with the Churches or religious bodies aforesaid, in this Province, whose deeds of trust heretofore executed, or Acts of incorporation heretofore obtained, made no provision for the filling up from time to time of trusteeships vacant by death, removal from the Province, or resignation of trustees, and whose property is held under a conveyance to the trustees and their heirs, or to the trustees and their successors, or otherwise, and to regulate in regard to the future acquisition of property as well by congregations, missions or societies, either already formed, or which may be hereafter formed, any such congregation, or the members composing such mission or society, may from time to time meet together upon notice by the minister from the pulpit, or at the requisition in writing of any ten persons entitled to vote as hereinafter mentioned (notice of the day, hour and place of such meeting, in either case, being first publicly made in the church or place of meeting for public worship, on two Sabbath days next before such meeting shall be held,) and then and there, at such meeting so convened, by a majority of those present and entitled to vote, to elect and appoint new trustees in the room of such trustees as shall have removed from the Province, resigned or died, and thereupon the property of the congregation shall *ipso facto* become vested in such newly-elected trustees jointly, and with the remaining trustees, if any; and such trustees and their successors to be appointed as aforesaid, shall have full power and authority to hold and administer the trust or corporate property of such congregation; provided always, that the said newly-elected trustees shall be members of the said united body in full communion therewith; and those entitled to vote where there is no provision on the subject as aforesaid, shall be all persons who are members in full communion with said congregation and Church.

6. Trustees or other administrators of corporate or trust property of any congregation in connection or communion with the said united body, may, with the consent of the congregation, or of a majority of those entitled to vote at a meeting convened to consider the matter (as provided either by their trust deed or by section number 5 of this Act, for the election of trustees in case of vacancies, as the case may be), mortgage, sell or exchange any real estate belonging to or holden for the use of or in trust for the said congregation, for the purpose of repairing or securing the debt on any building thereon erected, or of erecting other or more suitable churches, manses or glebes, or schools, in any other locality that they may deem best, or of purchasing other and more suitable churches, manses, glebes or schools; provided, nevertheless, that such mortgage, sale or exchange be first sanctioned by the Presbytery under whose care such congregation is placed.

7. Clergymen of said united Church shall have the right to solemnize marriage, and to keep registers of civil status, and therein to record births, marriages and deaths, in conformity to the provisions of the Civil Code in this behalf. Any such registers at present in use by any of the clergymen of the religious bodies so to be united, may be continued after the union for the current year, as if this Act had not been passed and no union had taken place; and the united body and the several clergymen thereof shall, besides, have, for the purpose of such registers, all the powers that either of the said bodies, or the respective clergymen thereof, had before the union.

8. All other property, real or personal, belonging to or held in trust for the use of any of the said Churches or religious bodies, or for any college or educational or other institution, or for any trust in connection with any of the said Churches or religious bodies, either generally, or for any special purpose or object, shall from the time the said contemplated union takes place, and thenceforth, belong to and be held in trust for and to the use

in like manner of "The Presbyterian Church in Canada," or for, or to the use in like manner of the said college, educational or other institution or trust in connection therewith.

9. But all such property, real or personal, as is affected by this Act, shall in all respects, save as aforesaid, be held and administered, as nearly as may be, in the same manner and subject to the same conditions, as provided by the deeds of trust, Acts of incorporation, or other instruments or authority under which the same is now held or administered.

10. As soon as the said union takes place, the corporation of the Presbyterian College of Montreal shall stand in the same relation to the Presbyterian Church in Canada, as it now stands to the Canada Presbyterian Church ; and the provisions of the Act of the late Province of Canada, 28 Vict., cap. 53, intituled : " An Act to incorporate the Presbyterian College of Montreal," shall continue to apply to said college and corporation ; and all the rights, powers and authorities by said Act vested in the Synod of the Canada Presbyterian Church shall be vested in, apply to, and be exercised by the Supreme Court of the Presbyterian Church in Canada. And in like manner the corporation of Morrin College shall stand in the same relation to the Presbyterian Church in Canada, as it now stands to the Presbyterian Church of Canada in connection with the Church of Scotland ; and all the provisions of the Act of the late Province of Canada, 24 Vict., cap. 109, intituled : "An Act to incorporate Morrin College at Quebec," shall continue to apply to said college ; and all the rights of the Synod of the Presbyterian Church of Canada in connection with the Church of Scotland shall be vested in the Supreme Court of the Presbyterian Church in Canada ; and all the rights, powers and authorities, vested by the said Act in the minister and congregation of St. Andrew's Church, Quebec, shall continue to be held and exercised by said minister and congregation in connection with the Presbyterian Church in Canada ; provided

always, that the said united Church shall not be required to elect trustees for any Arts department in Morrin College aforesaid.

11. Whereas the ministers of the said Presbyterian Church of Canada in connection with the Church of Scotland are entitled to receive incomes from a fund called the Temporalities Fund, administered by a board incorporated by statute of the heretofore Province of Canada, and it is proposed to preserve to them, and to their successors, even if the congregation over which they preside do not enter into the union, the income which they derive from the said fund; it is therefore enacted that the present members of the said board shall continue in office and manage the said fund on behalf of the said ministers now deriving revenue therefrom, and the income to said ministers shall be continued to them and to their successors, as aforesaid, so long as such Presbyterian ministers are in good standing in the Dominion of Canada, whether exercising their ministry or retired, or whether they are, or are not, in connection with the united Church: provided that the successors of ministers of congregations in the Province of Quebec existing at the time of the union, which do not enter into such union, shall retain the same rights to the benefits of the Temporalities Fund, which they would have had if such union had not taken place. So soon as any part of the revenue accruing from said fund is not required to meet the payment of said incomes and other vested rights in the fund, and expenses therewith, the same shall pass to and be subject to the disposal of the said united Church; and any part of said fund that may remain to the good after the death of the last survivor of the said ministers, shall thereupon pass to and be subject to the disposal of the Supreme Court of said united Church, for the purpose of a Home Mission Fund for aiding weak charges in the united Church; and vacancies in the meantime occurring in said board shall not be filled up in the manner hitherto observed, but shall be filled up in the manner provided by an Act passed during the present session, intituled "An Act to

amend the Act intituled, an Act to incorporate the Board for the management of the Temporalities Fund of the Presbyterian Church of Canada in connection with the Church of Scotland."

12. And whereas "The Canada Presbyterian Church" and "The Presbyterian Church of Canada in connection with the Church of Scotland," have each of them a fund for the benefit of widows and orphans of ministers pertaining to them respectively, and it is not deemed desirable that two such funds should long exist separately after the union, nor that that there should be two separate organizations for the management thereof: it is therefore enacted that the said two funds shall be kept separate, and the separate and distinct management and administration thereof continued by the boards respectively having the management and control thereof at the time of the union, so long only, and until the Supreme Court of said united Church shall have made provision for the amalgamation of said two funds and the management thereof, whereupon the said two separate organizations shall become extinct, and the said two funds shall pass to and vest in the trustees, body or persons indicated for the management thereof by the said Supreme Court; and until such provision is made, vacancies occurring in either of said respective organizations shall not be filled up as hitherto, but shall be filled up by the remaining members of each of said organizations for their respective bodies.

13. As soon as the said union takes place, the Presbyterian Church in Canada, and any college, educational or other institution or trust in connection with the said Church, and any of the religious, educational or charitable schemes of the said Church, and any congregation of the said Church, may by the name thereof, or by the trustees, from time to time take or hold by gift, devise or bequest, any lands or tenements, or interests therein, other than what may be required for the site of any church, chapel, meeting-house, school, manse, glebe, burial-ground, or appurtenances, if such gift, devise or

bequest be made at least six months before the death of the person making the same; but no lands, tenements or interests therein so acquired by gift, devise or bequest, other than what may be required or destined for the site of any church, chapel, meeting-house, school, manse, glebe, burial-ground or appurtenances, shall be held for a longer period than seven years after the acquisition thereof, and any part or portion thereof, or interest therein, which may not within the said period have been alienated or disposed of shall revert to the party from whom the same was acquired, his heirs or other representatives, and the proceeds of such property as shall have been disposed of during said period may be invested in public securities, municipal debentures, stocks of the chartered banks, or other approved securities.

14. The union of the said four Churches shall take place so soon as a notice shall have been published in the Quebec Official Gazette to the effect that the Articles of said union have been signed by the Moderators of the said respective Churches.

15. In so far as it has authority to do so, the Legislature of the Province of Quebec hereby authorizes the Dominion Legislature, and the several Legislatures of the other Provinces, to pass such laws as will recognise and approve of such union throughout and within their respective jurisdictions.

NEW BRUNSWICK.—38 Vict. cap. 48.—An Act concerning the congregations of churches connected with the Church of Scotland in this Province. (*Passed 10th April, 1875.*)

Whereas negotiations have been entered into between the Churches known as the Canada Presbyterian Church, the Presbyterian Church in Canada in connection with the Church of Scotland, the Presbyterian Church of the Lower Provinces, and the Presbyterian Church of the Maritime Provinces in connection with the Church of Scotland, to effect a union under the title of "The Presbyterian Church of Canada;" (a) and the terms of said union have been finally assented to by the Supreme Courts of those Churches respectively; and whereas, it is advisable, before the union of the negotiating Churches is consummated to protect the property and rights of the congregations connected with the Church of Scotland in this Province, who may enter into such union: Be it therefore enacted &c., as follows:—

1. All property, real or personal, now belonging to, or held in trust for, or to the use of any congregation heretofore and now connected with the Church of Scotland, whether the same shall have been organized under the Revised Statutes, or under deeds of trust, or under Acts of incorporation, or as union, or as joint stock churches, or otherwise howsoever, shall continue, on and after the consummation of said union, to be possessed and held by, and shall be used for the benefit of the same congregation, to the same extent as heretofore, after it shall have entered into said union.

2. Where in any Act of incorporation or deed of trust or conveyance, operating as such, or in any will, any congregation connected with the Church of Scotland is mentioned, or intended to be benefited, such Act, deed of trust, conveyance, or will, shall be understood and construed as referring to the same congregation or church, so soon as it shall have entered into connection or communion with the said united body.

3. Where in the Act of incorporation or deed of trust of any congregation or church heretofore connected with the Church of Scotland, or in any conveyance in the nature of a trust, or in any will, no provision has been made for the filling up, from time to time, of trusteeships, vacant by death, removal from the Province, incapacity to act, or resignation of the trustees, such congregation or church, so soon as the same shall be in connection or communion with the said united body, may

(a) *Sic* in the original Act.

at any regular meeting, held in accordance with their Act of incorporation or deed of trust, by a majority of those present and entitled to vote, elect and appoint new trustees in place of such trustees as shall have removed from the Province, become incapable to act, resigned or died, or shall have ceased to be adherents of the said united body; and such newly appointed trustees and their successors so to be appointed shall have full power and authority to hold and administer the trust or corporate property of such congregation.

4. Conveyances heretofore made of any lands or real estate, with a view to the erection of any church, or any school in connection with the church, or of any manse or parsonage thereon, and whereon such church, schoolhouse, manse or parsonage shall have been erected, and be now, or at any time hereafter, owned by any congregation in connection with the said united body, shall be held notwithstanding any want of form therein, to pass the fee simple in such land to the trustees of such church, duly appointed under any deed or will, or under any statute of this Province or under this Act.

5. Conveyances of any lands or real estate, heretofore made to trustees, or to trustees and their successors, for the use of any congregation, or any church, now or hereafter to be in connection or communion with the said united body, shall be deemed valid conveyances in fee simple, notwithstanding that the heirs of the trustees are not named, and notwithstanding that the manner of appointing successors is not provided in such conveyances, or in any will devising such lands.

6. Nothing in this Act contained shall abridge or take away the rights or privileges of any pew-holder, (a) or any other person or persons whomsoever, without just compensation being first made to such person or persons, to be ascertained, in case of disagreement, by arbitrators to be mutually chosen.

(a) For a discussion as to the rights of pew-holders, see *Johnston* v. *Minister and Trustees, St. Andrew's Ch., Montreal*, 1 Supreme Court Rep., 285.

7. This Act shall not be construed so as in anywise to repeal, alter, affect or vary any of the provisions in any special Act or charter of incorporation or deed of trust referring to any particular congregation, college, educational or other institution or trust connected with the Church; but any additional rights or privileges conferred by this Act shall be construed as supplementary to the provisions contained in any such special Act, charter of incorporation or deed of trust.

NEW BRUNSWICK.—38 Vict. cap. 99.—An Act respecting the union of certain Presbyterian Churches therein named. (*Passed 10th April, 1875.*)

Whereas the Canada Presbyterian Church, the Presbyterian Church of Canada in connection with the Church of Scotland, the Church of the Maritime Provinces in connection with the Church of Scotland, and the Presbyterian Church of the Lower Provinces, have severally agreed to unite together and form one body or denomination of Christians, under the name of "The Presbyterian Church in Canada;" and the Moderators of the General Assembly of the Canada Presbyterian Church, and of the Synods of the Presbyterian Church of Canada in connection with the Church of Scotland, and the Church of the Maritime Provinces in connection with the Church of Scotland and the Presbyterian Church of the Lower Provinces, respectively, by and with the consent of the said General Assembly and Synods, have, by their petitions, stating such agreement to unite as aforesaid, prayed that for the furtherance of this their purpose, and to remove any obstructions to such union which may arise out of the present form and designation of the several trusts or Acts of incorporation by which the property of the said Churches and of the colleges and congregations connected with the said Churches, or any of them respectively, are held and administered or otherwise, certain legislative provisions may be made in reference to the property of the said

Churches, colleges and congregations situated within New Brunswick, and other matters affecting the same in view of said union; Be it therefore enacted, &c., as follows :—

1. As soon as the union takes place, all property, real or personal, within New Brunswick, now belonging to or held in trust for or to the use of any congregation in connection or communion with the Presbyterian Church of New Brunswick, now united with the aforesaid Presbyterian Church of the Lower Provinces, shall thenceforth be held, used and administered for the benefit of the same congregation in connection or communion with the united body, under the name of "The Presbyterian Church in Canada."

2. Provided always, that if any congregation in connection or communion with any of the said Churches shall, at a meeting of said congregation regularly called according to the constitution of the said congregation or practice of the Church with which it is connected, and held within six months after the said union takes place, decide by a majority of the votes of those who by the constitution of the said congregation or the practice of the Church with which it is connected, are entitled to vote at such a meeting, not to enter into the said union, but to dissent therefrom, then and in such case, the congregational property of the said congregation shall remain unaffected by this Act or any of the provisions thereof; but in the event of any congregation so dissenting as aforesaid, at any future time resolving to enter into and to adhere to the said united Church, then from the time of such resolution being come to, this Act and the provisions thereof shall apply to the property of such congregation.

3. Congregations may, from time to time, alter or vary any of the provisions contained in the trust deeds under which their property is held, or in their constitutions, which relate to the mode in which their affairs and property shall be managed or regulated, and to the persons who shall be entitled to take part in such management

or to vote at meetings of the congregation on questions affecting the affairs and property of the congregation or the management thereof; but the sanction of the Presbytery within whose bounds such congregation is placed shall be obtained before any such alteration or variation shall take effect.

4. The several clauses and provisions of the Act of the General Assembly of New Brunswick, 22nd Victoria, chapter 6, intituled "An Act for incorporating the Synod of the Church known as the Presbyterian Church of New Brunswick, and the several congregations connected therewith." shall apply, except in those cases where such clauses and provisions are inconsistent with the provisions of this Act, to the various congregations of said Church in New Brunswick, in connection or communion with the Presbyterian Church in Canada; provided always, that before any of the powers of leasing, if for a period exceeding seven years, selling, exchanging or mortgaging, be exercised by any congregation or by the trustees thereof, the sanction of the Presbytery within whose bounds such congregation is placed shall be obtained.

5. All other property, real or personal, belonging to or held in trust for the use of any of the said Churches or religious bodies, or for any college or educational or other institution, or for any trust in connection with any of the said Churches or religious bodies, either generally or for any special purpose or object, shall from the time the said contemplated union takes place, and thenceforth, belong to and be held in trust for and to the use in like manner of "The Presbyterian Church in Canada," or for or to the use in like manner of the said college, educational or other institution or trust in connection therewith.

6. But all such property, real or personal, as is affected by this Act, shall in all respects, save as aforesaid, be held and administered as nearly as may be in the same manner and subject to the same conditions as provided by the deeds of trust, Acts of incorporation, or other

instruments or authority, under which the same is now held or administered.

7. As soon as the said union takes place, the Presbyterian Church in Canada, and any of the trusts in connection with the said Church, and any of the congregations or religious, or charitable schemes of the said Church, may by the name thereof, or by trustees, from time to time, take by gift, devise or bequest, any lands or tenements, or interests therein; but the said Church or congregation, or the said religious or charitable schemes of the said Church, shall at no one time take by gift, devise or bequest, lands or tenements, or any interest therein, the annual value of which shall exceed in the whole $3000; nor shall the said Church, or any of the congregations, or religious or charitable schemes of the said Church, at any time take by gift, devise or bequest, lands or tenements the annual value of which and of all the other real estate of the said Church in the Province of New Brunswick, or of the particular scheme in favour of which the gift, devise or bequest is made, shall together exceed $10,000.

8. The union of the said four Churches shall be held to take place as soon as the Articles of such union shall have been signed by the Moderators of the said respective Churches.

NEW BRUNSWICK.—39 Vict., cap. 13.—An Act relating to the Presbyterian Church in Canada. (*Passed 13th April, 1876.*)

Whereas an Act was passed in the 38th year of the reign of Her present Majesty, intituled An Act concerning the congregations of churches connected with the Church of Scotland in this Province, and also another Act intituled An Act respecting the union of certain Presbyterian Churches therein named; and whereas union of the said Churches was consummated at Montreal on the 15th day of June last, according to the tenor of the said Acts ; and whereas doubts have arisen regarding the ministers eligible to be elected by congregations under the said Act ; Be it therefore enacted as follows :—

1. Notwithstanding anything contained in any Act of Assembly, charter, trust, deed, conveyance or will, any probationer or minister of the Presbyterian Church in Canada, or any minister of any other Church holding the same doctrine, government and discipline, who may be willing to become a minister of the Presbyterian Church in Canada, under such terms and regulations as the said Presbyterian Church in Canada has agreed, or may from time to time agree upon, shall be eligible for election as minister for any church in connection with the Presbyterian Church in Canada, although such probationer or minister may not belong to the Church or denomination specified in such Act, charter, trust, deed, conveyance or will.

2. All Acts or parts of Acts inconsistent herewith, in so far as they are inconsistent, are hereby repealed, and the provisions of this Act shall be read and construed as if it had been inserted in and formed part of each of the Acts referred to in the recital hereto.

NEW BRUNSWICK.—47 Vict., cap. 36—An Act in addition to and in explanation of chapter 99 of the Acts of the General Assembly of the Province of New Brunswick, passed in the 38th year of the reign of Her present Majesty, intituled "An Act respecting the union of certain Presbyterian Churches therein named. (*Passed 1st April, 1884.*)

Whereas in and by chapter 6 of the Acts of the General Assembly of this Province passed in the 22nd year of the reign of Her present Majesty, certain persons therein named, their associates and successors, were under the name of " The Synod of the Church known as the Presbyterian Church of New Brunswick," and the several congregations connected therewith, incorporated a body politic and corporate in deed and name, and were to be known as a corporate body under that name; and whereas the several ministers and elders constituting the said Synod and the several congregations connected therewith, united with and became merged in the body or Church then known as the Presbyterian Church of the Lower Provinces, and ceased to be known as "The Church known as the Presbyterian Church of New Brunswick," without any legislation being had repealing the said Act of Assembly, chapter 6, of the 22nd year of the reign of Her present Majesty; and whereas the said Presbyterian Church of the Lower Provinces did unite with and became merged in the Church now known as the Presbyterian Church in Canada, and the several churches and congregations in the Province of New Brunswick adhering to and under the ecclesiastical control of the said Presbyterian Church of the Lower Provinces formerly constituting the Synod of the Church known as the Presbyterian Church of New Brunswick, and now yield allegiance to the said Presbyterian Church in Canada, and are under its ecclesiastical supervision and control; and whereas doubts exist as to the effect and scope of said Act of Assembly, chapter 99, passed in the 38th year of Her present Majesty's reign, and to remove all such doubts so far as the Synod of the Church known as the Presbyterian Church of New Brunswick is concerned: Be it therefore enacted as follows:—

1. That the said Synod of the Church known as the Presbyterian Church of New Brunswick, and the several ministers, elders and congregations now or formerly constituting the same, is hereby declared to be merged in and subject to the ecclesiastical control of the said Presbyterian Church in Canada; and the said incorporated Synod shall after the passing of this Act cease to exist as a corporate body, and so much of said Act as relates to the existence and constitution of said incorporation as aforesaid is hereby repealed.

2. That all the powers, duties and legal rights formerly held, used, exercised and enjoyed by the said Synod

of the Church known as the Presbyterian Church of New Brunswick shall be held, used, exercised and enjoyed by the Synod of the Maritime Provinces in connection with the Presbyterian Church in Canada: and that all the rights, duties and trusts which might, could or had been held, used, exercised and enjoyed by the said incorporated Synod, shall be held, used, exercised and enjoyed by the said Synod of the Maritime Provinces in connection with the Presbyterian Church in Canada.

3. Any grant, devise, gift or bequest made, or which shall hereafter appear to have been made to the said Synod of the Church known as the Presbyterian Church of New Brunswick upon any trust or condition, or for any purpose whatever, shall be held and enjoyed for the like purposes and upon the like trusts by the said Synod of the Maritime Provinces in connection with the Presbyterian Church in Canada, and which Synod is hereby declared to be the legal successors of the said Synod of the Church known as the Presbyterian Church of New Brunswick; and it is hereby enacted and declared that all the property, securities for money, estate and effects of the said Presbyterian Church of New Brunswick shall be vested in and held by the said Presbyterian Church in Canada, and subject to the regulations and control of the said Synod of the Maritime Provinces in connection with the said Presbyterian Church in Canada, anything heretofore existing or law heretofore in force to the contrary notwithstanding.

4. This Act shall come into force and take effect on the 1st day of October, 1884.

PRINCE EDWARD ISLAND.—38 Vict. cap. 27.—An Act concerning the Congregations of Churches connected with the Church of Scotland and the Presbyterian Church of the Lower Provinces in this Province. (*Passed 27th April, 1875.*)

Whereas negotiations have been entered into between the Churches known as the Canada Presbyterian Church, the Presbyterian Church in Canada in connection with the Church of Scotland, the Presbyterian Church of the Lower Provinces, and the Presbyterian Church of the Maritime Provinces in connection with the Church of Scotland, to effect a union under the title of " The Presbyterian Church of Canada ;" (a) and the terms of said union have been finally assented to by the Supreme Courts of those Churches respectively ; and whereas it is advisable, before the union of the negotiating Churches is consummated to protect the property and rights of the congregations connected with the Church of Scotland and the Presbyterian Church of the Lower Provinces respectively in this Province, who may enter into such union : Be it enacted &c., as follows :—

1. All property, real or personal, now belonging to, or held in trust for, or to the use of any congregation heretofore and now connected with the Church of Scotland or the Presbyterian Church of the Lower Provinces respectively, whether the same shall have been organized under any statute passed by the Legislature of this Province or under deeds of trust, or under Acts of incorporation, or as union, or as joint-stock churches, or otherwise howsoever, shall continue, on and after the consummation of said union, to be possessed and held by, and shall be used for the benefit of the same congregation, to the same extent as heretofore, after it shall have entered into such union.

2. Where in any Act of incorporation or deed of trust or conveyance, operating as such, or in any will, any congregation connected with the Church of Scotland or the Presbyterian Church of the Lower Provinces is mentioned, or intended to be benefited, the Act, deed of trust or conveyance, or will, shall be understood and construed as referring to the same congregation or Church, so soon as it shall have entered into connection or communion with the said united body.

3. Where in the Act of incorporation or deed of trust of any congregation or Church heretofore connected

(a) *Sic* in the original Act.

with the Church of Scotland or the Presbyterian Church of the Lower Provinces, or in any conveyance in the nature of a trust, or in any will, no provision has been made for the filling up, from time to time, of trusteeships, vacant by death, removal from the Province, incapacity to act, or resignation of the trustees, such congregation or Church, so soon as the same shall be in connection or communion with the said united body, may at any regular meeting, held in accordance with their Act of incorporation or deed of trust, by a majority of those present and entitled to vote, elect and appoint new trustees in place of such trustees as shall have been removed from the Province, become incapable to act, resigned or died, or shall have ceased to be members in communion with the said united body, and such newly appointed trustees and their successors so to be appointed shall have full power and authority to hold and administer the trust or corporate property of such congregation.

4. Conveyances heretofore made of any lands or real estate with a view to the erection of any Church, of any school in connection with a Church, or of any manse or parsonage thereon, and whereon such Church, school-house, or parsonage shall have been erected, and be now, or at any time hereafter owned by any congregation in connection with the said united body, shall be held, notwithstanding any want of form therein, to pass the fee simple in such land to the trustees of such Church duly appointed under any deed or will, or under any statute of this Province, or under this Act.

5. Conveyances of any lands or real estate, heretofore made to trustees, or to trustees and their successors, for the use of any congregation or any Church now or hereafter to be in connection with the said united body, shall be deemed valid conveyances in fee simple, notwithstanding that the heirs of the trustees are not named, and notwithstanding that the manner of appointing successors is not provided in such conveyance, or in any will devising such lands.

6. Nothing in this Act contained shall abridge or take away the rights or privileges of any pew-holder (a) or any other person or persons, whosoever without just compensation being first made to such person or persons to be ascertained, in case of disagreement, by arbitrators to be mutually chosen.

7. This Act shall not be construed so as in anywise to repeal, alter, affect or vary any of the provisions in any special Act or charter of incorporation, or deed of trust referring to any particular congregation, college, educational or any other institution or trust connected with the Church of Scotland or the Presbyterian Church of the Lower Provinces, respectively, but any additional rights or privileges conferred by this Act shall be construed as supplementary to the provisions contained in any such special Act, charter of incorporation or deed of trust.

Nova Scotia.—38 Vict. cap. 99.—An Act concerning the Congregations of Churches connected with the Church of Scotland in Nova Scotia. (*Passed 6th May, 1875.*)

Whereas negotiations have been entered into between the Churches known as the Canada Presbyterian Church, the Presbyterian Church in Canada in connection with the Church of Scotland, the Presbyterian Church of the Lower Provinces of British North America, and the Presbyterian Church of the Maritime Provinces in connection with the Church of Scotland, to effect a union under the title of "The Presbyterian Church in Canada; and the terms of such union have been finally assented to by the Supreme Courts of those Churches respectively; and whereas, it is advisable before the union of the negotiating Churches is consummated to protect the property and rights of the congre-

---

(a) As to rights of a pew-holder, &c. *Johnston v. Minister and Trustees, St. Andrew's Church, Montreal,* 1 Supreme Court Rep. 235.

gations connected with the Church of Scotland in this Province who may enter into such union; Be it therefore enacted, &c., as follows:—

1. All property, real and personal now belonging to, or held in trust for or to the use of any congregation, heretofore and now connected with the Church of Scotland, whether the same shall have been organized under the Revised Statutes or under deeds of trust, or under Acts of incorporation, or as union, or as joint stock churches, or otherwise however, shall continue, on and after the consummation of such union, to be possessed and held by and shall be used for the benefit of the same congregation, to the same extent as heretofore, after it shall have entered into such union.

2. Where, in any Act of incorporation, deed of trust or conveyance operating as such, or in any will, any congregation connected with the Church of Scotland is mentioned, or intended to be benefited, such Act, deed of trust, conveyance, or will shall be understood and construed as referring to the same congregation or church, so soon as it shall have entered into connection or communion with such united body.

3. Where in the Act of incorporation or deed of trust of any congregation or church heretofore connected with the Church of Scotland, or in any conveyance in the nature of a trust, or in any will, no provision has been made for the filling up, from time to time, of trusteeships, vacant by death, removal from the Province, incapacity to act or resignation of the trustees, such congregation or church so soon as the same shall be in connection or communion with said united body may at any regular meeting held in accordance with the Act of incorporation or deed of trust by a majority of those present and entitled to vote, elect and appoint new trustees in place of such trustees as shall have removed from the Province, become incapable to act, resigned or died, or shall have ceased to be members in communion with the united body, and such newly appointed trustees and their successors, to be appointed, shall have full power and

authority to hold and administer the trust or corporate property of such congregation.

4. Conveyances heretofore made of any lands or real estate, with a view to the erection of any church, or any school in connection with a church, or of any manse or parsonage thereon, and whereon such church, schoolhouse, manse or parsonage shall have been erected, and be now, or at anytime hereafter, owned by any congregation in connection with such united body, shall be held notwithshanding any want of form therein, to pass the fee simple in such land to the trustees of such church, duly appointed under any deed or will, or under any statute of this Province or under this Act.

5. Conveyances of any lands or real estate, heretofore made to trustees, or to trustees and their successors, for the use of any congregation, or any church, now or hereafter in connection or communion with such united body, shall be deemed valid conveyances in fee simple, notwithstanding that the heirs of the trustees are not named and notwithstanding that the manner of appointing successors is not provided in such conveyances, or in any will devising such lands.

6. Nothing in this Act contained shall abridge or take away the rights or privileges of any pew-holder, or any other person whomsoever, without just compensation being first made to such pew-holder or other person. Such compensation in case of disagreement, shall be ascertained by arbitrators, chosen as follows: one by the trustees or managing committee of the church or congregation, and one by such pew-holder or other person, and (in case of a difference of opinion between such two arbitrators) a third to be chosen as umpire by such two arbitrators. The award of any two of the persons so chosen shall be final.

7. This Act shall not be construed so as in anywise to repeal, alter, affect or vary any of the provisions in any special Act or charter of incorporation or deed of trust referring to any particular congregation, college, educa-

tional or other institution or trust connected with the Church; but any additional rights or privileges conferred by this Act shall be construed as supplementary to the provisions contained in any such special Act, charter of incorporation or deed of trust.

8. No vested rights or freehold property of any congregation or church shall be transferred or converted, except on the vote of two-thirds of the pew-owners, passed at a public meeting called for the purpose after due notice.

9. This Act shall come into force so soon as the union of the four Churches named in the preamble shall have been consummated, and the Articles of such union shall have been signed by the Moderators of such respective Churches.

10. So much of the existing law as is inconsistent with this Act is repealed.

NOVA SCOTIA.—38 Vict. cap. 100.—An Act concerning the Presbyterian Church of the Lower Provinces of British North America. (*Passed 6th May. 1875.*)

Whereas negotiations have been entered into between the Churches known as the Canada Presbyterian Church, the Presbyterian Church in Canada in connection with the Church of Scotland, the Presbyterian Church of the Lower Provinces of British North America, and the Presbyterian Church of the Maritime Provinces in connection with the Church of Scotland, to effect a union under the title of "The Presbyterian Church in Canada;" and the terms of such union have been finally assented to by the Supreme Courts of those Churches respectively; and whereas, it is advisable, before the union of the negotiating churches is consummated to protect the property and rights of the congregations connected with the Presbyterian Church of the Lower Provinces of British North America in this Province, who may enter into such union, and also to protect the various funds and property of such Church held by its Board of Education: Be it therefore enacted, &c., as follows:—

1. As soon as the union takes place, all property, real or personal, within Nova Scotia, now belonging to or held in trust for or to the use of any congregation in connection or communion with the Presbyterian Church of the Lower Provinces of British North America, shall thenceforth be held, used and administered for the benefit of the same congregation in connection or communion with the united body, under the name of "The Presbyterian Church in Canada."

2. Provided always, that if any congregation in connection or communion with such Church shall, at a meeting of such congregation, regularly called according to the constitution of such congregation, or the practice of the Church with which it is connected, and held within six calendar months after such union takes place, decide by a majority of the votes of those who, by the constitution of the congregation, or the practice of the Church with which it is connected, are entitled to vote at such a meeting, not to enter into such union, but to dissent therefrom; then, and in such case, the congregational property of such congregation shall remain unaffected by this Act, or by any of the provisions thereof; but in the event of any congregation so dissenting, at any future time resolving to enter into and adhere to such united Church, then, from the time of such resolution being come to, this Act and the provisions thereof shall apply to the property of such congregation.

3. Congregations may from time to time alter or vary any of the provisions contained in the trust deeds under which their property is held, or in their constitutions, which relate to the mode in which their affairs and property shall be managed or regulated, and to the persons who shall be entitled to take part in such management, or to vote at the meetings of the congregation on questions affecting the affairs and property of the congregation or the management thereof; but the sanction of the Presbytery within whose bounds such congregation is

placed shall be obtained before any such alteration or variation shall take effect.

4. All other property, real or personal, belonging to or held in trust for or to the use of such Presbyterian Church of the Lower Provinces, or for any college or educational or other institution, or for any trust in connection with such Church or religious body, either generally or for any special purpose or object, shall, from the time the said contemplated union takes place, and thenceforth, belong to and be held in trust for and to the use in like manner of "The Presbyterian Church in Canada," or for and to the use in like manner of such college, educational or other institution or trust in connection therewith. All such property, real and personal, as is affected by this Act, shall in all respects, save as aforesaid, be held and administered, as nearly as may be, in the same manner, and subject to the same conditions as provided by the deeds of trust, Acts of incorporation, or other instruments or authorities under which the same is how held and administered; provided always, that the relation now subsisting between such Presbyterian Church of the Lower Provinces of British North America and the Governors of Dalhousie College in Halifax, whereby such Church contributes towards the support of the institution the salaries of two professors, shall remain in force as heretofore, until the same be altered or revoked by the Presbyterian Church in Canada, or by the Board of Governors of such College.

5. The several funds of the Presbyterian Church of the Lower Provinces, held by any boards or committees in connection therewith, for the benefit of widows and orphans of ministers, for the benefit of aged and infirm ministers, for the support of the home and foreign mission schemes of the Church, and the fund known as the Geddie Memorial Fund, shall bear the same relation in all respects to the General Assembly of the Presbyterian Church in Canada that they now bear to the Synod of the Presbyterian Church of the Lower Provinces; and until such General Assembly shall provide or otherwise direct, such several funds shall be managed and directed

by the boards or committees now having charge thereof: and until such provision is made vacancies occurring in any of such respective organizations shall not be filled up as hitherto, but shall be filled up by the remaining members of each of such organizations for their respective bodies, and the General Assembly of such Presbyterian Church in Canada shall have power to unite any of such funds with the funds held by any other of the uniting Churches for similar objects.

6. All the funds and property in the possession or under the control of the Board of Education of the Presbyterian Church of the Lower Provinces, as incorporated by chapter 68 of the Acts of this Province for the year 1861, shall, until the General Assembly of the Presbyterian Church in Canada shall otherwise provide for the management thereof, remain in the charge of such board and its officers as heretofore; and all their acts in relation thereto shall be as valid as if this Act had not passed.

7. So much of the existing law as is inconsistent with this Act is repealed.

8. This Act shall come into force so soon as the union of the four Churches named and mentioned in the preamble shall have been consummated, and the Articles of such union shall have been signed by the Moderators of such respective Churches.

MANITOBA.—38 Vict., cap. 47—An Act respecting the Union of certain Presbyterian Churches therein named. (*Assented to 14th May, 1875.*)

Whereas the Canada Presbyterian Church, the Presbyterian Church of Canada in connection with the Church of Scotland, the Church of the Maritime Provinces in connection with the Church of Scotland, and the Presbyterian Church of the Lower Provinces, have severally agreed to unite together and form one body or denomination of Christians, under the name of "The

Presbyterian Church in Canada," and the Moderator of the General Assembly of the Canada Presbyterian Church, by and with the consent of the said General Assembly, has by petition, stating such agreement to unite as aforesaid, prayed that for the furtherance of this their purpose, and to remove any obstructions to such union which may arise out of the present form and designation of the several trusts or Acts of incorporation by which the property of the said Canada Presbyterian Church, of the college and of the congregations connected with the said Church, is held and administered or otherwise, certain legislative provisions may be made in reference to the property of the said Church, college and congregations situate within Manitoba, and other matters affecting the same in view of said union ; Therefore Her Majesty, &c., enacts as follows :

1. As soon as the union takes place, all property, real or personal, within Manitoba, now belonging to or held in trust for or to the use of any congregation in connection or communion with the said Canada Presbyterian Church, shall thenceforth be held, used and administered for the benefit of the same congregation in connection or communion with the united body, under the name of " The Presbyterian Church in Canada."

2. Where the trust deed or conveyance under which any property is held within this Province, by or for the use or in trust for any congregation in connection or communion with the said Canada Presbyterian Church before the union, sufficiently provides for the case of such a union as that contemplated by the present Act, and stipulates for any consent thereto by such congregation or the members or adherents thereof, or any specified proportion of such congregation or the members or adherents thereof, nothing in this Act shall be construed to affect the right of such congregation, or the members or adherents thereof, in that behalf, or to change the conditions on which they may have consented to come into the union.

3. Congregations may from time to time alter or vary any of the provisions contained in the trust deeds under

which their property is held, or in their constitutions, which relate to the mode in which their affairs and property shall be managed or regulated, and to the persons who shall be entitled to take part in such management, or to vote at meetings of the congregation on questions affecting the affairs and property of the congregation or the management thereof; but the sanction of the Presbytery under whose care such congregation is placed shall be obtained before any such alteration or variation shall take effect.

4. All other property, real or personal, belonging to or held in trust for the use of the said Church, or for any college or educational or other institution, or for any trust in connection with the said Church, either generally or for any special purpose or object, shall from the time the said contemplated union takes place, and thenceforth belong to and be held in trust for and to the use in like manner of "The Presbyterian Church in Canada," or for or to the use in like manner of the said college, educational or other institution or trust in connection therewith.

5. But all such property, real or personal, as is affected by this Act, shall in all respects, save as aforesaid, be held and administered, as nearly as may be, in the same manner and subject to the same conditions as provided by the deeds of trust, Acts of incorporation, or other instruments or authority under which the same is now held or administered.

6. As soon as the said union takes place, the Presbyterian Church in Canada, and any college, educational or other institution or trust in connection with the said Church, and any of the religious, educational or charitable schemes of the said Church and any congregation of the said Church in the Province of Manitoba, may by the name thereof, or by the trustees, deacons or managers, from time to time, take or hold by gift, devise or bequest, any lands or tenements, or interests therein, other than what may be required for the site of any church, chapel, meeting-house, school, manse, glebe,

burial-ground, or appurtenances, if such gift, devise or bequest be made at least six months before the death of the person making the same; but no lands, tenements, or interests therein so acquired by gift, devise or bequest, other than what may be required or destined for the site of any church, chapel, meeting-house, school, manse, glebe, burial-ground, or appurtenances, shall be held for a longer period than seven years after the acquisition thereof, and any part or portion thereof, or interest therein, which may not within the same period have been alienated or disposed of shall revert to the party from whom the same was acquired, his heirs or other representatives, and the proceeds of such property as shall have been disposed of during said period, may be invested in public securities, municipal debentures, stocks of the chartered banks, or other approved securities, not including mortgages on lands.

7. The union of the said four Churches shall be held to take place as soon as the Articles of such union shall have been signed by the Moderators of the said respective Churches, and a notice published in the Manitoba Official Gazette, to the effect that the Articles of said union have been signed by the Moderators of the said respective Churches, shall be deemed *prima facie* evidence of such signature.

8. In so far as it has authority to do so, the Legislature of the Province of Manitoba hereby authorizes the Dominion Legislature and the several Legislatures of the other Provinces to pass such laws as will recognize and approve of such union throughout and within their respective jurisdictions.

ACTS OF ASSEMBLY.

Act Constituting the General Assembly.

(1.) The General Assembly shall consist of one-fourth of the whole number of ministers whose names are on the rolls of the several Presbyteries of the Church, and an equal number of elders.

(2.) When the number of names on the roll of a Presbytery is not divisible by four; the fourth shall be reckoned from the next higher multiple of four.

(3.) Each Presbytery shall elect its representatives at an ordinary meeting, held at least twenty-one days before the meeting of the General Assembly. If any one thus elected resigns his commission, the Presbytery may, at any subsequent meeting, held not less than eight days before the meeting of the General Assembly, appoint another in his stead.

(4.) A Presbytery may appoint as its commissioner to the General Assembly an elder belonging to any other Presbytery of the Church, provided, always, that the person so appointed is at the time an acting member of some session.

(5.) Ministers whose names are on the roll of a Presbytery as ministers shall not be eligible to hold commissions as elders from their own or any other Presbytery.

(6.) Each Presbytery shall, through its Clerk, transmit to the Clerk of Assembly, at least ten days before the Assembly meets, a certified roll of the commissioners appointed at its ordinary meeting. A separate report of any commissions afterwards given to ministers or elders in place of such as may have resigned their commissions, shall be presented to the General Assembly by the Presbyteries as soon as convenient after the Assembly has been constituted.

(7.) The roll to be called at the opening of the Assembly shall be made up from the rolls of the several Presbyteries, as transmitted to the Clerk of Assembly, containing the names of commissioners appointed at least twenty-one days before. At its first session the Assembly shall appoint a "Committee on Commissions", to which shall be referred the reports of Presbyteries regarding commissions issued at a later date and all matters affecting the roll. On the report of this Committee the Assembly shall order such changes to be made in the roll as may be required. The roll thus amended shall be the permanent roll of the General Assembly.

(8.) Forty commissioners, of whom twenty-one are ministers, shall constitute a quorum for the transaction of business. But twenty commissioners who were appointed twenty-one days before, being met at the place and time appointed, may constitute the court, and adjourn from time to time until a full quorum is present.

(9.) Presbyteries should make suitable provision for defraying the expenses of commissioners when attending the General Assembly.

The Barrier Act.—(a).

Minutes, 1877, p. 22. (1.) No proposed law or rule relative to matters of doctrine, discipline, government or worship, shall become a permanent enactment until the same has been submitted to Presbyteries for consideration. Such consideration shall be given by each Presbytery, at an ordinary meeting, or a special meeting held for the purpose; and an extract minute of the Presbytery's judgment shall be sent to the Clerk of the General Assembly, before the next meeting of that court.

(a) "Soon after the abolition of Episcopacy in 1638, the fathers of the Church saw the necessity of guarding against innovations on the laws of the Church, and in 1639 and 1641, acts were passed which required the consultation of Synods and Presbyteries in the framing of new laws. Notwithstanding those impediments, however, a further check became necessary on rash legislation, and on the 25th December, 1695, an overture was brought in on the subject, for the consideration of the Church in its subordinate judicatories. On the 8th January, 1697, in consequence of that overture, an Act was passed, which is termed The Barrier Act, and which fixed permanently the mode of legislating in the General Assemblies of the Church." *Introduction to Compendium of the Laws of the Church of Scotland, Vol. 2.* "It is the right and duty of every Presbytery of the Church to take its part in the legislation of the Church, by approving or disapproving of overtures transmitted by the General Assembly, with a view to such overtures being passed into Standing Laws, in terms of what is called The Barrier Act." *Moncrieff's Practice of the Free Church of Scotland, 66.* And see *Hodge's What is Presbyterian Law, 272; Morris' Presbyterian Digest, 325.*

(2.) The Assembly, if it sees cause, may, by a majority of two-thirds of those present, pass such proposed law or rule into an Interim Act, which shall possess the force of law, (*b*) until the Presbyteries have, as herein required, reported their judgment upon it to the next General Assembly.

(3.) If a majority of the Presbyteries of the Church express their approval, the Assembly may pass such proposed law or rule into a standing law of the Church. If a majority of the Presbyteries express disapproval, the Assembly shall reject such proposed law or rule, or again remit it to the Presbyteries.

ADMISSION OF MINISTERS AND LICENTIATES FROM OTHER CHURCHES.

Minutes 1880, p. 52. (1.) Any minister who is a settled pastor or a professor of Theology, or who is employed by special appointment in some department of the work of the Church, in a Church which holds the same doctrine, government and discipline as this Church, if regularly called by a congregation of the Church, may be received by a Presbytery, on presenting a Presbyterial certificate; but the Presbytery, if it sees cause, may refer the case to the Assembly.

(2.) Ministers and licentiates expressly designated or commissioned by the Presbyterian Churches in Great Britain and Ireland may, on producing their commissions, be admitted by Presbyteries as ministers or probationers of this Church.

(3.) In all cases in which an applicant for admission does not come in the manner provided above, but with a

---

(*b*) "When the immediate enactment of the new law proposed in an overture, appears essential for the good of the Church, the General Assembly exercises the power of converting the overture into what we are accustomed to call an Interim Act; and it is acknowledged by all who understand our constitution, that till the meeting of the next Assembly, such temporary enactments are binding upon all the members of the Church." *Hill's Practice of the Church of Scotland*, 101; and see *Moncrieff's Practice, &c.*, 96. But no overture may be converted into an Interim Act which involves an essential alteration of the existing law or practice of the Church. *Hill's Practice, &c.*, 101.

Presbyterial certificate only, he cannot be received into full standing as a minister or probationer of this Church without permission of the General Assembly.

The Presbytery, at an ordinary meeting, holds private conference with the applicant for the purpose of ascertaining his doctrinal views, his literary attainments and other particulars. If satisfied, the Presbytery records its judgment, and agrees to transmit the application, with extracts of its proceedings thereon, and relative documents, to the next General Assembly, and instructs its Clerk to issue circular letters forthwith to the other Presbyteries.

If the Presbytery is unanimous in transmitting the application, it may, in the meantime, avail itself of the applicant's services.

If the Assembly grants permission, the Presbytery may, on the applicant's satisfactorily answering the questions appointed to be put to ministers or probationers, and on his signing the formula, receive him as a minister or probationer of this Church.

(4.) When the Church from which the applicant comes is not a Presbyterian Church, he is required to apply to the Presbytery within whose bounds he resides, and to produce documentary evidence of his good standing as a minister in that Church. If the Presbytery is satisfied with such evidence, they proceed to confer with him, and answers are required to the following questions:

(*a.*) What course of study has he passed in Arts and Theology?

(*b.*) When, where and by whom was he ordained to the ministry?

(*c.*) Has he ever been connected with any other Church than that from which he brings documents, and if so, in what capacity?

(*d.*) What are his reasons for applying for admission to this Church, and what has led to his change of views?

(*e.*) How long has he resided within the bounds of the Presbytery?

The Presbytery further enquires as to the degree of success which has attended the previous ministry of the applicant, and if satisfied as to the probability of his usefulness in the Church, and as to his Christian character and good report, the Presbytery records its judgment on the whole case, and resolves to apply for leave to admit him. The answers given and the information obtained are embodied in a report which is transmitted to the General Assembly, with extract minutes and other documents.

A duly certified extract of the Assembly's deliverance in the matter is sent to the Presbytery, which thereupon takes such further action as is called for. (See preceding sub-section, last clause.)

(5.) All applicants for admission to the Church, except those referred to in sub-section 2, should appear personally before the General Assembly.

Minutes 1887, p. 54.—Direct Presbyteries to adhere strictly to the provisions of the Act of the General Assembly, passed in 1880, anent the reception of ministers from other Churches, in dealing with all applicants, and especially to avoid entering into engagements with such applicants, or giving them ground for expectations that may be inconsistent with the fullest freedom on the part of the General Assembly in finally disposing of their applications. Further, that care be taken in every case to ascertain that the literary and theological training of applicants is such as is required by the Church of our own students.

Minutes 1896, p. 19.—The following recommendations of the committee on the reception of ministers, were adopted:—

(*a*) That the attention of Presbyteries be drawn to the propriety of exercising extreme caution in dealing with applicants who are desirous of being received as ministers of this Church.

(*b*) That Presbyteries do not entertain any application where the applicant has not pursued a course of study in all respects similar or equivalent to that required of our own students.

Representation of Mission Stations in Church Courts.

Minutes 1893, p. 46.—The committee appointed at last Assembly to deal with the reference from the Presbytery of Guelph, and the overture from the Presbytery of Toronto, as to the question, whether Mission Stations have a right to representation in the Church Courts gave in a report, which was adopted, the recommendations in it enacted as law *ad interim* and sent down to Presbyteries under the Barrier Act.

That a change be made in the law of the Church, by allowing representation to Mission Stations in which are organized sessions whether the Station be a single one or consisting of a group.

Minutes 1894, p. 43.—With regard to the representation of Mission Stations in Presbyteries and Synods, that in view of the desire expressed in the returns made by Presbyteries, the *interim* Act become the law of the Church.

Formula to be Signed by all Office Bearers.

Minutes 1876, p. 71.—I hereby declare that I believe the Westminster Confession of Faith, as adopted by this Church in the basis of Union, and the government of the Church by Sessions, Presbyteries, Synods and General Assemblies, to be founded on and agreeable to the Word of God; that I own the purity of worship at present authorized by this Church; and that I engage to adhere faithfully to the doctrine of the said Confession, to maintain and defend the said government, to conform to the said worship, and to submit to the discipline of this Church, and to follow no divisive course from the present order established therein.

Standing Orders and Regulations Anent Records of Church Courts.

In 1876 the Assembly adopted certain Standing Orders, and Regulations anent the Records of Church Courts (*Minutes 1876, pp. 71-72*). In the "Rules and Forms of Procedure" adopted by the General Assembly in 1889, these matters are dealt with more in detail. The Standing Orders there appear as, Sections 125 to 137; and the Regulations anent the Records, as Sections 179 to 188. There are also given, General Rules of Church Courts, and Rules of Debate, Sections 138 to 172.

PART II.—THE COLLEGES.

(1) Queen's College, Kingston.

ROYAL CHARTER.—Victoria, by the Grace of God of the United Kingdom of Great Britain and Ireland, Queen, Defender of the Faith.

To all to Whom these Presents shall come, Greeting:

Whereas, the establishment of a college within the Province of Upper Canada, in North America, in connection with the Church of Scotland, for the education of youth in the principles of the christian religion; and for their instruction in the various branches of science and literature, would greatly conduce to the welfare of our said Province. *And Whereas* humble application hath been made to us by The Rev. Robert McGill, Moderator of the Synod of the Presbyterian Church of Canada in connection with the Church of Scotland, and The Rev. Alexander Gale, clerk of the said Synod, and the several other persons hereinafter named, to make them a body corporate and politic for the purposes aforesaid and hereinafter mentioned; by granting to them our Royal Charter of Incorporation, and to permit them to use our Royal Title in the name or style thereof.

Now Know Ye, that We having taken the premises into our Royal consideration, and duly weighing the great utility and importance of such an institution, have of our special grace, certain knowledge, and mere motion, granted, constituted, declared and appointed, and by these Presents for Us, Our Heirs and Successors, Do grant, constitute, declare and appoint the said Robert McGill and Alexander Gale, The Rev. John McKenzie (*and others, naming them*), ministers of the Presbyterian Church of Canada in connection with the Church of Scotland, The Honble. John Hamilton, The Honble. James Crooks (*and others, naming them*), members of the said Church, and all and every such other person and persons as now is or are, or shall or may at any time or times hereafter be ministers of the Presbyterian Church of Canada in connection with the Church of Scotland—or members of the said Presbyterian Church in such connection, and in full communion with the said Presbyterian Church—shall be and be called, one body Corporate and Politic, in Deed and in Law by the name and style of "Queen's College at Kingston," and them by the name of "Queen's College at Kingston," *We do for* the purposes aforesaid and hereinafter mentioned, really and fully for Us, Our Heirs and Successors, make, erect, create, ordain, constitute, establish, confirm, and declare by these presents, to be one body politic and corporate in deed and in name: And that they and their successors by that name shall and may have perpetual succession as a college—with the style and privileges of an university, for the education and instruction of youth and students in arts and faculties; and shall also have and may use a common seal, with power to break, change, alter or make new the same seal, as often as they shall judge expedient. And that they and their successors, by the name aforesaid, shall and may forever hereafter be able, in Law and in Equity, to sue and be sued, implead and be impleaded, answer and be answered unto, defend and be defended, in all courts and places whatsoever: and also to have, take, receive, purchase, acquire, hold, possess, enjoy and maintain in law, to and for the use of the said college, any messuages, lands, tenements and hereditaments, of what kind, nature or quality soever, so as that the same do not exceed in yearly value, above all charges, the sum of £15,000 sterling : and also that they and their successors shall have power to take, purchase, acquire, have, hold, enjoy, receive, possess and retain all or any goods, chattels, monies, stocks, charitable or other contributions, gifts, benefactions or bequests whatsoever : and to give, grant, bargain, sell, demise, or otherwise dispose of, all or any part of the same, or of any other property, real, personal, or other they may at any time or times possess or be entitled to, as to them shall seem best for the interest of the said college. *And We do further Will,* Ordain and Grant that the said college shall be deemed and taken to be an university ; and that the students in the said college shall have liberty and faculty of taking the degrees of Bachelor, Master and Doctor in the several arts and faculties at the appointed times ; and shall have liberty within themselves of performing all scholastic exercises for conferring such degrees, in such manner as shall be directed by the statutes, rules and ordinances of the said college. *And We do further Will,* Ordain and Appoint that no religious test or qualification shall be required of, or appointed for any persons admitted or matriculated as scholars within our said college ; or of or for persons admitted to any degree in any art or faculty therein, save only that all persons admitted within Our said college to any degree of Divinity, shall make such and the same declarations and subscriptions as are required of persons admitted to any degree of Divinity in our University of Edinburgh. *And for the better execution* of the purposes aforesaid, and for the more regular government of the said corporation, We do Declare and Grant that the said corporation and their successors shall forever have twenty-seven trustees, of whom twelve shall be ministers of the said Presbyterian Church of Canada, and fifteen shall be laymen in full communion with the said Church. And that the said several persons hereinbefore named and the Principal of the said college for the time being, shall be the first and present trustees of the said corporation, and shall respectively continue in such office until others shall be appointed in their stead, in pursuance of these Our Letters Patent. *And We further Will* that the said trustees, of the said corporation hereinbefore particularly named, shall continue in and hold the office of trustees until the several days in the manner hereinafter mentioned, that is to say, three ministers and four laymen whose names stand lowest in these Our Letters Patent, shall retire from the said board of trustees on the first day of the annual meeting of the said Synod in the year 1843, and their room be supplied by the addition of seven new members in manner hereinafter mentioned. Three other ministers and four other laymen whose names stand next to those in these Our Letters Patent, who shall have previously retired, shall retire from the said board of trustees on the first day of the annual meeting of the said Synod in the year 1844, and their room be supplied by the addition of seven new members in manner hereinafter mentioned. Three other ministers and four other laymen whose names stand next to those in these Our Letters Patent who shall have previously retired, shall retire from the said board of trustees on the first day of the annual meeting of the said Synod in the year 1845, and their room be supplied by the addition of seven new members in manner hereinafter mentioned; and the two remaining ministers and the three remaining laymen whose names stand next to those in these Our Letters Patent, who shall have previously retired, shall retire from the said board of trustees on the first day of the annual meeting of the said Synod in the year 1846, and their room be supplied by the addition of five new members in manner hereinafter mentioned. And on the first day of each succeeding annual meeting of the said Synod, three ministers and four laymen whose names stand lowest in the future roll of ministers and laymen composing the said board of trustees, shall retire from the same, excepting in every fourth year, when two ministers only, instead of three, and three laymen only, instead of four, shall so retire. And the new members of the board to be appointed from time to time in succession to those who retire, shall be appointed in manner following, that is to say: The three ministers or two ministers, as the case may be, shall be chosen by the said Synod on the first day of every annual meeting of the same, in such manner as shall seem best to the said Synod; and the four laymen or three laymen, as the case may be, shall be chosen also on the first day of every annual meeting of the said Synod, by the lay trustees remaining after the others shall have retired; and shall be so chosen from a list of persons made up in the following manner, that is to say: each congregation admitted on the roll of the said Synod, and in regular connexion therewith, shall, at a meeting to be specially called from the pulpit for that purpose in every third year, nominate one fit and discreet person, being a member in full communion with the said Church, as eligible to fill the office of trustee of the said college; and the persons' names so nominated being duly intimated by the several congregations to the secretary of the board of trustees in such form as the said board may direct, shall be enrolled by the said board, and constitute the list from which lay trustees shall be chosen to fill the vacancies occurring at the board during each year. And the names of members thus added to the board of trustees, shall be placed from time to time at the top of the roll of the board, the names of the ministers chosen as new trustees being first placed there in such order as the said Synod shall direct. And the names of the laymen chosen as new trustees being placed in such order as their electors shall direct, immediately after the names of the said ministers. *Provided always* that the retiring trustees may be re-elected as heretofore provided, if the Synod and remaining lay trustees respectively see fit to do so. *And Provided always*, that in case no election of new trustees shall be made on the first day of the annual meeting of the said Synod, then in such case the said retiring members shall remain in office until their successors are appointed at some subsequent period. *And Provided always* that every trustee, whether minister or layman, before entering on his duties as a member of the said board, shall have solemnly declared his belief of the doctrines of the Westminster Confession of Faith, and his adherence to the standards of the said Church in government, discipline and worship; and subscribed such a formula to this effect as may be prescribed by the said Synod; and that such declaration and subscription shall in every case be recorded in the books of the said board. *And We further Will* that the said trustees and their successors shall forever have full power and authority to elect and appoint for the said college a Principal, who shall be a minister of the Church of Scotland, or of the Presbyterian Church of Canada in connexion with the Church of Scotland; and such professor or professors, master or masters, tutor or tutors, and such other officer or officers as to the said trustees shall seem meet, save and except only, that the first Principal of the said college, who is also to be professor of Divinity, and likewise the first professor of Morals in the said college, shall be nominated by the committee of the General Assembly of the Church of Scotland. *Provided always* that such person or persons as may be appointed to the office of Principal or to any professorship or other office in the Theological department in the said college shall, before discharging any of the duties, or receiving any of the emoluments of such office or professorship, solemnly declare his belief of the doctrines of the Westminster Confession of Faith, and his adherence to the standards of the Church of Scotland, in government, discipline and worship, and subscribe such a formula to this effect as may be prescribed by the Synod of the Presbyterian Church of Canada, in connection with the Church of Scotland, and that such declaration and subscription be recorded in the books of the board of trustees: *And provided always*, that such persons as shall be appointed to professorships, not in the Theological department in the said college, shall before discharging any of the duties, or receiving any of the emoluments of such professorships, subscribe such a formula, declarative of their belief of the doctrines of the aforesaid Confession of Faith as the Synod may prescribe. *And We Further Will*, that if any complaint respecting the conduct of the Principal, or any professor, master, tutor, or other officer of the said college, be at any time made to the board of trustees, they may institute an enquiry, and in the event of any impropriety of conduct being duly proved, they shall admonish, reprove, suspend, or remove the person offending, as to them may seem good. (*a*) *Provided always*, that the grounds of such admonition, reproof, suspension or removal be recorded at length in the books of the said board. *And We further Will*, that the said trustees and their successors shall have full power and authority to erect an edifice or edifices for the use of the said college. *Provided always*, that such edifice or edifices shall not be more than three miles distant from St. Andrew's Church in the town of Kingston in the Province of Upper Canada. *And We further Will* that the said trustees and their successors shall have power and authority to frame and make statutes, rules and ordinances touching and concerning the good government of the said college, the performance of Divine service therein, the studies, lectures, exercises, and all matters regarding the same; the number, residence and duties of the professors thereof, the management of the revenues and property of the said college, the salaries, stipends, provision and emoluments of, and for the professors, officers and servants thereof, the number and duties of such officers and servants, and also touching and concerning any other matter or thing which to them shall seem necessary for the well being and advancement of the said college, and also from time to time by any new statutes, rules or ordinances, to revoke, renew, aug-

---

(*a*) In a suit brought against the trustees by a professor who had been removed from his office, the Court of Chancery held that the professorships were offices of freehold, held *ad vitam aut culpam*; that the trustees could not at their discretion, without inquiry, remove a professor, and that the Court would by injunction prevent the trustees from improperly interfering with professors. But on appeal the decision was reversed, the Court of Appeal holding that there was no jurisdiction in equity to interfere for the restoration of the complainant, and that, under the charter, a sufficient number of trustees might remove in their discretion. *Weir v. Matheson*, 11 Grant 383; 3 Error & Appeal Reports 123.

ment or alter, all, every or any of the said statutes, rules and ordinances as to them shall seem meet and expedient : *Provided always* that the said statutes, rules and ordinances, or any of them, shall not be repugnant to these presents or to the laws and statutes of the said Province. *Provided also,* that the said statutes, rules and ordinances, in so far as they regard the performance of Divine service in the said college, the duties of the professors in the Theological department thereof, and the studies and exercises of the students of Divinity therein, shall be subject to the inspection of the said Synod of the Presbyterian Church, and shall forthwith be transmitted to the clerk of the said Synod and be by him laid before the same at their next meeting for their approval; and until such approval duly authenticated by the signatures of the moderator and clerk of the said Synod is obtained, the same shall not be in force. *And We further Will,* that so soon as there shall be a Principal and one professor in the said college, the board of trustees shall have authority to constitute under their seal the said Principal and professor together with three members of the board of trustees, a court to be called "The College Senate," for the exercise of academical superintendence and discipline over the students, and all other persons resident within the same, and with such powers for maintaining order and enforcing obedience to the statutes, rules, and ordinances of the said college, as to the said board may seem meet and necessary :—*Provided always,* that so soon as three additional professors shall be employed in the said college, no trustee shall be a member of the said college senate, but that such Principal and all the professors of the said college shall for ever constitute the college senate, with the powers just mentioned. *And We further Will,* that whenever there shall be a Principal and four professors employed in the said college, the college senate shall have power and authority to confer the degrees of Bachelor, Master, and Doctor, in the several arts and faculties. *And We further Will,* that five of the said trustees, lawfully convened as hereinafter directed, shall be a quorum for the dispatch of all business, except for the disposal and purchase of real estate, or for the choice or removal of the Principal or professors, for any of which purposes there shall be a meeting of at least thirteen trustees. *And We further Will*, that the said trustees shall have full power and authority, from time to time to choose a secretary and treasurer; and also once in each year or oftener, a chairman who shall preside at all meetings of the board. *And We further Will*, that the said trustees shall also have power by a majority of voices of the members present, to select and appoint in the event of a vacancy in the board by death, resignation or removal from the Province, a person whose name is on the list from which appointments are to be made to fill such vacancy, choosing a minister in the room of a minister and a layman in the room of a layman, and inserting the name of the person so chosen in that place on the roll of the board in which the name of the trustee in whose stead he may have been chosen stood; so that the persons so chosen may be as to continuance in office and in all other respects as the persons would have been by whose death, resignation or removal the vacancy was occasioned. *And We further Will*, that the first general meeting of the said trustees shall be held at Kingston, upon such a day within six calendar months after the date of these our Letters Patent, as shall be fixed for that purpose by the trustee first named in these presents, who shall be then living; of which meeting thirty days' notice at least shall be given by notification in writing to each of the trustees for the time being, who shall be resident at the time within the Provinces of Upper and Lower Canada; and the same shall also be notified at the same time by advertisement in one or more of the public newspapers of the said Provinces. *And* the said trustees shall also afterwards have power to meet at Kingston aforesaid, or at such other place as they shall fix for that purpose upon their own adjournment, and likewise so often as they shall be summoned by the chairman, or in his absence by the senior trustee, whose seniority shall be determined in the first instance by the order in which the said trustees are named in these presents, and afterwards by the order in which they shall be subsequently arranged pursuant to the powers hereinbefore contained. *Provided always*, that the chairman or senior trustee shall not summon a meeting of the trustees unless required so to do by a notice in writing from three members of the board : *And provided also*, that he cause notice of the time and place of said meeting to be given in one or more of the public newspapers of the Provinces of Upper and Lower Canada, at least thirty days before such meeting; and that every member of the board of trustees resident within the said Provinces shall be notified in writing by the secretary to the corporation of the time and place of such meeting. *And We Will*, and by these presents for Us, Our Heirs and Successors do Grant and declare that these Our Letters Patent or the enrolment or exemplification thereof shall and may be good, firm and valid, sufficient and effectual in the law, according to the true intent and meaning of the same, and shall be taken, construed and adjudged in the most favorable and beneficial sense for the best advantage of Our said college, as well in Our courts of record as elsewhere ; and by all and singular judges, justices, officers, ministers and others, subject whatsoever of Us, Our Heirs and Successors, any unrecital, non-recital, omission, imperfection, defect, matter, cause, or anything whatsoever, to the contrary thereof in any wise notwithstanding. In witness whereof, we have caused these Our Letters to be made patent. Witness Ourself, at Our Palace at Westminster, this Sixteenth day of October, in the Fifth year of our Reign.

By Writ of Privy Seal.—Edmunds.

38 Vict. cap. 76 (O.) An Act respecting Queen's College at Kingston. (*Assented to 21st Dec., 1874.*)

> This Act was got from the Legislature of Ontario before the union in 1875, but doubts having arisen as to its validity in consequence of the decision of the Judicial Committee of the Privy Council in *Dobie* v. *Temporalities Board*, 7 Appeal Cases 136, a further Act was got from the Dominion Parliament. The provisions of that Act being the same as those of the Ontario Act the latter is not printed here, except sections 9 and 10, and they are given because the Dominion Act without repeating them *in extenso*, declares the University Council of Queen's College to be duly constituted "according to the terms and provisions of and with the powers conferred by the said Act," and further provides that the Council "may be continued in the manner and exercise all powers and functions mentioned and set forth" in that Act.

9. There shall be in connection with the said Queen's College a council which shall be called the University Council of Queen's College, and the said council shall, as to membership, consist of all the trustees of the said college, for the time being, and their successors, and of all the members of the college senate, for the time being, and their successors, and of as many graduates or alumni as shall be equal in number to these aforesaid members taken together; and the members of the council other than the trustees and members of the college senate, shall be appointed, in the first instance by the trustees and members of the college senate, at a meeting thereof to be convened by the chairman of the board of trustees causing a written or a printed notice to be mailed to each of them at least fifteen days before the meeting, and within one year after this Act shall come into force; but the successors of the graduates and alumni so appointed shall be elective members of the council, and shall be elected in the manner following, that is to say :—Within one year after the holding of the aforesaid meeting and appointing of the aforesaid members, the chairman of the board of trustees shall convene a meeting of the council constituted in the manner aforesaid by causing a written or printed notice to be mailed to each member at least fifteen days before the meeting, and at

the said meeting, or any meeting adjourned therefrom, or held subsequent thereto, the members present, provided their number be not less than fifteen, shall have power and authority to frame and pass by-laws for the following purposes, that is to say:—(1.) For the obtaining of a registration of such graduates and alumni of Queen's College as may desire to vote for elective members of the council and for a Chancellor of the University of Queen's College as hereinafter provided, and to be considered eligible for election to membership in the council, and such registration shall be a condition of any graduate or alumnus voting or being elected; provided always that the council shall not admit to such registration any alumnus actually attending classes in Queen's College, or any alumnus who may have left Queen's College without being a matriculant of two years' standing, or any graduate who has not matriculated at least once as an alumnus or student of Queen's College, or any alumnus who shall matriculate after the year 1879, until such alumnus shall become a graduate of said college. (2.) For the retiring annually of a certain number, not being less than five nor more than eight of the elective members, and for the election of their successors by graduates and alumni duly registered as hereinbefore provided, and also for the election of persons to fill vacancies that may occur from time to time by death, resignation, or otherwise. (3.) For the appointment and removal of a secretary and such other officers as the council may deem necessary or expedient. (4.) For the election of a Chancellor, who shall be chosen without respect to his ecclesiastical connection except that he must be a Protestant, who shall be designated the Chancellor of Queen's University, who shall be the highest officer of the university and college, who, as such highest officer, shall preside at all meetings of convocation and of the university council, and all statutory meetings of the college senate at which he may be present, who shall have both a deliberative and a casting vote on all motions submitted to any such meetings, and who shall hold office for three years from the date of his election and longer if need be, until his successor be chosen; provided always that if two or more candidates for the office of Chancellor be at any time nominated at the meeting of the council called for the nomination of a Chancellor, the election of one of the candidates shall be referred to the graduates and alumni registered as aforesaid, and shall be decided by a majority of their votes taken according to such by-laws as may be framed and passed by the council.

10. The university council, constituted in the manner hereinbefore provided, shall have and may exercise the powers following, that is to say:—(1) The power of discussing any matter whatsoever relating to the said college, and of declaring the opinion of the council on such matter; (2) The power of taking into consideration all questions affecting the well-being and prosperity of the said college, and of making representations from time to time on such questions to the board of trustees and the college senate, or either of the said bodies, who shall consider the same and return to the council their conclusions thereon; (3) The power of deciding upon such terms as the board of trustees shall propose in writing as to the affiliation of any college or school with the University of Queen's College aforesaid; (4) The power of determining all matters pertaining to the calling of meetings of the council and of convocation, whether the same be annual, adjourned, or special meetings, of fixing the number of members that shall be a quorum for the despatch of business at all such meetings, or any or either of them, and of deciding upon and regulating the mode of conducting its own proceeding and the proceedings of convocation; (5) The power of framing a declaration of fidelity to his office on the part of the Chancellor, and of determining what shall be the form of his assent thereto, and also of appointing the ceremonies to be observed at his installation and the manner of their observance; (6) The power of requiring fees to be paid by members of the council as a condition of member-

ship, and by graduates and alumni as a condition of registration or voting as hereinbefore provided; and (7) The power of framing and passing by-laws touching and concerning all matters whatsoever appertaining to the powers and functions of the council and the lawful exercise thereof, and also from time to time by new by-laws to revoke, renew, augment, or alter any of the said by-laws as to the council shall seem meet and expedient; provided always that any such by-laws shall not be repugnant to the provisions of the Letters Patent aforesaid, or of this Act, or of the laws of the Province of Ontario or of the Dominion of Canada; provided always that except as in this Act expressly provided the council shall not be entitled to interfere in or have any control over the affairs of the university or college.

45 VICT. CAP. 123 (D)—An Act respecting Queen's College at Kingston. (*Assented to 17th May, 1882*).

Whereas Queen's College at Kingston, in the Province of Ontario, was incorporated and founded under and by virtue of Royal Letters Patent, bearing date the 16th day of October, in the Fifth year of Her Majesty's reign; and whereas by the said letters patent, the ministers and members in full communion of the Presbyterian Church of Canada in connection with the Church of Scotland, constitute and compose the said corporation, and provision is made for the appointment from time to time by the said corporation, of trustees for the government of its affairs in the manner directed by the said letters patent; and whereas the said corporation have represented that the said the Presbyterian Church of Canada in connection with the Church of Scotland has become united with certain other Presbyterian Churches, to wit: "The Canada Presbyterian Church," "The Church of the Maritime Provinces in connection with the Church of Scotland," and "The Presbyterian Church of the Lower Provinces," and the said Churches now form one united Church under the name of "The Presbyterian Church in Canada;" and whereas it is desirable and the said corporation has, by petition, prayed that an Act be passed to enable the said College to stand towards the said "The Presbyterian Church in Canada" in relations similar to those which it lately held to the Presbyterian Church of Canada in connection with the Church of Scotland, and to provide for the mode of appointment of trustees of the said corporation, and to enable the said trustees and their successors to continue the administration of its affairs, and to enable the said College to continue its functions on terms and conditions like to those which have heretofore existed; and whereas an Act was passed by the Legislature of the Province of Ontario in the 38th year of Her Majesty's reign, and chaptered 76, entitled "An Act respecting Queen's College at Kingston," for the purposes above recited; and whereas doubts have arisen regarding the validity of the said Act, and it is desirable to confirm all things which have been properly done, relying upon the validity thereof; and whereas under and by virtue of the said Act there was constituted in the said College a council called the "University Council," consisting of all the trustees of the said college, and all the members of the college senate for the time being and their successors, and of as many graduates or alumni as should be equal in number to the number of the aforesaid members, to be chosen as provided by the said Act; and whereas certain powers were, by the said Act, conferred upon the said council, and it is desirable to confirm all acts and proceedings of and connected with the said council, done and taken under the said Act, and to confirm the constitution and the powers of the said council as set forth and provided by the said Act: Therefore Her Majesty, &c., enacts as follows:—

1. At and by virtue of the union of the said Churches on the 15th day of June, 1875, the ministers and members in full communion of the said united Church called

the Presbyterian Church in Canada, became and thenceforth continued to be and now are the only corporators of the said corporation called "Queen's College at Kingston," and from and after the said 15th day of June, 1875, all the provisions of the said Letters Patent which theretofore applied to the Church of Scotland, or to the Presbyterian Church of Canada in connection with the Church of Scotland, became and are and shall be applicable thereto in the same sense, for the same purposes, and to the same extent as they were applicable to the said Church of Scotland, or the said Presbyterian Church of Canada in connection with the Church of Scotland : and all the powers, rights and privileges formerly exercised and enjoyed by the ministers and members of the Presbyterian Church of Canada in connection with the Church of Scotland, as corporators of the said college, and by the Synod of the said Presbyterian Church of Canada in connection with the Church of Scotland, in virtue of their relations respectively to Queen's College at Kingston, shall be exercised and enjoyed by the ministers and members of the Presbyterian Church in Canada, and by the General Assembly or other Supreme Court of the said Presbyterian Church in Canada, respectively, except as hereinafter provided.

2. The number of trustees, both ministers and laymen, who by the said Letters Patent are required to retire annually on the first day of the annual meeting of the Synod of the Presbyterian Church of Canada in connection with the Church of Scotland, shall retire annually on a day which the trustees shall have power from time to time to appoint for the purpose, and on the same day the board of trustees, duly convened and met, shall elect successors to the members so retiring, whether such members be ministers or laymen.

3. When, at any time after this Act shall come into force, the chairman of the board of trustees, or, in his absence, the senior trustee, shall receive a notice in writing from three members of the board, requesting him to

summon a meeting of the trustees, such meeting shall be legally convened by the chairman or such senior trustee causing the secretary to the board to notify every member of the board of the time, place and purpose of such meeting, and by the secretary mailing notices of the meeting at least fifteen days before it shall take place.

4. The board of trustees may appoint a Vice-Principal of the said college, and such Vice-Principal shall, in the absence of the Principal, take the place and discharge the duties of the Principal.

5. The chairman of the board of trustees shall have the right to vote the same as other members of the board on all motions submitted to any meeting of the trustees; and in case of an equality of votes upon any motion, he shall also be entitled to a second casting vote.

6. The power hitherto vested in the corporation of Queen's College, at Kingston, to take, purchase, acquire, have, hold, enjoy, receive, possess and maintain in law, to and for the use of the said college, any messuages, lands, tenements and hereditaments, goods, chattels, moneys, stocks, charitable or other contributions, gifts, benefactions or bequests whatsoever, shall be continued in and enjoyed by the said corporation.

7. The college senate shall have power to pass by-laws touching any matter or thing pertaining to the conditions on which degrees in the several arts and faculties may be conferred, whether the said degrees be such as are gained in course, or such as are honorary, or whether they be conferred on matriculants of Queen's College or other persons; but any such by-law shall be reported to the first meeting of the board of trustees after being passed, and shall cease to be in force if disapproved of by the board.

8. The trustees, lecturers, tutors, fellows, graduates, and alumni or students being undergraduates of the said college, shall have power and authority to meet in con-

vocation for the public conferring of degrees and other honours and distinctions awarded or granted by the college senate, for the installation of the Chancellor hereinafter mentioned, the Principal, or any professor duly elected or appointed according to the provisions of the aforesaid Letters Patent, and for such other purposes as the University Council, constituted as hereinafter provided, shall, from time to time, determine.

9. The University Council of Queen's College, constituted under and by virtue of the said Act of the Legislature of the Province of Ontario, intituled "An Act respecting Queen's College, at Kingston," is hereby declared to be duly constituted according to the terms and provisions of and with the powers conferred by the said Act; and all acts and proceedings of the said council, taken under and by virtue of the said Act, are hereby confirmed and declared to be valid; and the said council may be continued in the manner, and may exercise all the powers and functions mentioned and set forth in the said Act of the Province of Ontario.

10. All provisions whatsoever contained in the aforesaid Letters Patent, except so far as any of them are modified or changed by the provisions of this Act, shall continue in force in like manner as if this Act had not been passed.

11. The Principal shall be Vice-Chancellor of the University, and in the absence of the Chancellor shall take his place and discharge his duties.

12. All acts and proceedings done and taken by "Queen's College, at Kingston," their board of trustees, senate, professors and other officers, agents and servants under and by virtue of the said Act of the Legislature of the Province of Ontario, intituled "An Act respecting Queen's College, at Kingston," are hereby confirmed and declared to be valid.

52 Vict. cap. 103 (D) An Act to amend the Act respecting Queen's College, at Kingston. (*Assented to 16th April, 1889.*)

Whereas Queen's College, at Kingston, has petitioned for an Act to amend the Act passed in the 45th year of Her Majesty's reign, chapter 123, so as to empower the University Council of the said University to elect a limited number of trustees of the University, and to provide for the prescribing of the religious test which shall be administered to trustees and professors, and to empower the said corporation to take, hold and sell real estate and other property in any part of Canada; and has further prayed for additional powers and privileges, with the view of increasing the efficiency and of extending the usefulness of the said University, and it is expedient to grant the prayer of its petition : Therefore Her Majesty, enacts as follows :—

1. Besides the trustees for whose election provision is made by the Royal Charter and by the Act cited in the preamble of this Act, other and additional trustees may be elected as hereinafter provided, who shall have the same powers, functions, rights and privileges as the trustees elected in terms of the charter and of the said Act.

2. The University Council of the said college may elect and appoint annually a member of the said council to be a trustee of the said college, and every trustee so appointed shall hold office for five years and no longer, unless re-elected.

3. It shall not be necessary that any trustee elected by the University Council be a member of the Presbyterian Church in Canada, or that any trustee of the said college hereafter elected make or subscribe any religious declaration or formula whatever before entering upon his duty as such trustee.

4. In case any trustee elected by the University Council shall die or resign his office of trustee, or cease

to be a member of the council, the council may at once elect some other member of the council to be trustee in the place and for the unexpired term of the trustee so dying, resigning, or ceasing to be a member of the council.

5. Any such trustee, if otherwise qualified, may be re-elected whenever and as often as his term of office expires.

6. All professors, other than those in the Theological faculty of the said college, shall subscribe only such formula, declaratory of their religious belief, as the Board of Trustees from time to time prescribe.

7. The said corporation may acquire, take, receive and hold real or personal estate in any part of Canada, by purchase, gift, devise or otherwise; subject, however, to the laws of any Province in which any real estate so acquired is situated, as to such acquisition and tenure by corporations.

8. The said corporation may, from time to time, on any terms it thinks fit, sell, alienate, exchange, demise, let or lease all or any such messuages, lands, tenements, hereditaments and immovable or leasehold property of or to which it is now or may hereafter be or become seized and possessed or entitled.

9. The said corporation may, for the purpose of investment lend money upon the security of real estate, purchase bonds or debentures of municipal or school or railway corporations, or Dominion or Provincial stock or securities, and may sell or dispose of any such securities, as to it seems advisable.

STATUTES, RULES AND ORDINANCES OF QUEEN'S UNIVERSITY AND COLLEGE.

(*Passed 26th Jan., 1863; amended 8th June, 1867, and 26th Oct., 1875.*)

Whereas the charter of the University of "Queen's College at Kingston" empowers the trustees of the said college to frame and make statutes, rules and ordinances, touching and concerning the good government of the said college; the performance of divine service therein, the studies, lectures, and exercises, and all matters regarding the same; the number, residence, and duties of the professors thereof; the management of the revenues and property of the said college; the salaries, stipends, provision and emoluments of and for the professors, officers and servants thereof; the number and duties of such officers and servants; and also touching and concerning any other matter or thing which to them shall seem necessary to the well being and advancement of the said college.

And whereas it is necessary and expedient to make such statutes, rules, and ordinances;

Therefore, at a meeting of the trustees of the said college, duly convened and holden held at Kingston, on the 26th day of January, 1893, whereat there were present the Hon. John Hamilton, chairman; the Rev. Principal Leitch, the Rev. Dr. Williamson, the Rev. Dr. Urquhart, the Rev. Duncan Morrison, Alexander McLean, Hugh Allan, Alexander Morris, M. P. P., John Paton, and Andrew Drummond, esquires, the said trustees, by virtue of the power and authority as aforesaid vested in them, do enact, frame, and make the following statutes, rules, and ordinances for the good government of the said college :—

Designation.

1. The designation of the University shall be 'QUEEN'S UNIVERSITY"—the legal designation of the college being "Queen's College at Kingston."

Rules for Meetings of the Board of Trustees, the College Senate, and all Other College Boards.

2. The order of business shall be—(1) Opening of the meeting with prayer by the Principal when present; (2) reading, amending and sanctioning the minutes of last meeting; (3) business remaining over since last meeting; (4) reading of letters received since last meeting; (5) reading reports of committees.

3. The chairman shall speak to and decide on all questions of order.

4. No member shall be entitled to speak except to a motion committed to writing.

5. No member shall be entitled to speak more than once to a motion except in the way of explanation. The introducer of the motion shall be entitled to reply.

6. Any member may require the yeas and nays to be recorded, but no one shall be entitled to have his dissent or grounds of dissent recorded.

7. The chairman shall have a casting and also a deliberative vote.

8. A member shall not be entitled to withdraw a motion except with the consent of the seconder and the meeting.

9. Amendment to a motion shall be put to the vote before the motion itself, and the voting shall be in the reverse order in which they have been moved.

Board of Trustees.

10. All officers shall be appointed, shall have their duties prescribed by, and shall hold office only during the pleasure of the trustees, except in cases where a special agreement may have been or may be made; and shall be entitled to such salaries or emoluments as may be from time to time agreed on.

11. All donations, grants and bequests to the observatory, museum, library, foundation of scholarships, particular faculties, or other college purposes, shall be administered by the board of trustees.

12. The trustees shall have the exclusive power of exercising discipline over the officers of the college.

13. When a complaint is made respecting the conduct of any officer, the complainant shall be required to act as prosecutor, and, in the event of any impropriety being duly proved, the grounds of the sentence shall be recorded at length in the books of the board of trustees. When the board has resolved to institute an inquiry, a summons, in the following form, shall be served on the accused :—

To A. B.,—---- of ------ ------, in the City of Kingston (Principal, Professor, or Janitor, &c.) in Queen's College at Kingston :

Whereas a complaint hath been duly entered in writing against you as such officer before the board of trustees of the said college, of which a true copy is hereunto annexed ; and whereas the said board hath resolved that the matter contained in the said complaint shall be further inquired into and adjudicated upon : You are therefore hereby required to file in the office of the secretary of the said board at the said college, within ten days after the service hereof, your answer to the matters in the said complaint contained ; and you are hereby notified and required to be and appear in your proper person before the said board, at a meeting to be held at the same college, on

———, the ——— day of ——— next, in order to your defence in the said matter of complaint.

In witness whereof the seal of the said college is hereto affixed.

(Signed) ————————,
Chairman Board of Trustees.

(Signed) ————————,
Secretary Board of Trustees.

14. The trustees may, on their own motion, and without any complaint being made, deal with the Principal, professors, janitor, or any other officer, when they see cause. In such case it shall not be necessary that the grounds of censure, suspension, or removal, be recorded —the recording of the grounds being warranted only in the case of a judicial process in which a complainant acts as prosecutor. An officer on being removed shall be entitled to claim salary up to the date of removal.

15. The board of trustees shall be a court of review and appeal with respect to the decisions of the college senate, and all other college boards.

16. The board of trustees shall annually print a report of the state and progress of the college, with such synopsis of their proceedings as to them may seem desirable, and an account of revenue and expenditure, copies of which report shall be distributed among the members of the board, and of the Synod of the Presbyterian Church of Canada in connection with the Church of Scotland at their annual meeting.

17. The board of trustees shall annually publish a calendar, copies of which shall be distributed, along with the annual report, among the trustees and the members of the Synod at their annual meeting.

18. The books and subjects prescribed by the Synod of the Presbyterian Church of Canada in connection with the Church of Scotland for candidates for license shall form part of the course of instruction in the respective classes, and the above books and subjects in the arts department shall be prescribed to candidates for degrees.

19. A regular meeting of the board of trustees shall be held on the last day of the session, when all suggestions for a change in the calendar made by the college senate or any of the college boards or officers shall be considered and decided upon. Grants for prizes, library books, and for other college purposes, shall be made at this meeting. The salaries of officers shall also be fixed or modified.

The Principal.

20. He shall have the ordinary superintendence of the internal affairs of the college, under such regulations as the board of trustees may prescribe.

21. He shall, as chief executive officer, see that the laws of the college are carried out and observed by officers and students, and he shall employ such discretionary measures as may be necessary to secure this end without judicial procedure; but should it be necessary at any time to enforce the laws or exercise discipline, the case shall be laid before the board of trustees, when relating to the officers of the college, and before the college senate when relating to the students.

22. He shall from time to time inspect the classes, museum, library, minute books, matriculation books, and class roll books, and offer such suggestions to the officers as he may deem expedient; and should any department require the special attention of the trustees, he shall report accordingly.

23. He shall, *ex officio*, preside at the college senate, and in the several faculty boards.

24. He shall preside at all examinations for degrees, and see that all examination papers are regularly set and valued.

25. He shall sign all diplomas for degrees, certificates of honours awarded by the college senate, and inspect all certificates of candidates for degrees, and report to the senate as to whether the requirements of the university have been complied with.

26. He shall sign all minutes of meetings of college senate; and should any meeting be held in his absence, the decision of the meeting shall not be valid till the minutes have received his signature or approval.

27. He shall sign all orders for necessary incidental expenses not authorized by the board of trustees, and shall superintend all entries in the college register.

28. He shall either personally, or by substitute appointed by him, deliver an address to the students at the opening of the college session, and on each occasion when degrees are conferred in convocation.

29. He shall see that proper arrangements are made for the conducting of divine service in the college on Sabbath.

30. He shall report to the meeting of trustees, to be held on the last day of the session, any changes in the calendar suggested by the senate, college boards or officers.

Professors.

31. They shall perform the duties of their office under such regulations as the board of trustees may from time to time prescribe, and shall not engage in any vocation which the trustees shall deem inconsistent with their office.

32. The roll shall be regularly called in each class, so that the attendance of each student may be accurately ascertained.

33. Each professor shall, at the close of the session, grant certificates of attendance, progress and attainments. No student however, shall be entitled to such certificate who has not paid the class fees unless he has been exempted from payment thereof.

34. They shall have regular *viva voce* and written examinations in the class.

35. The professors of the arts and theological faculties shall examine, when required, candidates for all scholarships founded by or tenable in Queen's College. They shall also visit and examine the county grammar school, which has been affiliated to the college, when required so to do.

36. When any professor cannot attend his class or other duty, he shall notify this to the Principal. In all such cases the Principal, on the fact coming to his knowledge, shall either officiate himself or take such steps as may be necessary to secure a temporary substitute.

37. Each professor, in the exercise of discipline in his class, shall have the power to admonish and fine—the fine in any one case not to exceed one dollar. Fines may be inflicted for lateness, absence, attending without cap and gown, and similar offences. In the case of graver offences, the professor shall bring the matter before the college senate. The fines shall be appropriated to the library.

38. No professor shall in his class, or in the discharge of any part of his duties, make any statement or do anything derogatory to religion or morals, injurious to his fellow professors, or disrespectful to the college authorities.

39. All professors, before they are publicly inducted to their office, shall answer affirmatively the following questions :—

(1.) Do you promise to observe the statutes, rules and ordinances of this university, and to submit to its constituted authorities ? (2.) Do you promise that you will follow no divisive courses from the present government and discipline of this university ? (3.) Do you promise that in the performance of the duties of your chair you will neither make any statement nor teach any doctrine derogatory to christian faith and morals? 4. Do you promise that, in the discharge of your duties as professor of———, you will invariably seek to promote the interests of the students under your charge, the welfare of this institution, and the glory of God?

Secretaries.

40. Secretaries shall, when requested by the party entitled to call meetings, send written notices of the meetings, specifying the business to be transacted.

41. They shall conduct the correspondence of the boards under the superintendence of the chairman, take minutes, and file all the papers in the order in which they have been read, with proper endorsements, keep them in order, and retain copies of all letters sent.

42. The matriculation books and the minute books of the college senate and of the several faculties shall be laid by the secretaries upon the table of the board of trustees at the meeting on the last day of the session, and the trustees shall appoint a committee to examine and report as to the manner in which they have been kept.

Deans.

43. The deans of faculties shall call meetings and preside in the absence of the Principal, and shall present students for graduation at meetings of convocation. The offices of dean and secretary may be combined.

Treasurer.

44. It shall be the duty of the treasurer to keep accurate books of account in such form as from time to time shall be ordered by the trustees, of all revenues, receipts, and expenditure of the university, with all requisite vouchers; to collect and receive all moneys and revenues of the university, from whatever source derivable, and forthwith to lodge the same to the credit of the college in such chartered bank as may be designated by the trustees; to submit at the general meeting of the trustees, held on the last day of the session, a minute of such collections and deposits, together with a statement of all moneys due to the university and not paid, and of all outstanding claims against the university; to pay all such claims, when ordered by the committee of finance or by the trustees, by his cheque, countersigned always by at least one trustee being of the committee of finance in the time being; to submit a full statement of his accounts to the trustees at each regular meeting of the trustees, held on the last day of the session, exhibiting in detail all revenues, receipts and disbursements of the university, as also to the trustees at such time as they shall specially direct, and generally to obey and carry out all

instructions of the finance committee and trustees. He shall enter into bonds, with security to the satisfaction of the trustees, in such sum, not less than $1000, as they may from time to time ordain, for the faithful accounting for all moneys collected or received by him, and the correct performance of his duty generally.

Finance and Estate Committee.

45. A finance and estate committee of four trustees, of whom the treasurer and Principal shall be *ex-officio* members, shall be appointed at the general meeting held on the last day of the session; they shall have power, and it shall be their duty, to inspect all lands, buildings, and other property of the university, and report promptly to the trustees all necessary repairs and expenditure thereon, and superintend, under their direction, the execution of such repairs as shall be ordered by the trustees; to take all necessary steps for the conservation thereof; to submit, at the meeting held on the last day of the session, a report exhibiting the state and condition of the real estate property of the college and its financial position; as also an estimate of the expenditure for the ensuing year, and the ways and means of meeting such expenditure; all accounts of necessary articles, of whatever nature, required by the faculties of arts and theology shall be paid by the treasurer of the college, but not until the ordering of the same shall have first been sanctioned by the committee, or the payment of the same shall have been expressly ordered by the committee; the finance committee shall have the right of inspection and audit of the books of any faculty, whose funds are managed by such faculty and do not fall into the general revenues of the college; and the said committee shall, subject to the supervision of the board of trustees, have the general care and conduct of all matters concerning the revenues, finances and expenditure of the college, except as may be otherwise herein provided, and shall have power from time to time, to make and alter investments, but the committee shall take the first opportunity of reporting to a meeting of the board all acts done by them in the exercise of this power. The elected members of the committee shall be appointed at the present meeting, and shall hold office until the last day of the session, and shall be eligible for re-election.

Registrar.

46. He shall keep the college register, and the secretaries of the several faculties shall annually supply him with lists of matriculated students, and with such particulars regarding them as the entries may require.

47. The registrar shall act as secretary of all college boards to which the trustees have not appointed secretaries: All diplomas shall be prepared and registered by him before they are issued.

48. He shall, under the superintendence of the Principal, conduct the general correspondence not devolving on the several secretaries.

49. He shall keep lists of all instruments, apparatus, class furniture, and other college property, and he shall annually give in to the trustees a report on the state of such instruments, &c., and for this purpose secretaries and professors shall furnish him with the requisite lists; The report to be given in on the last day of the session.

50. The registrar shall, under the direction of the Principal, give notice in the newspapers of the opening of the session, and the notices shall be inserted a month at least before the opening.

51. All accounts of college expenditure shall be examined by the registrar before being paid to the treasurer. All incidental expenses of the various classes shall be ordered through the registrar, and he shall present the accounts to the finance committee.

Students.

52. Every student shall, before matriculation, produce a certificate of character from his minister, or some respectable party competent to grant such certificate.

53. Every student at the time of his matriculation shall subscribe the following declaration: I, ————, being now admitted a student of Queen's College, do hereby sincerely and solemnly declare and promise that I shall at all times render due respect and obedience to the Principal, professors, and other authorities of the university, and strictly observe the laws and statutes thereof; that I shall give a regular attendance at my classes, and shall apply myself carefully and diligently to the studies in which I am engaged, and perform to the utmost of my power the exercises prescribed; that I shall conduct myself in a courteous and peaceable manner towards my fellow students; and that I shall always maintain and defend the rights and privileges of the university, and never seek in any way or manner the hurt or prejudice thereof.

(To be signed) ————
Student.

54. Students shall attend morning prayers within the college. Exemptions in special cases may be granted by the Principal or senatus.

55. Students shall regularly attend divine service in the churches to which they belong.

56. Students receiving free education with a view to the ministry, or holding church scholarships or bursaries, shall sign an engagement to repay the money should they change their intention of applying for license as preachers of the Presbyterian Church of Canada in connection with the Church of Scotland.

57. Graduates and under-graduates in arts, when attending prayers, their several classes, or any college meeting, shall wear the academic costume prescribed by the college senate.

College Senate.

58. The college senate, constituted of all the professors of the college, a majority of members to be a quorum, shall exercise academic superintendence and dicipline over the students and others (not officers) resident therein, with the following powers for maintaining order and enforcing obedience to the statutes, rules, and ordinances of the college.

59. On any complaint being made regarding the conduct of any student, they shall, if they see fit, make inquiry, and if the charge be proved to their satisfaction, they shall record the sentence, and the grounds on which it has been passed, in their minutes.

60. Insubordination, immoral conduct, either in or out of college, gross neglect of study, refusal to perform the appointed exercises, breach of college regulations, injury to college property, and all offences of a similar kind, shall render a student liable to the infliction of a penalty proportionate to the offence. The penalties which the college senate may inflict shall be such as the following:—(1.) Fines not exceeding in any one case more than ten dollars. (2.) A note of disapprobation in the class certificate. (3.) Rustication for a definate period. (4.) Forfeiture of right to a degree. (5.) Degradation from the rank of graduate. (6.) Expulsion.

61. The senate shall appoint all examiners whether belonging to the teaching staff of the college or not.

62. The oral examinations for degrees shall be conducted in the presence of the college senate, and any member shall be entitled to put questions.

63. In each of the departments of examination, written questions shall be set, to which written answers shall be given in presence of the examiners.

64. No degrees shall be granted except at the regular meetings of the college senate appointed for that purpose.

65. The college senate shall, after hearing the reports of the examiners, decide on the claims of the candidates proposed for degrees, and the Principal shall, in name of the university, and in convocation, confer the degrees on the successful candidates.

66. The college senate shall have power from time to time to confer honorary degrees in the several faculties, except arts and medicine, for literary, scientific and professional distinction.

67. Meetings shall be called by order of the Principal ; or, in his absence, at the request of two members, by the secretary. Two days' notice shall be given, by circular, of all meetings of the college senate for the appointment of examiners and the granting of degrees. Meetings shall be held only during the college session.

68. In the absence of the Principal, the senior professor shall take the chair.

69. The following regular meetings shall be held annually : One on the second Friday of January, to elect a hospital governor and curators of library ; one on Tuesday before the last Thursday in March, to grant medical degrees ; and one on Tuesday before the last Thursday of April, to grant degrees in art and theology.

70. The senate shall award all scholarships by examination, subject only to the conditions of the founders, and the regulations of the board of trustees.

71. No student shall hold two scholarships, but a church student may have a scholarship supplemented out of the bursary fund.

72. The college senate may draw up by-laws, consistent with the statutes, rules, and ordinances of the university, which shall be submitted to the trustees for approval, modification, alteration, or rejection, and shall be subject to their revision at any time.

Faculty Boards.

73. The professors, lecturers and fellows of each faculty shall have power to meet as a separate board, and to administer the affairs of the faculty under such regulations as the board of trustees may prescribe.

74. Faculty boards shall be entitled to draw up by-laws consistent with the statutes, laws, and ordinances of the university, which shall be submitted to the board of trustees for approval, modification, alteration, or rejection, and shall be subject to the revision of the trustees at any time. The Principal shall be, *ex officio*, president and a member of all the faculty boards.

The Observatory.

75. The professor of mathematics shall be director.

76. In order to fulfil the conditions of the deed of conveyance, the director shall deliver four lectures annually in the observatory, and the Principal shall provide for two lectures in the city hall.

77. Its affairs shall be managed by a board consisting of the Principal, the director, and the secretary of the board of visitors.

78. It shall not be entitled to receive any sum from the ordinary revenue of the college, but all special grants, donations and bequests, shall be applied exclusively to its support.

79. All expenditure by the observatory board shall first be sanctioned by the board of trustees.

80. An observer shall be appointed as soon as the funds permit, who shall make regular observations, and fulfil the conditions of the deed by which the observatory was conveyed to the college.

81. The observatory board shall be entitled to draw up by-laws, to be approved by the board of trustees.

The Library.

82. The librarian shall be appointed by the trustees, and his duties shall be :—(1) To keep a list of all books given out and returned ; and no books shall be taken out of the library by any person without the knowledge of the librarian ; (2) To keep a list of all new books, entering them in the order in which they are received ; (3) To keep an alphabetical catalogue of all new books, each book being entered into its place in the catalogue as it is received ; (4) To keep a classed catalogue, each book being entered under the subject to which it belongs ; (5) To attend daily during the session to give out and receive books—the attendance during the recess being at least once a week ; (6) To recall all books at least twice a year; (7) To supply the *Presbyterian* newspaper from time to time with a list of books received as donations, with the donors' names, and to write to the donors, acknowledging the donation ; (8) To send in to the curators on the sixth day before the last day of the session, and on the tenth day after the opening of the Theological Hall, each year a return of the number of books added to the library, and of the number lost or missing, with the names of the parties to whom such books were delivered ; (9) To keep a list of the prices paid for the books ; (10) To observe any by-laws that may be drawn up by the curator and sanctioned by the trustees.

83. The library shall be managed by a board of curators, consisting of the Principal and a member appointed annually by the college senate from each of the faculties of theology and arts.

84. The board of curators shall order all purchases of books from the matriculation fees, and each faculty shall be entitled to books in that department amounting in value to the matriculation fees contributed by it to the library. The whole of the matriculation fees in the faculties of arts and theology shall be devoted to the purchase of books.

85. The curators shall furnish an annual report to the board of trustees and the college senate.

86. The curators shall draw up by-laws to be submitted to the board of trustees for approval.

87. The library shall be open to all students who have paid their matriculation fees, and to all professors, trustees and graduates, under such regulations as the curators may frame.

Museum.

88. The professor of natural history shall be the curator of the museum, and shall manage its affairs under such regulations as the board of trustees may prescribe.

89. The curator shall give in to the board of trustees an annual report of the state of the museum, and an account of the receipts and expenditure.

90. Such grants as may from time to time be voted for the purchase and preservation of specimens shall be applied by the curator under the direction of the board of trustees.

91. The curator shall draw up a classified catalogue of all the articles in the museum. The names of the donors shall be entered in the catalogue and affixed to the articles.

92. All donations shall be deposited in the museum immediately on their arrival, and shall be duly acknowledged by the curator, by writing to the donor and by inserting a notice in the *Presbyterian*.

93. The museum shall be open to students and the public under such regulations as may be prescribed.

94. The curator shall supply the professors with such specimens as they may require for the illustration of their lectures, and shall enter in a book kept for the purpose the times when such specimens are given out and returned.

Convocation.

95. The convocation shall consist of the board of trustees, the Principal, professors, lecturers, tutors, fellows and graduates of the university.

96. Meetings of convocation shall be held on the days fixed, for the public conferring of degrees, under the authority vested in the senate, and for the induction of professors to the chairs to which they have been appointed. Due notice of such meeting shall be given, by order of the Principal.

97. The Principal, or in his absence a member of senate elected by the senate for the purpose shall preside, and shall perform the ceremony of induction and laureation.

98. Four fellows shall be annually elected by the members of convocation, at their last meeting of the session, and after the degrees of the session have been conferred, viz.: one from the graduates of each of the four faculties of arts, theology, law, and medicine. The fellows shall hold office for one year and be entitled to sit in the boards of their respective faculties. The fellows shall rank with professors, in meetings of convocation. No student shall be eligible.

99. No change shall be made in the code of statutes, rules and ordinances, unless at a general meeting of trustees, called specially for the purpose, on a requisition to the chairman, in writing, of three trustees, and the notice calling such meeting shall state the time and place of such meeting and the nature of the changes proposed to be enacted. The changes that may be made in the calendar by the meeting of the board of trustees, on the last day of the session, must be consistent with the code of statutes, rules and ordinances.

Minutes 1878, p. 46. The Assembly sanction the institution of a preparatory department in connection with the theological work of the college. In doing so, the Assembly renew a former recommendation to the colleges to use all legitimate means to induce students to take the regular arts' course in some approved university.

Degree of Bachelor of Divinity.

1. Candidates for the degree of Bachelor of Divinity (B.D.) must be Graduates in Arts of this University, or of a University whose degrees are recognized by the senate.

2. The degree shall not be conferred until the candidate has completed the theological curriculum, with a view to the ministry in the church to which he belongs, and has passed a satisfactory examination in the branches of Theology taught in the University.

3. The subjects of examination shall be in two departments : The first embracing (1) Hebrew and Chaldee, (2) the Evidences of Religion, Biblical Introduction and the Inspiration of Scripture ; the second embracing—(1) Church History, (2) Biblical Criticism, (3) Systematic Theology. (*a*).

4. Candidates who have completed the theological course may be examined in either of these departments, and may defer their examination in the other department, provided there be not a greater interval than two years between their two examinations.

5. Students may be admitted to examination in the first department, at the end of the second session of their theological course.

6. A candidate may, subject to the preceding regulations, appear at any University examination in Theology, provided he gives two weeks' notice of his intention to the Registrar.

MINUTES OF BOARD OF TRUSTEES—27TH APRIL, 1892.

1. That there shall be and there is hereby established in the University of Queen's College a Faculty of Medicine, which shall be known as "The Medical Faculty of the University."

2. The Faculty shall consist of Professors, Lecturers and Demonstrators in medicine and of such members of the Staff in the Faculty of Arts, who shall be known as Associate Professors of both faculties, as shall be needed to give full instructions in the subjects that may from time to time be prescribed for the curriculum in medicine.

3. The Trustees shall appoint, from among the Professors of the Medical Faculty, a Dean. His duties shall be to preside, in the absence of the Principal, at all meetings of the Faculty ; to keep the records of the Faculty, or cause them to be duly kept by some other member of the Faculty ; to register the students in medicine and collect from them the registration fee ; and (under the Principal) to take general superintendence of the affairs of the Faculty.

4. The Teaching Staff, as defined in enactment No. 2, shall meet at the call of the Principal of the University or the Dean of the Faculty.

5. The Professors in the Medical Faculty, as in the other Faculties, shall be members of the University Council.

6. The Professors, Lecturers, Demonstrators, or other Instructors may be required to act as Examiners at University Examinations in medicine without additional remuneration.

7. All class fees shall be paid to the Registrar of the University.

(*a*) The particular subjects of examination, and information as to books to be consulted, will be found each year in the College Calendar.

8. The fees for the Classes of Associate Professors, or those who are appointed by the Board of Trustees directly and who devote their whole time to the work prescribed by the Trustees, shall form part of the regular income of the University.

9. Fees for all other Classes in the Medical Faculty shall be divided into two parts : One part, consisting of two-thirds of the amount, shall be used to pay the salaries of the Professors, according to a scale to be hereinafter determined, the other part, consisting of one-third, shall be used to pay the general expenses of the Medical Faculty, including the due maintenance of the building and appliances and necessary equipment.

10. As regards appointments to chairs in the Medical Faculty and changes and dismissals, the Board of Trustees shall act, on the recommendation of a joint committee, consisting on the one part of the Dean and four members elected by the Medical Faculty, and on the other part of five members of the University Council elected by the Council, and also of the Principal, who shall be chairman *ex officio*. The Faculty shall elect its members for four years, except in the first case when one shall be elected for four years, one for three years, one for two years and one for one year. Any member, on either part, on the expiry of his term of office, shall be eligible for re-election.

11. The Professors in the Medical Faculty shall hold office on the same terms as the Professors in the other Faculties of the University, but every Professor in the Medical Faculty hereafter appointed shall not hold office for a term longer than five years from the date of his appointment, but shall be eligible for re-appointment.

12. There shall be a committee, consisting of the Principal, the Dean and a member annually elected by the Faculty, who shall determine from time to time the sums that are needed for equipment and general expenses, and the Registrar shall pay these out of the portion of the fees referred to in enactment No. 9, on the written order of the Dean. To this committee all recommendations of the Faculty shall be referred by the Secretary.

13. The Registrar shall also hold the other fees referred to in enactment No. 9, and pay them on the written order of the Dean.

14. The faculty shall from time to time frame Regulations, as occasion may require, touching the details of the course of study and teaching and examinations, the admission of students, the amount and payment of fees and the discipline and internal government of the Faculty ; and shall duly enforce such Regulations, and may alter or repeal the same or any of them ; and shall hear and determine all

complaints as to the violation thereof. Provided always, that such Regulations, or such alteration or repeal thereof, be first approved by the Trustees, and that such Regulations shall be further subject to alteration or repeal by the Trustees.

15. The Faculty shall constitute an integral portion of the College Senate, for the purpose of receiving and deciding on the reports of the examiners in medicine and especially for determining on whom degrees in medicine shall be conferred, at a meeting of senate called for the purpose by the Registrar; and also for any other purpose affecting the study of medicine or the Medical Professors or Students.

(2.) KNOX COLLEGE.

22 Vict. cap. 69 (C).— An Act to incorporate Knox College.—(*Assented to 24th July, 1858.*)

Whereas a Theological Institution has been for some time, and is now, in operation in Toronto, in this Province, under the authority of the Synod of the Presbyterian Church of Canada ; and whereas, the property now held in trust for the said institution has been acquired or granted from persons who granted or conveyed the same for the purpose of creating an educational establishment, wherein the theological principles and doctrines of the Presbyterian Church of Canada should be taught, and the said Synod has petitioned the Legislature for an Act to incorporate the said Institution under the name of "Knox College," and whereas it is expedient to comply with the said petition : Therefore, Her Majesty, &c., enacts as follows :—

1. James Gibb, of Quebec ; Michael Willis, D.D., the Rev. William Reid, of Toronto, (*and others, naming them*), and all and every such other person or persons as now is or are or shall at any time hereafter be ministers of the Presbyterian Church of Canada, or members of the said Church in full communion therewith, shall henceforth be a body corporate under the name of "Knox College," and shall continue to be a body corporate, with perpetual succession, and a common seal,

with the powers vested in corporate bodies by the "Interpretation Act," and also with power under the said corporate name, and without license in mortmain, to hold all property, now held by the said institution, or by any one or more persons in trust for the benefit of the said institution, and to purchase, acquire, have, take, hold and enjoy, by gift, grant and conveyance, devise, bequest or otherwise, to them and their successors, any estate or property, real or personal, to and for the use of the said College, in trust for the promotion of theological learning and education of youth for the holy ministry, under the authority and according to the principles and standards of the Presbyterian Church of Canada aforesaid, and also with power to let, convey or otherwise dispose of such real or personal estate, from time to time, as may be deemed expedient, with the written consent of the Synod; provided always, that such real estate so held by the said College hereby incorporated, shall be such and such only as may be required for the purposes of college buildings and offices, residences for the professors, tutors, students and officers, with gardens or pleasure grounds pertaining thereto; provided also, that the said college may acquire any other real estate, or any interest therein, by gift, devise or bequest, if made at least six months before the death of the party making the same, and the college may hold such estate for a period of not more than three years, and the same or any part or portion thereof, or interest therein, which may not, within the said period, have been alienated and disposed of, shall revert to the party from whom the same was acquired, his heirs or other representatives; and provided also, that the proceeds of such property as shall have been disposed of during the said period, may be invested in the public securities of the Province, stocks of the chartered banks or other approved securities, for the use of the said college.

2. It shall be lawful for the Synod of the Presbyterian Church of Canada, at its next ordinary meeting after the passing of this Act, to declare, by a resolu-

tion or a by-law to that effect, recorded in the register of proceedings of the said Synod, the theological doctrines and principles which shall be taught in the said college, or what are the books and documents in which the said principles and doctrines are contained ; and such declaration so made and recorded shall be irrevocable in so far as the said college shall be concerned, and shall be held at all times thereafter to contain the theological doctrines and principles to be taught in the said college, and for the propagation of which the property now held for the said college, or hereafter acquired for the same, shall be appropriated, and to no other.

3. And the said Synod of the Presbyterian Church of Canada shall have power at its next or any subsequent meeting to appoint and remove professors and tutors in such way and manner as to them shall seem good ; and shall also have power to make rules and by-laws for the government of the said college, and to alter, amend and annul the same and make other rules instead thereof, and also to constitute a senate for the said college, with such powers as they may deem from time to time expedient ; also to constitute a board of management for the financial and other affairs of the said college not otherwise provided for, in such manner and with such powers and under such conditions as to the said Synod shall from time to time seem expedient ; provided always, that such by-laws, rules or regulations be not contrary to this Act or repugnant to the laws of the Province.

4. In case the body of christians known under the name of the Presbyterian Church of Canada, shall at any time or times hereafter, under that or any other name, unite itself with any other body or bodies of Presbyterians adhering to the principles and doctrines mentioned in the declaration to be made according to the second section of this Act, or in the books and documents therein mentioned as containing the said principles and doctrines, or take such other body or bodies of Presbyterians into union with itself, and in case such united body of Presbyterians shall agree to hold and

shall hold a Synod once or oftener in each year according to the manner now in use in the said Presbyterian Church of Canada, then and in every such case this Act shall apply to such united body of Presbyterians under whatever name they shall have formed such union, and all rights, powers and authorities by this Act vested in the Synod of the Presbyterian Church of Canada shall be vested in and apply to the Synod of such united body under whatever name or designation such united body may be known.

5. In case the said Presbyterian Church of Canada, or such united body as aforesaid, shall determine to form itself into two or more Synods, and to form one General Assembly, which shall have supreme jurisdiction in such church or united body, then all the rights, powers and authorities by this Act vested in the Synod of the Presbyterian Church of Canada, or in the Synod of such united body as aforesaid, shall be diverted from the said Synod and be applied to and be vested in such General Assembly; and for the purposes of this Act such General Assembly or Supreme Court shall thenceforth exclusively exercise all the right, powers and authorities conferred by this Act on the Synod of the Presbyterian Church of Canada.

44 VICT. CAP. 82 (O.)   An Act to amend the Act to incorporate Knox College. (*a*)   (*Assented to 4th March, 1881.*)

Whereas Knox College, by its petition, represents that the said college is an institution for the theological education of students for the ministry of the Presbyterian church in Canada, and has been incorporated for that purpose by chapter 69 of the statutes of the then Province of Canada, passed in the session held in the 22d year of the reign of Her Majesty Queen Victoria; that since the foundation of the said college between

---

(*a.*) **The matter of Theological degrees was brought before the Assembly by an overture from the Synod of Hamilton and London, when a resolution was passed empowering the Boards and Senates of the Colleges in Toronto and Montreal to take such steps in the matter as they might deem advisable.** *Minutes, 1880, pp. 48, 49.*

three and four hundred students have received in it their theological education; that nearly all the students of said college have received the greater part of their literary education at University College, Toronto; that the students of Knox College will to a great extent seek their education in arts at said University College; that neither the University of Toronto nor said Knox College has power to confer degrees in divinity, and the said students are thus precluded from obtaining such degrees from the institutions where they have received their literary and theological education; that the said college has a staff of professors and tutors, and a valuable theological library, and has erected large and expensive buildings at Toronto, in proximity to said University College, for the purpose of affording a thorough education to the said students for the ministry of said Presbyterian Church: and that said Knox College is already partially endowed, and is constantly receiving further sums towards completing said endowment; and whereas the said Knox College has prayed that in order to promote a higher standard of theological learning, and to prevent its students from being compelled to resort to other colleges for degrees in divinity, power might be granted to it to confer such degrees; and whereas it is expedient to grant the prayer of said petition: Therefore, Her Majesty, &c., enacts as follows:—

1. The senate of Knox College shall have power to confer the degrees of Bachelor of Divinity and Doctor of Divinity upon graduates in Arts of such Universities as the said senate shall recognize for that purpose, as well as upon such students of the said college as are now taking the regular course of study therein, or have before the passing of this Act completed the said course, and are now ordained ministers of the Presbyterian Church in Canada, subject however, in either case, to such regulations as to examination or otherwise as may, from time to time, be prescribed by by-law of the said senate.

2. The said senate shall also have power to confer the honorary degree of Doctor of Divinity, and may

make by-laws and regulations touching any matter or thing pertaining to the conditions on which said degree may be conferred.

---

47 Vict. cap. 87. (O)—An Act to amend the Act to Incorporate Knox College. (*Assented to 25th March, 1884.*)

Whereas by an Act of the Parliament of the late Province of Canada, passed in the 22nd year of Her Majesty's reign, chapter 69, entitled "An Act to Incorporate Knox College," certain persons therein named, and all and every such other person or persons as then were or should at any time thereafter be ministers of the Presbyterian Church of Canada, or members of the said church, in full communion, should thenceforth be a body corporate under the name of "Knox College," with perpetual succession and a common seal, and with the powers vested in corporate bodies by "The Interpretation Act," and also with power among other things to purchase, acquire, have, take, hold, and enjoy by gift, grant, conveyance, devise, bequest or otherwise, to them and their successors, any estate or property, real or personal, to and for the use of the said college in trust for the promotion of theological learning, and the education of youth for the holy ministry according to the principles and standards of the Presbyterian Church of Canada, and also with power to let, convey, or otherwise dispose of such real or personal estate from time to time as might be expedient; and whereas it was thereby among other things enacted that the college might acquire any real estate, other than what was required for the purposes of college buildings, offices and residences, for professors, tutors, students and officers, with gardens or pleasure grounds pertaining thereto, or any interest therein by gift, devise, or bequest, if made at least six months before the death of the party making the same, and the said college might hold such estate for a period of three years, and invest the proceeds of the sale of such property in the public securities of the said Province, stocks of chartered banks or other approved securities, for the use of the said college; and whereas the said college, under the authority of the General Assembly of the Presbyterian Church in Canada, has established an endowment fund, the annual income and proceeds whereof are to be applied towards payment of the salaries of the professors, lecturers and tutors of said college, and of the annual expenses connected with the maintenance of the said college; and whereas the said college has represented that it would be for the advantage of said college if the term during which the college may hold real estate or any interest therein, not required for buildings, offices, residences, or gardens as aforesaid acquired by gift, devise or bequest as aforesaid, should be extended to seven years; and whereas the said college has also represented that it would be for the benefit of the college and tend to the security and permanence of said endowment fund if the college were authorized to invest the moneys of said college, whether appropriated for said endowment fund or otherwise, in the securities mentioned in said Act of incorporation, and also in mortgage and other securities, as hereinafter provided by this Act; and whereas it is expedient to grant the prayer of the said petition; Therefore, Her Majesty, &c., enacts as follows:—

1. Knox College may hold lands, tenements or interests acquired by gift, devise, bequest or purchase, and not required for the purposes specified in the said Act passed in the 22nd year of Her Majesty's reign, and chartered 69, for a period not longer than seven years from the acquisition thereof, and within such period they shall be absolutely disposed of by the said corporation, which shall have power to grant and convey the said lands to any purchaser, and the proceeds of said sales, and all or any part of the moneys of the said corporation appropriated to the said endowment fund or otherwise, may be invested from time to time in the securities mentioned in the said Act, and also in mortgage securities over real estate, whether freehold or leasehold, and

also in municipal debentures or the debentures of any society or company in which any trustee under section 1 of chapter 21 of the Act passed in the 42nd year of Her Majesty's reign, may invest any trust fund; provided always that no lands, tenements, or interests therein, which may be acquired by the said corporation by gift, purchase, devise, bequest, foreclosure, or otherwise, and not required by the corporation for the purposes specified by the said Act, shall be held by the said corporation for a period longer than seven years after the acquisition thereof, and within that period they shall be absolutely disposed of by the said corporation, and such lands, tenements or interest therein as have not within the said period been so disposed of shall revert to the person from whom the same were acquired, his heirs, executors, administrators and assigns.

The following Act, which gives the college extended powers for conferring degrees in Divinity, has been passed in the Legislative Assembly of Ontario, but has not yet (29th March, 1897) received the assent of the Lieutenant-Governor:

An Act to amend the Act incorporating Knox College.

Whereas by an Act of the Legislative Assembly of the Province of Ontario passed in the 44th year of the reign of Her Majesty Queen Victoria, chaptered 82, intituled "An Act to amend the Act to incorporate Knox College," the senate of the said college was empowered to confer the degrees of Bachelor of Divinity, and Doctor of Divinity, on graduates in Arts of such Universities as the said senate should recognize for that purpose; and whereas Knox College has by its petition represented that it is desirable to encourage ordained ministers of the Presbyterian Church in Canada not having obtained degrees in Arts, to prosecute their studies in theological and other literature in order to proceed to a degree in divinity; and whereas it is expedient to grant the prayer of the said petition; Therefore Her Majesty, &c., enacts as follows:—

1. Section 1 of the said Act passed in the 44th year of Her Majesty's reign, chaptered 82, is repealed and the following section substituted therefor;—

1. The senate of Knox College shall have power to confer the Degrees of Bachelor of Divinity, and Doctor of Divinity, upon graduates in Arts of such Universities as the said senate shall recognize for that purpose, and also upon such ordained ministers of the Presbyterian Church in Canada as the senate shall determine to be possessed of the necessary qualifications, subject, however, in either case, to such regulations as to examination or otherwise as may from time to time be prescribed by by-law of the said senate.

DECLARATION OF PRINCIPLES.

Presbyterian Church of Canada, Minutes 1859, p. 27.—That the principles and doctrines to be taught in Knox College by the professors and tutors, or other persons who shall from time to time, and at all times hereafter, be employed or appointed in giving instruction in the said college shall be such and such only as are consistent with and agreeable to the "Confession of Faith," the "Larger and Shorter Catechisms," and the "Form of Church Government," all of which are called "The Westminster Standards," and shall comprise all theological learning consistent with said standards; provided always, that the said "Confession of Faith" be understood and taken with the explanatory note thereto, agreed upon by the Synod of the Presbyterian Church of Canada, met at Toronto in the year of our Lord, 1854; provided also that the said "Westminster Standards" be taken and understood with such other, or further directions and rules as to church government, discipline, or worship, as may from time to time be prescribed or ordained by the Synod of the said Presbyterian Church of Canada, with the concurrence of a majority of the Presbyteries of the said Church, to be ascertained in such manner as the Synod shall prescribe, and that such regulations and rules be duly recorded in the minute book of the said Synod and signed by the moderator and clerk for the time being of such Synod.

The Synod further instruct their clerk to register this resolution and declaration in the records of the Synod and in the public records of the City of Toronto.

BY-LAWS.

Presbyterian Church of Canada Minutes, 1860, p. 26.—1. There shall be a board of management, composed of thirty-five persons, ordained ministers and elders of the Church, of whom seven shall be a quorum for transaction of all business. The said board shall be aunually appointed by the Synod (*a*) and its members shall hold office until their successors be appointed. They shall appoint their own secretary and treasurer, (*b*) who shall keep records and accounts, which shall be open to the inspection of the Synod. The chairman of the board shall be appointed annually by the Synod, and in the event of no such appointment being made, or of the death, removal or resignation of said chairman, his place shall be supplied by the board itself

2. The board shall be convened by the chairman at least three times a year, and at such time and in such manner as may be determined by the Synod or by the board itself.

3. The board shall have the whole management of the financial affairs of the said college, shall receive and disburse all its moneys, keep and manage all its property, and transact all its business relating to property and money committed to its care, by the Synod or otherwise, and shall exercise all the powers in regard to property and money vested in the corporation of Knox College by the Act 22 Victoria, chapter 69. In cases where special instructions shall be given by the Synod, in writing under the hand of their clerk, it shall be the duty of the said board to act according to such instructions.

4. The board shall receive annual reports from the senate in reference to the departments under the care of said senate, and shall transmit the same to the Synod, along with a report on all matters entrusted to said board, and an audited balance sheet of the property and financial affairs of the college.

5. The board shall further take general cognizance of all matters pertaining to the interest of the college, and co-operate with the senate in maintaining its discipline. They shall also take charge of the boarding department of the college, and make such regulations for its management as they may see fit, and shall appoint all subordinate servants, and dismiss and remove the same as they shall see fit.

(*a*) The expression "Synod" is used throughout these by-laws, but the General Assembly can exercise all the powers and authorities given the Synod, either by the Act of Incorporation or these by-laws. *See* 22 *Vict.* c. 69, s. 5, (C.) In 1887 there was presented to the Assembly a memorial from the Alumni Association of the college praying that they should be represented in the Senate, by three members, nominated by the Association, and subject to appointment by the Assembly, and the prayer of the memorial was granted. *See Minutes 1887, p. 22.*

(*b*) When, in 1876, the General Assembly defined the duties of the Agent of the Western section of the Church, it was provided that he should act as secretary and treasurer of Knox College, *Minutes 1876, p. 77*, but this by-law was not varied. In the Report of the Board of Management of the College in 1896, *Minutes 1896, App. No. 11*, attention was called to this matter, and the Board recommended, "that the resolution of 1876 be amended so that no question should arise as to the authority of the Board to appoint its own officers;" stating at the same time that they had appointed Rev. Dr. Warden (the agent of the Western section) as their treasurer, and Rev. Wm. Burns, as their secretary. This report was received and adopted, *Minutes 1896, p. 23*, but this matter was not further dealt with.

6. The board shall have power to appoint an acting sub-committee, with such powers as they may deem requisite.

7. (*As amended, see Minutes 1896, p. 33.*) That the chairman of the board shall have the custody of the seal of the corporation, and shall affix it to all discharges of mortgages required to be executed by the college, and that the execution of all such discharges shall be attested both by the chairman and treasurer of the college without special instructions from the board, and also that all such other instruments as may require to be executed by the college shall be executed by affixing the corporate seal thereto, attested by the signature of the chairman and treasurer, or in his absence by the secretary, whenever directed by the board, or any sub-committee or executive committee thereof, and that it shall not be necessary to prove the giving of any such special instructions.

8. The Principal and professors of the college, together with seven members of Assembly, shall be annually appointed by the Synod as a "College Senate," to whom shall be entrusted the reception, academical superintendence, and discipline of the students, and of all other persons within the said college. The senate shall take a general inspection of the whole internal arrangements of the college, and of the studies of the students, and shall place said students in that year of the curriculum to which they may be certified by Presbyteries, or by such other body as the Synod may determine, and shall have charge of the library and museum.

9. The senate shall at the close of each college session hold an examination of the students, and present to the board of management a report on the studies of the classes, and on any other matters under its supervision.

The Principal.

10. The title of the Principal shall be "The Reverend the Principal of Knox College."

11. He shall preside in all meetings of the college senate, and summon such meetings at stated or convenient times. In the unavoidable absence or inability of the Principal, the senior professor shall summon and preside at necessary meetings of the senate with the consent of the other professors. In case of a division, the Principal shall only have a casting vote.

12. He shall preside at the public opening and closing of the college session.

13. He shall be the medium of communication with, and conduct the official correspondence of, the college senate.

14. He shall have a general superintendence of the studies of the students in accordance with the instructions of the senate; it being understood that the other professors shall be responsible only to the Synod for the discharge of the duties entrusted to them.

Professors and Tutors.

15. No person shall at any time be employed, or inducted into office, as professor of theology who is not at the time of his employment or induction an ordained minister of the Presbyterian Church of Canada; and if a licentiate shall at any time be appointed, he shall, before induction, be ordained to the holy ministry in the usual manner by the Presbytery of Toronto, or by a commission specially appointed for that purpose by the Synod; and all persons, if any, who shall be appointed or employed as tutors, shall at the time of their entrance into office be members of the said Church in full communion therewith, and said professors and tutors shall sign *the formula* appointed to be signed by ministers, &c., of the Church.

16. All professors and tutors who shall hereafter be appointed or employed in the said college, shall be appointed by the said Synod at its ordinary annual session, or at any special meeting of the said Synod, to be called for the purpose of making such appointments or appointment by notice from the moderator of Synod for the time being, to be sent to each member of Synod, at least fifteen days before the day appointed for such special meeting, such appointment to be made by open vote of the majority of members present, at the sederunt of the Synod at which the appointment shall be made, or in such other manner as the said Synod shall from time to time by resolution determine, and direct to be pursued in making such appointments; provided always that any such professor or tutor may resign, or may by the said Synod be removed, suspended or deposed from office, according to the laws of the Church; and in case of any such tutor resigning or ceasing to be such as aforesaid, or in case of any such professor being removed or being deposed from the ministry in due process of discipline, such tutor or professor so resigning, ceasing to be a member, or being removed or deposed as aforesaid, shall, *ipso facto*, cease to be a professor or tutor in the said college, and cease to have any emolument or privilege belonging to the said college, and his office shall be vacant.

Sessions; Admission and Attendance of Students.

17. The session or academical year shall commence on the first Wednesday of October, and end on the first Wednesday of April. There shall be such recess at the end of December, as may be fixed by the senate.

18. No person shall be entitled to rank as a student, who has not been certified to the senate by some Presbytery of the Church, or such other body as the Synod may appoint, and who has not signed the Album of the college, and agreed to submit to its discipline in such form as may be determined by the senate.

19. Every student shall, at the end of each session, apply to the professors on whose instructions he has attended, for certificates attesting the regularity of his attendance, his proficiency, diligence and general conduct, which certificates shall be presented to the Presbytery of the Church, by whom the said student may be examined for license, or to the board of examiners (c) for entrance upon the next year of the curriculum ; and before any student shall be taken on trials for license, he shall present to his Presbytery a certificate from the senate signed by the Principal, attesting that he has attended all the classes and performed all the duties required by the Church.

20. Cases of an urgent or peculiar nature of attendance on, or absence from, the classes of any particular year shall be adjudged upon by the senate according to the circumstances of each case.

THE DEGREE OF BACHELOR OF DIVINITY.

1. Candidates for the degree of B. D. must be graduates in Arts of some approved university ; but students who have already completed the literary course in Knox College, and are now in the ministry of the Presbyterian Church in Canada, and also students who are now (1881) taking the regular course in Knox College, may become candidates.

2. Candidates must have completed a course of theological study in this college, or in some theological school approved by the senate.

3. The degree of B. D. cannot be conferred earlier than one year after the completion of the ordinary theological course.

4. The subjects of examination shall be arranged in two departments, as follows :—First Department—Latin, Greek, Hebrew, Apologetics, Church History and Church Government, Systematic Theology, Textual Criticism and Canon. Second Department—Greek, Hebrew and Chaldee, Church History, Systematic Theology, Exegetics, Homiletics and Pastoral Theology. (d)

5. Candidates may take, at one examination, the whole of the work in both departments, but not earlier than the month of March, after the completion of the ordinary theological course.

6. The examinations in the two departments may be taken at different times. In this case the examination in the first department

(c) In the report of the college board presented to the Assembly in 1887 (*Minutes 1887, App. No. 7*), there was a recommendation that the board of examiners be discontinued, and their functions assigned to the senate. The recommendation was adopted by the Assembly. See *Minutes 1887. p. 21*.

(d) The particular subjects are published each year in the College Calendar

shall not usually be taken earlier than the month of March next following the completion of the ordinary theological course; but students who shall have averaged not less than sixty per cent. of the maximum number of marks in the examinations of the second year shall be allowed to take this examination at the close of their ordinary course. The examination in the second department cannot be taken earlier than the March following, and cannot be deferred beyond three years from the date of the first examination.

7. Candidates are required to communicate their names, together with attestations of their qualifications, as specified in the foregoing regulations, to the secretary of the senate, at least two months before the day appointed for the examination.

8. The fee for the degree of B. D. shall be ten dollars to be paid to the secretary, previous to conferring the degree.

(3) The Presbyterian College, Halifax.

24 Vict., cap. 68., (N. S.)—An Act to incorporate the Board of Education of the Presbyterian Church of the Lower Provinces of British North America.—(*Passed, 15th April, 1861.*)

Whereas the two bodies of Christians known as the Presbyterian Church of Nova Scotia and the Free Church of Nova Scotia have lately been united into one, by the name of "The Presbyterian Church of the Lower Provinces of British North America," and they are desirous that the two educational institutions incorporated in this Province, by the Acts 9 Vict., chap. 36, and 19 Vict., chap. 81, should be consolidated and incorporated into one by the name given in this Act: Be it therefore enacted, &c., as follows:—

1. The Act 9 Vict., chap. 36, entitled "An Act to incorporate the Educational Board of the Presbyterian Church of Nova Scotia," and the Act 19 Vict., chap. 81, entitled "An Act to incorporate the College and Academy Board of the Free Church of Nova Scotia," are hereby repealed.

2. The Rev. Andrew King, the Rev. John Logan Murdoch (*and others, naming them*) together with the

moderator and clerks, for the time being, of the Synod of such united body, and all other person or persons who shall or may hereafter be duly appointed by such Synod as hereafter provided for, and their successors in office shall and are hereby declared to be a body politic and corporate, by the name of "The Board of Education of the Presbyterian Church of the Lower Provinces of British North America."

3. The board shall not at any one time, hold lands, tenements, and hereditaments, goods, chattels, or effects, of greater value than $200,000.

4. All and singular the lands and premises, wherever situate, now vested in the Educational Board of the Presbyterian Church of Nova Scotia, and the College and Academy Board of the Free Church of Nova Scotia, or in trustees for either of those corporate bodies, with all the right, title, interest, use, trust, inheritance and demand, of such corporate bodies and trustees, or any of them; and also all the incomes, goods, chattels, and other personal property of every kind now belonging to such corporate bodies, or held by any trustees for them, or either of them, or belonging to the united Synod, and the two several bequests mentioned in the 2nd section of the Act, 9th Vict., chap. 36, shall be and are hereby declared to be vested in, and shall be and become, and are hereby declared to be the absolute property of the board hereby incorporated, and of their successors in office, and shall be held for the purpose of promoting classical, literary and theological education in the institutions in connection with and under the control of the united body, as fully and effectively, to all intents and purposes, as if the same had been originally conveyed by deed, assignment, or otherwise; and all mortgages and other securities held by any parties in trust for the purposes contemplated by the Acts hereby repealed, or either of them, or by the Synods of such original bodies now united into one, shall be and are hereby declared to be vested in the board hereby incorporated, whether such securities be in this Province or elsewhere: pro-

vided that the original intentions of the donors of any part of such funds or securities, and the conditions annexed thereto, shall not be infringed, but such funds shall be applied and expended for promoting the objects originally contemplated, and all such conditions shall be substantially observed.

5. It shall be the duty of the board, from time to time, as may be necessary, to assume the management and control of the real estate, and also of the moneys or other personal property hereby vested in them, or which may hereafter be acquired by the board, or shall come into their possession, to and for the purposes contemplated by the Synod, and, as often as occasion may require, to meet together and consult upon the state of the property entrusted to their care, the safe investment of the funds belonging to the board, and the expenditure of moneys for any necessary purposes, and generally to exercise a due and watchful supervision over the affairs of the board, for the purpose of preserving the property and funds from loss or destruction, and of increasing the value thereof; any five members of the board to form a quorum for the transaction of business.

6. The members of the board shall be duly chosen and appointed by the united Synod at its regular meetings; and it shall be lawful for the Synod to remove or displace any member of such board, and to substitute the names of any members to fill their places, or to add to the number of the board; and any member may be at liberty to resign his seat at such board, and by his resignation he shall cease to be a member thereof: provided that the Synod shall have the power of nominating and appointing any person or persons to fill the place of those who may so resign, and that no person shall be appointed a member of such board unless he be at the time of his appointment in full communion with the Presbyterian Church of the Lower Provinces of British North America.

7. If at any time hereafter the Synod shall unite with any orthodox body of christians, either in this or in any

of the adjoining Provinces, so as to form one Ecclesiastical Synod, the property and funds hereby vested in the board shall be deemed and be the property and funds of the united body, upon such terms and conditions as the uniting parties may agree to, and notwithstanding any change or difference in the name assumed by the united body from that by which the Synod is now known: provided that the funds shall be applied and expended in promoting the objects originally contemplated by the donors, and that the united body shall profess and adhere to the constitution and principles of the Westminster standards as set forth in the basis of union of the united bodies; and if at any future time, a division or separation shall take place, or be agreed upon, in the united Synod or Presbyterian Church of the Lower Provinces, that then, and in such case, the new Synod which shall adhere most closely to the standards of the united church, as set forth in its basis of union in government, doctrine and discipline, shall be and is hereby declared to be the true, rightful, and legal owner of such funds and property, of whatever nature or kind, vested in or belonging to the board, and appertaining to or forming any part of the trust funds then held and enjoyed by them for the purposes aforesaid.

8. In case of any such union being hereafter effected, it shall be lawful for the united body, at any regular meeting of the Synod, from time to time, to nominate and appoint a new board of trustees, who shall represent the interests of the whole united body, or to add to the existing board the names of any person or persons belonging to the body or bodies with whom such united bodies may unite.

9. If at any time hereafter, upon such a union being effected, the united body shall see fit to constitute themselves into the higher Ecclesiastical Court, usually known in Scotland as a General Assembly, the property and funds hereby vested in the Board of Education of the Presbyterian Church of the Lower Provinces of British North America shall be held by the board to and for

the use of the General Assembly; and such General Assembly shall have, possess, and enjoy, the same rights, powers and authorities, for all the purposes of this Act, as are now held and enjoyed by the Synod, anything herein contained to the contrary notwithstanding: provided that such General Assembly shall profess and hold to the same doctrines or principles as required of the Synod under the 7th section of this Act.

10. Any bequests that have been made to the Education Board of the Presbyterian Church of Nova Scotia, or in trust for the Church in aid of its mission schemes, shall be vested in the board hereby incorporated, and be by them applied for the uses and purposes in such bequests set forth, and the conditions thereof as near as may be fulfilled; and it shall be lawful for the board to receive, hold, and dispose of, in accordance with the will of the donors, and subject to the direction of the Synod, any bequests or contributions, in lands, moneys, or other securities, made for the promotion of any of the schemes or religious objects of the Presbyterian Church of the Lower Provinces of British North America.

11. This Act shall go into operation on the third day of the meeting of the united Synod, in the month of June next.

---

42 Vict., cap. 82 (N. S.)—An Act to amend an Act to incorporate the Board of Education of the Presbyterian Church of the Lower Provinces of British North America. (*Passed 17th April, 1879.*)

Whereas by chapter 68 of the Acts of 1861, the Board of Education of the Presbyterian Church of the Lower Provinces of British North America became duly incorporated for the purposes therein described, and whereas, by reason of the union of the said Church with other Presbyterian Churches in Nova Scotia and the other Provinces of the Dominion under the title of "the Presbyterian Church in Canada," the present name of the said corporation is inapplicable, and it is desirable to change the same, and otherwise to amend the said Act ; Be it therefore enacted, &c., as follows :

1. The corporation incorporated by the said chapter 68 of the Acts of 1861, and heretofore known as the Board of Education of the Presbyterian Church of the Lower Provinces of British North America, shall hereafter be called and known under the corporate name of " The Board of the Presbyterian College, Halifax."

2. The Rev. Robert F. Burns, D.D., the Rev. Peter Gordon McGregor, D.D., the Rev. Alex. McKnight, D.D., (*and others, naming them*) shall, for the time being, be the members and constitute the said board, and shall hold such appointment subject to the will of the General Assembly of the Presbyterian Church in Canada, and the said General Assembly shall have power to remove or displace any member of such board, and to substitute the names of any persons to fill their places, and to add to or reduce the number of the board : provided, however, that no person shall be appointed a member of such board unless he be at the time of his appointment a member of, and in full communion with the Presbyterian Church in Canada.

3. All the real and personal estate now vested in or held or owned by the Board of Education of the Presbyterian Church of the Lower Provinces of British North America are hereby declared to be absolutely vested in and owned by the Board of the Presbyterian College, Halifax.

4. Such corporation may effectually convey any real estate by deed, signed by the chairman and secretary of the said board for the time being, and having the corporate seal of the said board affixed thereto.

5. The said board may hold property to the value of $400,000, and shall in all other respects hold, possess, and enjoy all the rights and privileges, and be subject to the same obligations as are granted to or imposed

upon the Board of Education of the Presbyterian Church of the Lower Provinces of British North America by the Act hereby amended.

6. So much of the chapter hereby amended, and chapter 99 of the Acts of 1875, entituled "An Act concerning the Presbyterian Church of the Lower Provinces of British North America," as is inconsistent with this Act is repealed.

---

45 Vict., cap. 28 (N. S.)—An Act to incorporate for certain purposes the Senate of the Presbyterian College, Halifax. (*Passed 27th Feb'y, 1882.*)

Be it enacted, &c., as follows :—

1. The senate of the Presbyterian College at Halifax, that is to say, the Rev. Alex. McKnight, D. D., Principal; the Rev. Allan Pollok, D. D., and the Rev. John Currie, Professors, (*and others, naming them*), appointed as such by the General Assembly of the Presbyterian Church in Canada, on the 15th day of June, A. D. 1881, and their successors in office, as such senate from time to time appointed by the General Assembly, are hereby created a body politic and corporate, under the name of the Senate of the Presbyterian College at Halifax, with power to have and use a common seal, and to confer upon the students attending such college, and upon such other persons as they may see fit, the degree of Bachelor of Divinity, and the degree of Doctor of Divinity, and to grant to them suitable certificates of the conferring of such degree under the common seal of the senate.

Rules, &c., of Procedure, Presbyterian Church of the Lower Provinces, p. 113.—1. A committee is appointed by the Synod to superintend the theological hall, with power to transact any business which may require to be attended to in fulfilling the Synod's engagements in connection with Dalhousie College. This committee of which the professors are members *ex officio*, is called the board of superintendence, and reports annually to the Synod.

Minutes, 1876, p. 76.—The General Assembly resolved :—1. That the length of the theological session be extended to six full months.

2. That the bursary committee be merged in the board of superintendence.

3. That a senate be appointed for the theological hall of the Maritime Provinces.

4. That the Assembly permit the board to sell the buildings in Halifax and Truro, provided such step should have the approval of the Synod of the Maritime Provinces.

Minutes, 1878, p. 46.—1. The Assembly authorize the committee of superintendence to obtain such legislation as may be necessary to have the name of "The Educational Board for the Presbyterian Church of the Lower Provinces" changed, and to amalgamate the said board and the committee of superintendence.

2. The Assembly sanction an effort to increase the number of bursaries and scholarships by inducing congregations, Sabbath schools, and wealthy members of the Church to found such.

3. The Assembly resolve to have a Principal for the theological hall, Halifax.

REGULATIONS— DEGREE OF BACHELOR OF DIVINITY.

1. Candidates for the degree of B. D. must be graduates in Arts of some approved university.

2. The degree may be obtained either in ordinary course or by special examination.

3. Candidates in ordinary course are required to make 50 per cent in each subject, and a general average of 70 per cent in the class examinations of each year.

4. Candidates for the degree by special examinations are required to make 50 per cent on each paper, and an average of 70 per cent on all the papers. This examination may be taken in the two parts prescribed on the following page.

5. Both classes of candidates are required, after fulfilling provisions 3 and 4, respectively, to pass a final examination, to which the same rule as to percentage of marks shall apply.

6. This examination may be taken in two parts. Students of the third year may take Part I in November or in April; Part II in April. Candidates for the degree who have already finished their course may take both parts of the final examination either in November or in April.

7. The special and final examinations shall not necessarily be limited to particular books; but a list of books shall be given in the calendar as a general guide.

8. Those who intend to present themselves for examination in November are required to notify the clerk of senate not later than the 15th October; in April, not later than 2nd February.

9. The fee for those who take the degree in ordinary course is $10; for those who take the degree by special examination, $15.

(4). MORRIN COLLEGE.

24 Vict., cap. 109 (C).—An Act to incorporate Morrin College at Quebec. (*Assented to 18th May, 1861.*)

Whereas by a certain deed of gift made by Joseph Morrin, of the City of Quebec, Physician and Surgeon, and passed before William Bignall and his colleague, notaries public, residing at the said city, and bearing date the 26th day of September, in the year of our Lord, 1860, it is expressed that the said Joseph Morrin gave, assigned and made over unto the Reverend John Cook, Doctor in Divinity, William Stewart Smith, Doctor of Laws, and James Dean, senior, merchant, all of the said city, and to the survivor or survivors of them, and the heirs and assigns of such survivor or survivors, certain immoveable properties and sums of money, therein described and mentioned; and whereas, by another deed, executed by the said parties, on the same day, and before the same notaries, the said parties,—after reciting that the said Joseph Morrin was desirous of leaving some permanent memorial of his regard for the City of Quebec, of which he had been a citizen for more than fifty years, and over which he had twice had the honor of presiding as chief magistrate, and at the same time of marking his attachment to the Church in which he was reared, and to which he had always belonged, and considered that none could be more suitable for both purposes than a provision for increasing and rendering more perfect the means of obtaining for the youth generally, and especially those who may devote themselves to the ministry of the said Church, the means of obtaining a liberal and enlightened education,

—declared that the said deed of gift was made in trust for the purpose of carrying into effect the wishes of the said Joseph Morrin, by providing and establishing within the City or *banlieue* of Quebec, under an Act of incorporation, for which the said donees should apply at the then next meeting of the Provincial Parliament, and which should contain, among others, certain provisions hereinafter made, a college for the instruction of youth in the higher branches of learning, and especially for young men intended for the ministry of the Church of Scotland in Canada ; and whereas the said donees have accordingly applied to the Legislature for such Act of incorporation, and it is expedient to grant their prayer : Therefore, Her Majesty, &c., enacts as follows :—

1. There shall be and there is hereby constituted and established in the City or *banlieue* of Quebec, in Lower Canada, a body politic and corporate, under the name of Morrin College, which corporation shall consist of the following members, who shall be called governors of the said college, that is to say : (1). The said Reverend John Cook, the present Minister of St. Andrew's Church at Quebec, who shall during his pleasure, and whether he be or be not then such minister, be the first principal of the said college, with the right to choose for himself and hold any professorship therein, and shall, when present at any meeting of the governors, be the chairman thereof ; (2). The Minister of St. Andrew's Church aforesaid for the time being ; (3). The said William Stewart Smith, who shall be the first professor of classical literature in the said college ; (4). Daniel Wilkie, of Quebec, Esquire, who shall be secretary-treasurer of the said college, with such remuneration as the governors see fit ; (5). Two ministers from the Synod of the Presbyterian Church of Canada, in connection with the Church of Scotland, to be chosen by the Synod, on the second day of its annual meeting, and to hold office one year, and until others are appointed in their stead ; (6). An elder of St. Andrew's Church aforesaid, to be elected by the session, and to hold office for life, or so long as he remains such elder ; (7). A

trustee of St. Andrew's Church aforesaid, to be elected by the trustees of the said church, for life, or so long as he remains such trustee ; (8). James Dean, Sr., Esq., Alexander Rowand, M.D., James Dean, Jr., Esq., Frost Wood Gray, Esq., Andrew Thompson, Esq., and John Wilson Cook, Esq., who shall be governors for life.

2. Vacancies among the governors who are not such *ex officio*, and for the election of whose successors no other provision is herein made, shall, as they occur, be filled up by the said corporation, who shall appoint proper persons as governors to fill such vacancies, but such persons shall be members of the Presbyterian Church of Canada in connection with the Church of Scotland, or in the event of the union of that church with any other Presbyterian body or bodies, then members of the united Church, and the number of governors shall never exceed fourteen.

3. Any governor, *ex officio*, shall cease to be such on his ceasing to hold an office to which such governorship is attached ; and any other governor may resign his office as such, by a resignation in writing under his hand addressed to the corporation.

4. The governors for the time being shall form the corporation, whose acts shall not be invalidated by any temporary vacancy therein ; and the said corporation shall have full power, from time to time, to make and establish such by-laws, rules and regulations (not being inconsistent with the laws of Canada, or with this Act), as they shall think proper, as well concerning the system of education in, as for the conduct and government of, the said college, or of any other school or institution connected with or dependent on the same, and of the corporation thereof, and for the superintendence and management of all the property, moveable or immoveable, belonging to the corporation, and shall have power to take under any legal title whatever, and to hold for the use of the said college, without any further authority, license, or letters of mortmain, all lands and other property, moveable or immoveable, which may hereafter

be sold, ceded, given, bequeathed, or otherwise granted to the said corporation, and the same to sell, alienate and convey, let or lease, whenever need shall be.

5. Such title to the property, moveable and immoveable, as was conveyed by the said Joseph Morrin, to the said John Cook, William Stewart Smith, and James Dean, senior, by the deed of gift hereinbefore mentioned, shall be, and is hereby transferred to, and vested in the said corporation, subject to the following conditions: —(1) The said trustees, John Cook, William Stewart Smith, and James Dean, senior, may purchase for the corporation, within the city or *banlieue* of Quebec, a site for the erection of proper buildings for the said college; (2) Ample accomodation shall be provided in the college building for the High School of Quebec, if the corporation thereof shall elect to receive the same free of all charge, on condition that the said High School shall be subject to the government of the corporation of the said college, and ancillary to it; but the governors of the said college may, at any future time, have the school and college in separate buildings, if they deem it for the advantage of the said institutions. (3) In case the said William Stewart Smith should, from ill-health or otherwise, be prevented from fulfilling the duties and receiving the emoluments of the office of first professor of classical literature of said college, the governors thereof shall, in accordance with the wish of the said Joseph Morrin, make such reasonable allowance for his support as his circumstances and the funds at their disposal may warrant.

6. The quorum of governors at meetings of the corporation may be from time to time fixed by the by-laws thereof, but shall not be less than five, which number shall be the quorum, unless and until it is otherwise provided by by-law; and a majority of such quorum may exercise all the powers of the corporation, except in so far as it is otherwise expressly provided by this Act or by by-law.

7. All the property at any time belonging to the said corporation, and the revenues thereof shall at all times

be exclusively applied and appropriated to the advancement of education in the said college, and to no other object, institution or establishment whatever unconnected with or independent of the same.

8. The said Morrin College may, at any time, become affiliated to the University of Queen's College, Kingston, or to the University of Toronto, or to the University of McGill College, upon such terms as the said college and such university may agree upon.

9. Nothing in this Act shall be so construed as to give to the deed of gift hereinbefore mentioned any validity which does not otherwise belong to it.

---

45 Vict., cap. 90 (Q.)—An Act to amend the Act 24 Victoria, chapter 109, to incorporate Morrin College, Quebec. (*Assented to 27th May, 1882.*)

Whereas it has been represented that Morrin College, Quebec, is hindered in its usefulness and its very existence imperilled by being unable to confer degrees in divinity upon its students, and that it would be materially assisted, in the purposes for which it was founded, if permission were granted to it to confer such degrees ; and whereas, by petition, it has prayed for an amendment to its charter to that effect, and it is expedient to grant the prayer of the said petition : Therefore Her Majesty, &c., enacts as follows :—

1. The Theological Faculty of Morrin College shall have power to confer the degrees of Bachelor of Divinity and Doctor of Divinity, subject to such regulations and examinations as may be imposed by the Faculty.

2. The said Theological Faculty shall have power to make by-laws and regulations touching any matter or thing pertaining to the conditions on which the said degrees of Bachelor of Divinity and Doctor of Divinity may be conferred whether the said degrees be such as are gained in course or by examination, or such

as are honorary, or whether they be conferred on matriculants of the said Morrin College, or other persons, and to repeal or amend such by-laws or regulations, and to make others in their stead, when and as the said Theological Faculty may see fit.

3. This Act shall be read and construed with the said Act 24 Victoria, chapter 109, hereby amended, as forming part thereof.

At present Morrin College is affiliated to the University of McGill College, and its course in Arts is governed by what is prescribed by that university. No by-laws seem, as yet, to have been passed for the government of the college.

REGULATIONS—FACULTY OF DIVINITY.

1. Students who desire to enter the Theological Department of Morrin College, with the view of studying for the ministry, must forward to the registrar, on or before November 1st, of each year:—(1.) Presbyterial certificate of church membership, and of recommendation to the Senate for admission. (2.) Evidence that they are graduates of some university recognized as such by the Presbyterian Church in Canada, or that they have completed their attendance on the first three years' course of study in such university, or in Morrin College.

2. Divinity students who have attended other Theological Seminaries will, on presenting Presbyterial certificates of standing and recommendation, be admitted *ad eundem*.

3. The course of study throughout is that recommended by the General Assembly of the Presbyterian Church in Canada.

Degree of D. D.

The degree of Doctor of Divinity is conferred *honoris causa*.

Degree of B. D.

1. Candidates for the degree of Bachelor of Divinity must be graduates of Arts of some university recognized by the Church, or ministers of five years' standing.

2. The examination will be held in the beginning of April each year. It will be divided into two parts, the first of which may be taken at the close of the Theological Curriculum, and the second after an interval of not less than one year, nor more than two years.

3. The following are the subjects of examination for this degree:—
Part 1. (1) Sacred Languages. (2) Exegetics. (3) Church History. Part 2. (4) Systematic Theology. (5) Apologetics. (6) Practical Theology.

A first class standing in the B. A., Arts and closing Theological examination, exempts candidates from examination in any of the subjects embraced in Sacred languages. For the text books prescribed reference must be made to the college calendar.

(5). Presbyterian College, Montreal.

28 Vict., cap. 58 (C).—An Act to incorporate the Presbyterian College of Montreal. (*Assented to 18th March, 1865.*)

Whereas petitions have been presented on behalf of the Canada Presbyterian Church, setting forth that the said Church is desirous of creating an educational establishment in Montreal, in connection with the same, and praying for an Act of incorporation, and it is expedient to comply with the said petition : Therefore Her Majesty, &c., enacts as follows :

1. John Redpath, George Rogers, Warden King, the Reverend William Taylor, D. D., (*and others, naming them*), and such persons as may, from time to time, be and become members of the Canada Presbyterian Church, within the limits of Lower Canada, shall henceforth be a body corporate, under the name of "The Presbyterian College of Montreal," and shall continue to be a body corporate, with perpetual succession, and a common seal, and with the powers vested in corporate bodies by the Interpretation Act, and also with power under the said corporate name, and without license in mortmain to hold and to purchase, acquire, have, take, and enjoy by gift, grant, conveyance, devise, bequest, or otherwise to them and their successors, any estate or property, real or personal, to and for the use of the said college, in trust for the promotion of theological learning and education of youth for the holy ministry, under the authority, and according to the principles and standards of the Canada Presbyterian Church aforesaid, and also with power to let, convey, or otherwise dispose of such real and personal estate, from time to time, as may be deemed expedient, with the written consent of the Synod : provided always, that such real estate, so held by the said college hereby incorporated, shall be such, and such only, as may be required for the purposes of college buildings and offices, residences for the professors, tutors, students and officers, with gardens and

pleasure grounds pertaining thereto, not exceeding in annual value the sum of $50,000 : provided, also, that the said college may acquire any other real estate, or any interest therein by gift, devise, or bequest, if made at least six months before the death of the party making the same, and the college may hold such estate for a period of not more than three years, and the same or any part or portion thereof, or interest therein, which may not, within the said period, have been alienated and disposed of, shall revert to the party from whom the same was acquired, his heirs or other representatives ; and provided also, that the proceeds of such property as shall have been disposed of during the said period, may be invested in the public securities of the Province, stocks of the chartered banks, or other approved securities, for the use of the said college.

2. It shall be lawful for the Synod of the Canada Presbyterian Church, at its next ordinary meeting after the passing of this Act, to declare, by resolution, or a by-law to that effect and recorded in the register of proceedings of the said Synod, the theological doctrines and principles which shall be taught in the said college, what are the books and documents in which the said principles and doctrines are contained, and such declaration, so made and recorded, shall be irrevocable in so far as the said college shall be concerned, and shall be held at all times thereafter to contain the theological doctrines and principles to be taught in the said college, and for the propagation of which the property acquired for the said college shall be appropriated, and to no other.

3. And the said Synod of the Canada Presbyterian Church shall have power, at its next or any subsequent meeting, to appoint and remove professors and tutors in such way and manner as to them shall seem good ; and shall also have power to make rules and by-laws for the government of the said college, and to alter, amend and annul the same and make other rules instead thereof, and also to constitute a senate for the said college, with such powers as they may deem from time to time ex-

pedient; also to constitute a board of management for the financial and other affairs of the said college, not otherwise provided for, in such manner and with such powers and under such conditions as to the said Synod shall from time to time seem expedient : provided always, that such by-laws, rules or regulations be not contrary to this Act or repugnant to the laws of this Province.

4. In case the body of christians known under the name of the Canada Presbyterian Church, shall at any time or times hereafter, under that or any other name, unite itself with any other body or bodies of Presbyterians adhering to the principles and doctrines mentioned in the declaration to be made according to the second section of this Act, or in the books and documents therein mentioned as containing the said principles and doctrines, or take such other body or bodies of Presbyterians into union with itself, and in case such united body of Presbyterians shall agree to hold and shall hold a Synod once or oftener in each year, according to the manner now in use in the Canada Presbyterian Church, then and in every such case, this Act shall apply to such united body of Presbyterians, under whatever name they shall have formed such union, and all rights, powers and authorities by this Act vested in the Synod of the Canada Presbyterian Church shall be vested in and apply to the Synod of such united body under whatever name or designation such united body may be known.

5. In case the said Canada Presbyterian Church, or such united body as aforesaid, shall determine to form itself into two or more Synods and to form one General Assembly, which shall have supreme jurisdiction in such Church or united body, then all the rights, powers and authorities by this Act vested in the Synod of the Canada Presbyterian Church, or in the Synod of such united body as aforesaid, shall be divested from the said Synod and be applied to and be vested in such General Assembly; and for the purpose of this Act such General Assembly or Supreme Court shall thenceforth exclusively

exercise all the rights, powers and authorities conferred by this Act on the Synod of the Canada Presbyterian Church.

6. The said Presbyterian College of Montreal may at any time become affiliated to the University of McGill College upon such terms as the said University and the said Presbyterian College of Montreal may agree upon.

---

43 & 44 Vict., cap. 66 (Q.)—An Act to amend the Statute of the Province of Canada, 28 Victoria, chapter 53. intituled "An Act to incorporate the Presbyterian College of Montreal. (*Assented to 24th July, 1880.*)

Whereas petitions have been presented by the Presbyterian College of Montreal praying for an amendment to the Act passed in the 28th year of Her Majesty's reign, intituled "An Act to incorporate the Presbyterian College of Montreal," and it is expedient to comply with the said petitions: Therefore, Her Majesty, &c., enacts as follows :—

1. The name of the corporation shall be hereafter, "The Presbyterian College, Montreal."

2. The senate of the said "The Presbyterian College. Montreal," shall have power to confer the degree of Bachelor of Divinity, subject to such regulations and examinations as may be imposed by the said senate, as well as to confer the honorary degree of Doctor of Divinity.

3. The said senate shall have power to make by-laws touching any matter or thing pertaining to the conditions on which the said degrees of Bachelor of Divinity. and Doctor of Divinity, may be conferred, whether the said degrees be such as are granted in course or by examinations, or such as are honorary, or whether they be conferred on matriculants of the said Presbyterian Col-

lege, Montreal, or other persons, and such by-laws to amend when the said senate shall see fit.

DECLARATION OF PRINCIPLES.

Canada Presbyterian Church, Minutes 1865, p. 30.—That the principles and doctrines to be taught in the Presbyterian College of Montreal by the professors and tutors, or other persons who shall from time to time, and at all times hereafter, be employed or appointed in giving instruction in the said college shall be such and such only as are consistent with and agreeable to the " Confession of Faith," the "Larger and Shorter Catechisms," and the " Form of Church Government," all of which are called " The Westminster Standards" and shall comprise all theoglogical learning consistent with the said standards : provided always, that the said standards be understood and taken in terms of the articles of union agreed upon by the Synod of the Canada Presbyterian Church at Montreal, in the year of our Lord 1861 : provided also, that the said "Westminster Standards" be taken and understood with such other or further directions and rules as to church government, discipline or worship, as may from time to time be furnished or ordained by the Synod of the said Canada Presbyterian Church, with the concurrence of a majority of the Presbyteries of the said church, to be ascertained in such manner as the Synod shall prescribe, and that such regulations and rules be duly recorded in the minute book of the said Synod, and signed by the moderator and clerk for the time being of such Synod.

The Synod further instruct their clerk to register this resolution and declaration in the records of the Synod.

BY-LAWS.

Canada Presbyterian Church, Minutes 1867, p. 48.—1. There shall be a board of management, composed of thirty-five persons, ordained ministers and elders of the Church, or members in full communion, of whom seven shall be a quorum for transaction of all business. The said board shall be annually appointed by the Synod (*a*) and its members shall hold office until their successors be appointed. They shall appoint their own secretary and treasurer, who shall keep records and accounts, which shall be open to the inspection of the Synod. The chairman of the board shall be appointed annually by the Synod and in the event of no such appointment being made, or of the death, removal or resignation of the said chairman, his place shall be supplied by the board itself.

(*a*) Throughout these by-laws the expression "Synod" is used, but the General Assembly can exercise all the powers and authorities given to the Synod either by the Act of Incorporation or these by-laws. *See 28 Vict., c. 53, s. 5. (C.)*

2. The board shall be convened by the chairman at least three times a year and at such time and in such manner as may be determined by the Synod or by the board itself.

3. The board shall have the whole management of the financial affairs of the said college, shall receive and disburse all its moneys, keep and manage all its property, and transact all its business relating to property and money committed to its care, by the Synod or otherwise, and shall exercise all the powers in regard to property and money vested in the corporation. In cases where special instructions shall be given by the Synod, in writing under the hand of their clerk, it shall be the duty of the said board to act according to such instructions.

4. The board shall receive annual reports from the senate in reference to the departments under the care of the said senate, and shall transmit the same to the Synod, along with a report on all matters entrusted to said board, and an audited balance sheet of the property and financial affairs of the college.

5. The board shall further take general cognizance of all matters pertaining to the interest of the college, and co-operate with the senate in maintaining its discipline. They shall also take charge of the boarding department of the college, and make such regulations for its management as they may see fit, and shall appoint all subordinate servants, and dismiss and remove the same as they shall see fit.

6. The board shall have power to appoint an acting sub-committee, with such powers as they may deem requisite.

7. The chairman of the board shall have charge of the corporation seal, and shall affix it to such documents as he may be directed by the special instructions of the board.

College Senate.

8. (*As amended, Minutes 1882, p. 38*). The Principal, professors and lecturers of the college, together with not less than twelve members of the Church, shall be annually appointed by the General Assembly as a college senate, to whom shall be entrusted the reception, academical superintendence, and discipline of the students, and of all other persons within the said college. The senate shall take a general inspection of the whole internal arrangements of the college, and of the studies of the students, and shall place said students in that year of the curriculum to which they may be certified by Presbyteries, or by such other body as the Assembly may determine, and shall have charge of the library and museum.

9. The senate shall at the close of each college session hold an examination of the students, and present to the board of management

a report on the studies of the classes, and on any other matters under its supervision.

The Principal.

10. The title of the Principal shall be "The Reverend the Principal of the Presbyterian College, Montreal."

11. He shall preside in all meetings of the college senate, and summon such meetings at stated or convenient times. In the unavoidable absence or inability of the Principal, the senior professor shall summon and preside at necessary meetings of the senate with the consent of the other professors. In case of a division, the Principal shall only have a casting vote.

12. He shall preside at the public opening and closing of the college session.

13. He shall be the medium of communication with, and conduct the official correspondence of, the college senate.

14. He shall have a general superintendence of the studies of the students in accordance with the instructions of the senate; it being understood that the other professors shall be responsible only to the Synod for the discharge of the duties entrusted to them.

Professors and Tutors.

15. No person shall at any time be employed, or inducted into office, as professor of theology, who is not at the time of his employment or induction an ordained minister of the Canada Presbyterian Church; and if a licentiate shall at any time be appointed, he shall, before induction, be ordained to the holy ministry in the usual manner by the Presbytery of Montreal, or by a commission specially appointed for that purpose by the Synod; and all persons, if any, who shall be appointed or employed as tutors, shall at the time of their entrance into office be members of the said church in full communion therewith, and said professors and tutors shall sign the formula appointed to be signed by ministers, &c., of the Church.

16. All professors and tutors who shall hereafter be appointed or employed in the said college, shall be appointed by the said Synod at its ordinary annual session, or at any special meeting of the said Synod, to be called for the purpose of making such appointment or appointments by notice from the Moderator of Synod for the time being to be sent to each member of Synod, at least fifteen days before the day appointed for such special meeting, such appointment to be made by open vote of the majority of members present, at the sederunt of the said Synod at which the appointment shall be made, or in

such other manner as the said Synod shall from time to time by resolution determine and direct to be pursued in making such appointments ; provided always, that any such professor or tutor may resign, or may by the said Synod be removed, suspended or deposed from office according to the laws of the Church, and in case of any such tutor resigning or ceasing to be such as aforesaid, or in case of any such professor being removed or being deposed from the ministry in due process of discipline, such tutor or professor so resigning, ceasing to be a member, or being removed or deposed as aforesaid, shall *ipso facto* cease to be a professor or tutor in the said college, and cease to have any emolument or privilege belonging to the said college, and his office shall be vacant.

Sessions ; Admission and Attendance of Students.

17. The session or academical year shall commence on the first Wednesday of October, and end on the first Wednesday of April. There shall be such recess at the end of December, as may be fixed by the senate.

18. No person shall be entitled to rank as a student, who has not been certified to the senate by some Presbytery of the Church, or such other body as the Synod may appoint, and who has not signed the Album of the college, and agreed to submit to its discipline in such form as may be determined by the senate.

19. Every student shall, at the end of each session, apply to the professors on whose instructions he has attended, for certificates attesting the regularity of his attendance, his proficiency, diligence and general conduct, which certificates shall be presented to the Presbytery of the Church, by whom the said student may be examined for license, or to the board of examiners (*b*) for entrance upon the next year of the curriculum ; and before any student shall be taken on trials for license, he shall present to his Presbytery a certificate from the senate signed by the Principal, attesting that he has attended all the classes and performed all the duties required by the Church.

20. Cases of an urgent or peculiar nature of attendance on, or absence from, the classes of any particular year shall be adjudged upon by the senate according to the circumstances of each case.

DEGREES IN DIVINITY.

1. Regulations Concerning the Degree of Bachelor of Divinity.

1. Those entitled to become candidates for the degree of B. D. must have completed a course of theological study in this, or some recognized institution.

(*b*) The Assembly adopted a recommendation " That the powers hitherto exercised by the board of examiners be henceforth retained in the senate." *See Minutes 1880, p. 22.* Since then no board has been appointed.

2. They must be graduates in Arts in some recognized university.

3. The final examination for B. D. cannot be passed, nor the degree conferred until the session following that in which the candidate has completed his ordinary course in theology, unless by special permission of the senate.

4. The curriculum contains the following subjects (*a*):—Latin, Greek, Hebrew, Introduction, Apologetics, Dogmatics, Church Government, Homiletics, Church History.

5. Candidates may proceed to the degree of B. D. in one of three methods :—

(*a*) They may take at one examination the whole of the work prescribed for the degree.

(*b*) They may divide the work into two portions, passing the examination in the first portion at any period of study, and the second after an interval of not more than three years. The following is the division :—First Examination—Greek, Hebrew, Introduction, Apologetics, Dogmatics, Church Government, Homiletics, Church History. Second Examination—Greek, Chaldee, Latin, Introduction, Apologetics, Dogmatics, Church Government, Church History.

(*c*) Students of this college may spread the work over the three years of the honor course and the final examination for B. D. The latter examination includes : Greek, Syriac, Latin, Introduction, Apologetics, Dogmatics, Church History.

6. Candidates who have already passed examinations in any part of the prescribed honor course, will not be subject to re-examination in the same.

7. The examinations will be held in October and March of each session, and the degree will be conferred at the college convocation, on the first Wednesday of April, or on such other occasion as the senate may direct.

8. Candidates for examination must send notice of their intention to present themselves, together with such fee and certification as may be necessary, to the registrar, at least a month before the examination.

9. The fee for the examination for the degree of B. D. to candidates who have not passed examinations during their ordinary course in the college shall be five dollars ; which fee must be paid to the registrar at the time of application. Candidates who fail to pass may present themselves again without further fee.

10. In order to pass for the degree of B. D., the candidate must obtain two-thirds of the whole number of marks assigned to all the papers, and not less than one-half of the number assigned to any single paper.

11. The fee for the degree of Bachelor of Divinity shall be ten dollars, which must be paid to the registrar prior to the conferring of the degree.

(*a*) For the prescribed text books reference should be made to the College Calendar.

12. Applications from those holding the degree of B. D. from any other college to be received *ad eundem gradum* in this college, will be considered on their merits. The fee for conferring such degree shall be five dollars.

11. Degree of Doctor of Divinity.

1. Bachelors of Divinity desiring to obtain the Doctorate must make application to the senate, which reserves the right to determine who are eligible for its highest honor.

2. The degree of D. D. in course shall be granted only to those who have taken the degree of B. D. in this college, either by examination or by admission *ad eundem gradum*, who have been at least ten years in the ministry, and, at the same time, five years in the possession of the lower degree.

3. The applicants must have attained excellence in one of the following departments of theological study, viz.: Theology, Ecclesiology, Ethics, Patrology, Biblical Antiquities and History, Old Testament Exegesis, New Testament Exegesis, Biblical Introduction, Oriental Languages, Apologetics, and must give evidence of the same by passing a general examination, without prescribed text books, in that department.

4. Having satisfactorily passed the said examination, candidates shall submit to the senate a printed thesis (twenty-five copies) exhibiting independent research on some special subject in their department, which being sustained by the senate, the degree shall be conferred upon them.

5. The examination shall be held and the degree conferred at the times already specified for B. D. (Examination in March and degree first Wednesday in April.)

6. The fee for examination for the degree of D. D. shall be ten dollars.

7. The fee for the degree of D. D. shall be fifty dollars.

---

(6). Manitoba College.

---

36 Vict., cap 33 (M.)—An Act to incorporate the College of Manitoba. (*Assented to 18th March, 1873.*)

Whereas the Hon. Donald A. Smith, the Hon. Andrew Graham B. Bannatyne (*and others, naming them*), have, by their petition represented that an educational institution has been for some time, and is now in operation in this Province in connection with, and under the authority of, the General Assembly of the Canada Presbyterian Church, and whereas it would tend to advance and extend the usefulness of the said institution and promote the purposes for which it has been established, that it should be incorporated: Therefore, Her Majesty, &c., enacts as follows:—

1. The Hon. Donald A. Smith, of Winnipeg; the Hon. Andrew Graham B. Bannatyne, of Winnipeg (*and others, naming them*), and such persons as may from time to time be and become members of the Canada Presbyterian Church within the limits of Manitoba, shall be and are hereby constituted a body politic and corporate by and under the name of "The College of Manitoba," for the education of youth and the promotion of classical and scientific knowledge.

2. The said corporation shall, by the name of the College of Manitoba, have perpetual succession, and a common seal, and by such name may, from time to time, and at all times hereafter, acquire, hold, possess and enjoy, and may have, take and receive for them and their successors, any lands, tenements, and hereditaments, and real and immovable property and estate within the Province necessary for actual use and occupation as college buildings and offices, residences for the professors, tutors, students and officers, with gardens or pleasure grounds pertaining thereto, and the same may sell, alienate, and dispose of, and others in their stead purchase, acquire, and hold for the uses and purposes aforesaid: provided always, that the annual value of such real estate so held as aforesaid does not exceed the sum of $10,000.

3. The said corporation may, by the name aforesaid, acquire any other real estate or interest therein by gift, devise or bequest, if made at least six months before the death of the party making the same, and may hold such estate or interest therein for a period of not more than seven years; and the same or any part thereof or interest therein, which may not, within the said period, have been alienated or disposed of, shall revert to the party

from whom the same was acquired, his heirs or other representatives; and the proceeds of such property as shall have been disposed of during the said period may be invested in the public securities of the Dominion of Canada or of this Province, or in other approved securities for the use of the said corporation.

4. The affairs of the said corporation shall be managed by a board of management consisting of fifteen members (*a*); and the Hon. Donald A. Smith, the Hon. A. G. B. Bannatyne (*and others, naming them*), shall constitute the first board of management, and shall continue to hold office until their successors are appointed as hereinafter mentioned.

5. The board of management shall be appointed by the General Assembly of the Canada Presbyterian Church, in such manner as the said General Assembly may from time to time by rule or by-law appoint.

6. The board of management shall have the whole management of the financial affairs of the said corporation, shall receive and disburse all its money, control, keep and manage all its property and transact all business relating to property and money committed to its care by the General Assembly or otherwise, and shall at all times and in all things observe and obey the orders and instructions of the said General Assembly.

7. The professors in the said college, together with three (*b*) members of the board of management nominated by the said board annually for that purpose, shall constitute the senate of the said college, to whom shall be entrusted the reception, academical superintendence and discipline of the students and of all other persons within the said college.

8. The power of appointing and removing professors and tutors in the said college shall be and the same is hereby vested in the General Assembly of the Canada Presbyterian Church : provided always, that the said

---

(*a*) Twenty-five since 40 Vict. c. 61.
(*b*). Seven since 40 Vict., c. 51.

General Assembly may by rule or by-law delegate to the board of management the power of appointing and removing professors and tutors, under such restrictions and regulations as the said General Assembly may from time to time deem expedient.

9. The said General Assembly may from time to time make rules or by-laws for the government of the said corporation and for the guidance of the said board of management, and may alter, amend and annul the said rules or by-laws from time to time : provided always, that such rules or by-laws be not contrary to this Act or repugnant to the laws of this Province.

10. The said rules and by-laws shall be entered in a book kept for such purpose and signed by the moderator of the General Assembly at which the same are adopted or passed, and by the clerk or clerks thereof, and such book shall be deposited among the records of the said General Assembly.

11. A copy of the said rules or by-laws certified under the hand of the clerk or one of the clerks (if more than one) of the said General Assembly shall be admitted and received as evidence of the said rules or by-laws and of the contents thereof in any court of this Province, and for all purposes, without proof of the signature of the said clerk.

12. The said General Assembly may at any future time make provision in connection with the said college and as part of the proper work thereof for the education of students in theology, under the authority and according to the principles and standards of the Canada Presbyterian Church : provided always, that any resolution or by-law passed by the General Assembly in pursuance of the power conferred by this section shall declare the theological doctrines and principles which shall be taught in the said college, or what are the books and documents in which the said principles are contained, and such declaration shall be irrevocable in so far as the said college shall be concerned, and shall be held at all

times thereafter to contain the theological doctrines and principles to be taught in the said college ; and a copy of the said resolution or by-law, certified under the hand of the moderator of the General Assembly at which the same may be adopted or passed, and of the clerk or clerks thereof shall be filed in the office of the secretary of this Province within six months after the same has been passed or adopted : provided always, in the event of a union taking place at any time or times hereafter between the Canada Presbyterian Church and any other body or bodies of Presbyterians as hereinafter set forth, the basis of union which shall or may be adopted by such Church and such other body or bodies of Presbyterians for such union, shall be held and taken to be and form part of such declaration of theological doctrines and principles, and to interpret the same in manner as fully and effectually to all intents and purposes as if the same had been originally incorporated therewith and had formed part thereof.

13. In case the body of christians known under the name of the Canada Presbyterian Church shall at any time or times hereafter, under that or any other name, unite itself with any other body of Presbyterians, and in case such united body of Presbyterians shall agree to hold and shall hold a General Assembly once or oftener in each year, according to the manner now in use in the said Canada Presbyterian Church, then, and in every such case, this Act shall apply to such united body of Presbyterians, under whatever name they shall have formed such union ; and all rights, powers and authorities vested in the General Assembly of the Canada Presbyterian Church shall be vested in and apply to the General Assembly of such united body, under whatever name or designation such united body may be known.

14. All and every the estate and property, real and personal, held by any person or persons as trustees, for or on behalf of the said educational institution mentioned in the preamble of this Act, and all debts, claims and rights whatsoever due to any person or persons for the purposes of the said institution, shall be and are hereby

vested in the corporation hereby established, and all debts due by and all claims against any person or persons, on behalf of the said institution, shall be paid, discharged and satisfied by the said corporation.

15. All existing rules and regulations for the government of the said educational institution shall be the rules and regulations for the government of the corporation hereby established until the General Assembly of the Canada Presbyterian Church shall pass rules and by-laws for the government thereof, and for the guidance of the board of management as hereinbefore provided.

---

44 Vict. (3rd Sess.), cap. 32 (M.)—An Act to amend the Act incorporating the College of Manitoba. (*Assented to 25th May, 1881.*)

The Legislative Assembly, &c., enacts as follows :—

1. The College of Manitoba shall have and is hereby given full power and authority to borrow any sum or sums of money upon the security of any lands, tenements or hereditaments purchased or held by the said college, under the 2nd or 3rd sections of the Act passed in the 36th year of Her Majesty's reign, chaptered 33, and to mortgage all or any such lands, tenements or hereditaments to any person or persons for securing any sum or sums of money so borrowed, or for securing any portion of the purchase money of any such lands, tenements or hereditaments.

2. The said College of Manitoba shall have full power and authority to invest all or any sums of money of or belonging to the said college, or given or bequeathed to it, in any bonds or securities of the Dominion or of any Province thereof, or of Great Britain and Ireland, or of any foreign state, or in any debentures of any of the municipalities of this Province, and also to loan and invest any such moneys upon the security of any real or personal property, and the said College of Manitoba

may, under its corporate name or in the name of any person or persons as trustee or trustees, take and hold any real or personal property, or any interest therein by way of mortgage to secure any such investment.

---

49 Vict., cap. 61 (M.)—An Act respecting the College of Manitoba. (*Assented to 19th April, 1886.*).

Her Majesty, &c., enacts as follows :—

1. The affairs of the College of Manitoba, incorporated by an Act passed in the 36th year of Her Majesty's reign, chapter 33, shall be managed by a board of management consisting of twenty-five members, instead of fifteen as provided for in the 4th section of the said Act.

2. The professors in the said college, together with seven members of the board of management, shall constitute the senate of the said college, instead of the professors and three members of the board of management as provided for in the 7th section of the said Act.

3. The board of management and senate of the said college respectively shall continue to be appointed in the manner provided for by the said Act.

Rev. Stat. of Manitoba, cap. 147—An Act respecting the University of Manitoba.

Inter alia.

31. All incorporated and affiliated colleges shall have the entire management of their internal affairs, studies, worship and religious teaching ; and members of any other university within Her Majesty's Dominions shall be exempt from the preliminary examination hereinbefore in this Act mentioned, and may be admitted by the council of the university *ad eundem statum* or *ad eundem gradum.*

32. The following colleges incorporated at the time of the passing of this Act, (c) shall be in connection with the University of Manitoba, for the purpose set forth in the last preceding section, that is to say :—The College of St. Boniface, the College of St. John, and the Manitoba College, and all other colleges heretofore lawfully affiliated with the said university; and the Lieutenant-Governor-in-Council may, from time to time, affiliate other incorporated colleges into such university, on being satisfied of such colleges being in operation and possessed of the requisite buildings, and a sufficient staff of professors and teaching officers, to entitle such colleges in his judgment thereto. (d)

33. (*As amended by 58 & 59 Vict., ch. 47.*) Any incorporated denominational college which is at the time of the coming into force of this Act affiiliated with the university, or which may hereafter become affiliated therewith shall, with the sanction of the governing body of the denomination to which it belongs, have the power of granting in any such manner as it may determine, the degrees of Bachelor of Divinity and Doctor of Divinity, and to this end shall have the power of forming a separate faculty in theology.

34. Such graduates in theology shall have in the university the same rights and privileges as other graduates.

35. It shall be the duty of the presidents of the said faculties in theology to report respectively, from time to time to the chancellor of the university, upon the organization of such respective faculties, the granting of the degrees, and such other matters as the chancellor of the university and the presidents of such faculties may have agreed to, for the mutual benefit of said university and faculties.

(c) The original University Act, 40 Vict., ch. 11 (M.), was passed 28th Feb. 1877.

(d) To the colleges named in this section there have been added: Manitoba Medical College, incorporated by 40 Vict., ch. 13 (M.); 57 Vict., ch. 18 (M.); and Wesley College, incorporated by 40 Vict., ch. 41 (M.); 49 Vict., ch. 72 (M).

By-Laws.

Canada Presbyterian Church Minutes, 1873, p. 71.—1. The board of management shall consist of fifteen members, as provided by the Act of incorportion, to be elected annually, five of whom shall form a quorum.

2. The chairman of the board shall be appointed annually by the Assembly; and in the event of no such appointment being made, or of the death, removal, or resignation of said chairman, his place shall be supplied by the board itself. The board shall appoint their own secretary and treasurer, who shall keep records and accounts, which shall be open to the inspection of the Assembly.

3. The board shall be convened by the chairman, at least three times a year, and at such time and in such manner as may be determined by the Assembly, or by the board itself.

4. The board shall receive an annual report from the senate, in reference to the departments under the care of said senate, and shall transmit the same to the Assembly, along with a report on all matters intrusted to said board, and an audited balance-sheet of the property and financial affairs of the college.

5. The board shall have authority to appoint an acting sub-committee, with such powers as to transacting business entrusted to the board as may be requisite.

6. The chairman of the board shall have charge of the corporation seal, and shall, under the special instructions of the board, affix it to official documents.

7. The senate shall, at the close of each college term, hold an examination of the students, and present to the board of management a report on the studies of the classes, and on any other matters under its supervision.

8. The senate shall appoint annually one of their number to be their chairman, who shall summon all meetings of the senate. In the absence of the chairman, the senate may appoint another of their number to preside. In case of a division, the chairman shall only have a casting vote.

9. The session, or academical year, shall commence on the first Tuesday of October, and end on the last Friday of June. There shall be such vacations as shall be fixed by the senate.

10. Certificates of attendance, and of having passed the required examinations, may be given by the senate, signed by the chairman.

11. The curriculum of study shall be such as may at any time be determined by the Assembly ; and in the meantime is that contained in the accompanying schedule, comprising Greek and Latin classics, mathematics, including trigonometry, Euclid, algebra, arithmetic, English grammar and literature, French, the elements of German, history and geography, and the natural sciences, including geology, zoology, botany and chemistry, with the principles of scientific agriculture. The course in commercial subjects includes penmanship, business correspondence, book-keeping and banking.

*Report of Board of Management of Manitoba College, Minutes, 1883, App. p. 158.--Inter alia.--*The board has heard with satisfaction that the Presbytery of Manitoba have agreed to memoralize the General Assembly for the appointment of a professor of theology in the college, and that they are prepared to guarantee the salary of such a professor. The board cordially endorses the action of the Presbytery, and hopes that the prayer of the memorial will be granted.

Minutes 1883, p. 30.—There was read . . . a memorial from the Presbytery of Manitoba setting forth, in substance, the desirableness, expediency, and necessity, in order to the better promotion of the interests of the Church in Manitoba and the Northwest, that there should be a theological department in Manitoba College . . . and praying that the General Assembly take steps to have such department instituted, and a principal and professor of divinity appointed without delay.

Page 31. That the General Assembly appoint a committee, to whom the report of the College of Manitoba, and the accompanying memorial shall be remitted, with instructions carefully to consider the important subjects therein referred to, and report tomorrow its judgment as to the action which the General Assembly should take

Page 46. The Assembly called for the report of the committee appointed to consider the report of the board of management of Manitoba College, and the memorial of the Presbytery of Manitoba, in regard to the instituting of a theological department in said college. The report was handed in and read.

Page 47. That in accordance with the recommendation of the report, the Assembly do now appoint the Rev. John M. King, D. D,, Professor of Theology and Principal of Manitoba College. The motion was unanimously agreed to, and the Assembly decerned and ordered in terms thereof. (*a*)

(*a*) In taking this action the Assembly entirely overlooked the fact that Manitoba College was not, by its Act of incorporation, a theological college. It was founded "for the education of youth and the promotion of classical and scientific knowledge." Section 12 of the Act empowered the Assembly "to make provision in connection with the said college, and as part of the proper work thereof for the education of students in theology," but it had never made such provision, and indeed, had on several occasions decided that theology should not be taught in the college. See *Minutes 1881, pp. 19, 50 ; Minutes 1882, pp. 27, 45, 46.* The Assembly should, in the first place, have passed a by-law to provide for the teaching of theology, accompanied by a declaration of the doctrines and principles to be taught, as required by the Act, and then appointed a professor.

Minutes 1885, p. 18.—The General Assembly receives and adopts the report of the Manitoba College . . . expresses its approval of the step taken to institute examinations for the degree of B. D. by the college, instructing the senate to make the work, as nearly as possible, equal to that required by the other colleges of the Church, and empowers the board of the college to make application to the Legislature for such a modification of the Act of incorporation as will give a board of 25 instead of 15, with a corresponding increase of the senate.

Minutes 1887, p. 21. The Assembly appointed a committee—To prepare a resolution or by-law making provision for the education of students in theology in connection with the College of Manitoba, in accordance with the requirements of section 12 of the Act incorporating the college, and submit the same to this Assembly. *Page 52.* The committee appointed at a former sederunt, submitted a paper containing resolutions to bring Manitoba College under similar sanctions as to the teaching of theology with those on which the charter is based in regard to literary subjects. The report . . . was received and adopted, and is as follows :—

The General Assembly of the Presbyterian Church in Canada, deeming it expedient to make provision in connection with the College of Manitoba, and as a part of the proper work thereof, for the education of students in theology, under the authority and according to the principles and standards of the Presbyterian Church in Canada, the General Assembly doth hereby, in pursuance of the power conferred by the 12th section of the Act passed by the Legislature of Manitoba in the 36th year of Her Majesty's reign, chaptered 33, and in pursuance of all other powers and authorities enabling it on this behalf, establish a Faculty of Theology in the said college, and the said General Assembly doth hereby declare the theological doctrines and principles, which shall be taught in the said college, or what are the books and documents in which the said principles are contained, as follows :—

DECLARATION OF PRINCIPLES.

That the principles and doctrines to be taught in the College of Manitoba by the professors and tutors, or other persons who shall from time to time, and at all times hereafter, be employed or appointed in giving instruction in the said college shall be such and such only as are consistent with and agreeable to the "Confession of Faith," the "Larger and Shorter Catechisms," and the "Form of Church Government," all of which are called "The Westminster Standards," and shall comprise all theological learning consistent with said standards : provided always that the said standards be understood and taken in terms of the basis of union agreed upon by the General Assembly of the Presbyterian Church in Canada, at Montreal, in the year of our Lord 1875 : provided also that the said "Westminster

Standards" be taken and understood with such further or other directions and rules as to church government, discipline or worship, as may from time to time be prescribed or ordained by the General Assembly of the said Presbyterian Church in Canada, with the concurrence of a majority of the Presbyteries of the said Church, to be ascertained in such manner as the General Assembly shall prescribe, and that such directions and rules be duly recorded in the minute book of the said General Assembly, and signed by the moderator and clerk, or clerks, for the time being, of such General Assembly.

SUMMER SESSION.

Minutes 1891, p. 26. There were presented and read, (1) An overture from the Presbytery of Toronto, to the effect that the Assembly should make such arrangements for a Summer Session for students as will both conserve the interests of theological education, and provide, as far as possible, continuous supply in all mission fields; (2) An overture on the same subject from the Presbytery of Brandon; (3) An overture on the same subject transmitted by the Synod of Manitoba and the North West Territories. It was agreed, that the overtures be received, and the proposal recommended in them remitted to a committee which shall consider it or any other plan which may be proposed for overtaking the admitted necessities of our great mission field.

The committee subsequently brought in a report which led to lengthened discussion with several motions and amendments. *See pp. 48, 49, 50, 51.*

An amendment was moved to a motion before the Assembly, (*p. 50*) That the motion be not now adopted, but that the whole question anent a Summer Session be referred to the Presbyteries of the Church for their consideration to report to the next General Assembly. The amendment was adopted, and the Assembly decerned accordingly.

Report of Board of Management of Manitoba College. Minutes 1892, App. No. 9.—The proposal brought forward at the last meeting of the General Assembly that a summer session for students in theology should be held in one of its colleges, has been taken under consideration by the board, and should it, in the opinion of the General Assembly, be considered advisable to institute such a session, and to select Manitoba College as the one at which such shall be carried on in summer, the board, while quite satisfied with existing arrangements, is prepared cordially to acquiesce in the resolution of the Assembly, and to do all that lies within its sphere to carry the proposed scheme into successful operation. The board, when considering the question, had before it certain resolutions come to by the senate of the college, the substance of which appears in the report of the senate transmitted herewith. After careful consideration of these, the board fully approves of the action taken by the senate, and endorses the views expressed in its report. The board would, however, call the attention of the Assembly to the fact that the college will be put to considerably increased outlay in carrying on such a scheme, and it would respectfully, but earnestly, urge the necessity for action being taken by the Assembly to secure for the college the further financial support required. Mere general resolutions commending the college to the liberality of the Church, however well meant, will be an insecure foundation for the board to build upon. Surely, if the college agrees to such a radical change being made in the mode of carrying on part of its work, with the attendant risk and expense, in order to supply what is believed by so many to be an absolute necessity in connection with the extension and upbuilding of the Church throughout a large part of the Dominion the Assembly should provide the means of support without throwing an increased burden upon any of the professors or officials of the college.

Report of the Senate of Manitoba College. Minutes 1892, App. No. 9.—The important question of a change in the season of the year, during which the classes in theology should be taught, has largely engaged the attention of the senate since the date of last report. In the interests simply of the institution the senate would have wished that this question had not been raised. In deference, however, to what appears to be a general desire of the Church that a summer session should be instituted at the seat of one of the colleges, under the Assembly, and in view of the fact that Winnipeg, especially because of its proximity to the largest mission field of the Church, appears to be the most suitable locality, the senate has agreed to recommend to the General Assembly to arrange that the theological classes in Manitoba College should hereafter, and until otherwise appointed, be held during the summer months, that the session should extend from the beginning of April to the end of August, and that the new arrangement should take effect in April, 1893.

Minutes 1892, p. 37. The Assembly took up the report of the special committee on the remit of the last General Assembly on a summer session in one of the theological colleges. It was moved, That a summer session be instituted in connection with Manitoba college, and that the senate of that college be instructed to arrange that the theological classes be, until otherwise appointed, held during the summer months,—that the session should extend from the beginning of April to the end of August, and that the new arrangement should take effect in April, 1893. It was moved in amendment, That taking all circumstances into consideration, the General Assembly does not see its way clear to sanction the establishment of a summer session in the Manitoba College, as set forth by those favoring that scheme ; but, in view of the pressing necessities of the North West, remit to the Home Mission committee of the western section to consider in what other way these necessities may be met, and report to the next General Assembly. The debate was adjourned.

Page 44. The discussion of the matter of a summer session in Manitoba College was again taken up, and when the vote was taken, the "yeas and nays" being called for there voted for the motion, "yea" 114, and "nay" 13. The motion accordingly became the judgment of the Assembly.

Page 47. A motion was made, as to the expenses in connection with the summer session, followed by an amendment. Leave having been given to withdraw the original motion, the following motion was carried as the judgment of the Assembly:—That the Assembly is of opinion that $1,500 may be required annually to meet the additional expense incurred in connection with the summer session, and agrees that congregations and individuals be asked to increase their contributions to the ordinary fund of Manitoba College by that amount.

Report of Board of Management of Manitoba College, Minutes App. No. 12. 1896.—In the report presented last year, the board said, it might be necessary to ask the General Assembly to reconsider the whole question of the work to be undertaken by the college. While still believing the summer session to be advantageous to the home mission work of the Church, the board now respectfully request the General Assembly to relieve the college from carrying it on any longer, as the condition on which it was undertaken by the board, the provision by the Church of the additional expense incurred, has never been fulfilled, and as it has become evident that in the absence of this additional contribution to income, it cannot be maintained without involving the college again in debt, from which it has been freed only by a great effort. All the members of the teaching staff are overworked, but especially is this so in the case of the principal. Besides discharging all the duties which necessarily devolve upon him as the head of the institution, he has now for some years, without intermission, been spending at least eleven months of every year in the laborious work of teaching. The Church has no right to impose upon him such heavy work, seriously impairing his health and shortening his life. To carry on a summer session he must be relieved from the larger part of his work in teaching during the winter. Owing to the failure of the Church to provide the increased financial support, on the faith of which the work of a summer session was begun, the board has been unable to relieve him. But that relief must be secured before another summer session can be undertaken.

That by great exertions the principal has freed the college from a heavy debt, and that by careful management, and the exercise of rigid economy, he has, up to the present time, kept it from again falling into debt, cannot be an argument to justify failure on the part of the Church to do its duty. If extra work is to be done by the college to assist the Church in carrying on home mission work, it is surely not asking too much, to ask the Church to meet the extra expense necessary for doing that work. But what are the facts? The college has never received the additional $1,500 a year, on the faith of which the work of the summer session was begun. On the contrary, there has been a steady decrease year by year, and the amount contributed in Ontario, Quebec and the Maritime provinces, towards the support of the college during the year 1895-6, has been nearly $500 less than it was during the year in which the college was asked to undertake the work. Any income from the investment of legacies left the college, and from increased liberality of friends in the Northwest, should be applied to the development of the college apart entirely from the work of the summer session.

Under these circumstances the board must respectfully ask to be relieved from carrying on a summer session during another year.

Minutes 1896, p. 22. The Assembly agrees to refer the request of the board of the college, for the discontinuance of the summer session, on the ground of insufficient support, with the whole subject thereby raised, to a committee to be named by the moderator. *Page 47.* The report of the committee was received and adopted, the report being as follows :—

The committee beg leave to report that it has very fully considered matters connected with Manitoba College, and the effect upon its finances, as well as the increased work laid upon the Rev. Principal, in consequence of the holding of summer sessions of the college. The committee has had the benefit of a full statement as to the manner of carrying on the various departments of the work connected with the college. The information thus gained has been most useful to the committee, a careful consideration of the whole matter has led your committee to the following conclusions : (1) That the management is most careful, thorough and economical. (2) That the financial pressure experienced by the board of the college has arisen solely from the additional charges upon the revenue by the holding of the summer sessions, and the failure of the Church to keep faith in maintaining congregational contributions, which have been steadily decreasing for the past few years. (3) That the holding of the summer sessions has entailed upon Principal King an amount of extra labor which it is unreasonable for the Church to expect him to discharge, and of which a due regard to his health and future usefulness demands that he shall be relieved.

The committee considered the question of the utility of the summer sessions, and the necessity for their continuance in the interests of the work of the Church, and came to a unanimous finding in favor of their being continued The holding of a summer session has evidently greatly aided in carrying on the home mission work of the Church, and will continue to be most helpful, at least for some years to come.

The sum estimated as sufficient to relieve the college finances and provide such help as will remove the undue burden of work entailed upon the Principal, is $1500. This is a comparatively small amount, considering the good accomplished, and the raising of it should not be burdensome on the eastern portion of the Church. It has to be borne in mind, however, that the estimate is based on the assumption that the $3000, or a little over, which has been contributed by the sections of the Church lying east of Manitoba, shall be continued, making a total sum of $4500.

The committee would point out that the expense connected with the summer sessions is for the benefit of the whole Church, and therefore the Church should pay the same ; while the work done by the college in relation to the large new territory to which it is ministering in an educational and religious way, makes it necessary that the college management should, as far as possible, be relieved from anxiety.

With a view to ensure the raising of the sum required, the committee recommends : That the Assembly direct that the above mentioned sum be raised, and that Presbyteries within the bounds of the Synods of Montreal and Ottawa, of Kingston and Toronto, and of Hamilton and London, be directed to appoint a member of each Presbytery to present the claims of the college within the bounds of the Presbytery, and correspond with the treasurer of the college, Dr. King. That Dr. Bruce, Rev. John McMillan and Mr. Robert Murray be appointed to present the claims of the college on the Church in the Maritime Provinces, through the Synod of the same, at its meeting in the autumn of the present year. It is also proposed to appeal directly to some of the well-to-do members of the Church in commercial centres, to guarantee a fixed amount for say each of three successive years.

In order to ensure that this appeal may be effective, the committee recommends that the following be appointed by the Assembly a committee to prosecute the same: Rev. Dr. Robertson. Rev. Dr. Warden, Messrs. J. K. Macdonald, George Rutherford and Hon E. Bronson.

DEGREE OF BACHELOR OF DIVINITY.

The senate, having obtained the power of conferring this degree from the General Assembly in 1885, has adopted the following regulations respecting it:

1. Candidates for the degree must be graduates in Arts of the Manitoba University, or of some other approved university; but ministers in the service of the Presbyterian Church in Canada *at this date* (1885), and also students who are *now* (1885) taking the course of preparation for the ministry in Manitoba College or in some approved theological college, *though not graduates in Arts*, may become candidates on passing the examination required by the University of Manitoba in Latin and Greek.

2. The subjects of examination shall be divided into two parts, of which the first may be taken by a student at the close of the ordinary theological course, provided the average marks attained by him in the terminal examinations of the second year shall not be below sixty per cent. of the maximum.

3. The second part of the examination shall not be taken sooner than one year after the close of the theological course.

4. Candidates for the degree shall make application to the Principal of the college not less than two months before the date of examination, which shall be held in the month of April of each year. The fee for the degree shall be $10.

5. The following are the subjects of examination: First part—Latin, Greek, Hebrew, Apologetics, Systematic Theology, Church History, Criticism and Canon. Second part—Greek, Hebrew and Chaldee, Systematic Theology, Exegetics and Hermeneutics, Church Government, Homiletics. (*a*)

APPOINTMENT OF THEOLOGICAL PROFESSORS.

Minutes 1892, p. 48. That the General Assembly appoint a committee to take into consideration the relation of all our colleges to the Church, to consider the practice which prevailed in the various branches of the now united Church prior to union, regarding the appointment of theological professors, to suggest some plan by which uniformity of practice shall be secured, and to report to the next Assembly.

(*a*) The particular subjects appear each year in the college calendar.

Minutes 1893, p. 30. The report of committee on the relation of the colleges to the Church was presented (*a*), and it was agreed to consider along with the recommendations of the report, the portion of the report of the trustees of Queen's College dealing with the matter. *Page 39.* The Assembly receives the report of Queen's University, and records its grateful appreciation of the conduct of the board of trustees in proposing to give to the Assembly the right of veto in the appointment of theological professors ; that, as the mode of appointment of theological professors in all the colleges is still under consideration, the Assembly defers, at this stage, its final decision in regard to this proposal ; and that the report of the committee on the relation of the colleges to the Church be referred to the board of trustees of Queen's University, with the request that they will give it careful consideration, and report their opinion of its recommendations to the next General Assembly.

The Assembly receives the report of the committee on the relation of the colleges to the Church, and expresses general approval of the recommendations as securing to the Church control over all appointments to theological chairs.

That in view of the importance of the subject, and the desirableness of ascertaining the mind of the Church regarding it, this report, and also that portion of the report of the trustees of Queen's University bearing upon the closer relations of the theological faculty of Queen's College to the Church, be sent down to Presbyteries, college boards and senates, with instructions to report to next General Assembly on the best method to be followed in making appointments to theological chairs in the colleges of the Church, and on the desirableness of prescribing the same method in all the colleges or of allowing diversity of practice in the mode of appointment, as long as no appointment shall be made of which the General Assembly does not approve.

Minutes 1894, p. 25. The report of Queen's University (*b*) was received, and a motion disposing of it was carried unanimously. *Inter alia.* That the proposal of the trustees anent "the question of closer relations to the Church" be accepted as satisfactory to this Assembly, viz.: ''The theological professors shall be appointed by the trustees, subject to the veto of the Assembly, and no such professor shall enter upon his duties until after the meeting of the Assembly next succeeding the date of his appointment."

Minutes 1894, p. 53. The committee to whom it was remitted to suggest a deliverance, in the line of the views expressed by the

---

(*a*) The report of the committee appears in *Minutes 1893, App. No. 28 ;* that of the trustees of Queen's College in *Minutes, App. No. 7.*

(*b*) For this report *See Minutes 1894, App. No. 7.*

returns of Presbyteries, on the subject of the appointment of theological professors, reported as follows :—(1) The General Assembly expresses its satisfaction that all the Presbyteries reporting on the remit *in re* the appointment of theological professors recognize the necessity, however appointments may be made, of vesting the control of such appointments in the General Assembly. (2.) In view of the returns to the Assembly's remit on this subject it is resolved : That in the appointment of a professor in any of the theological colleges of the church, the board of management of said college shall nominate to the Assembly the person whom they deem suitable for the position, and that the appointment rest with the Assembly. This shall be the mode of appointment in all the colleges unless when the Assembly has specially determined otherwise. Further, that when an appointment falls to be made in any of our theological colleges, where nomination is required, intimation thereof shall be made by the board of said college, so that Presbyteries may have the opportunity of submitting names to the governing body of the college in question, and that in the case of all the theological colleges the name to be presented to the Assembly by the college board or governing body, shall, if possible, be made known to the Church at least four weeks before the General Assembly is called to decide upon any nomination or appointment. This report, with the addition that this deliverance of the General Assembly be transmitted to the governing bodies of the various theological colleges was adopted. *See Minutes 1891, p. 58.*

Resolutions as to Students.

Minutes 1890, pp. 32, 33. The Assembly took up the memorial of the senate of Knox College, when the following resolution was adopted :—The General Assembly receives the overture and approves of the steps being taken by the board and senate of Knox College to make the preparatory course more complete and thorough, and in accordance with the prayer of the overture from the senate, instructs Presbyteries to determine whether young men applying for certification to our colleges, with the view of entering the preparatory course, should take that course rather than a complete university course, and also to co-operate with the senates of the colleges in sustaining and increasing the efficiency of the preparatory course, by declining to certify to the senate those whose literary attainments are manifestly insufficient to enable them to pass the entrance examination, and that the clerk be instructed to transmit this resolution to the clerks of the Presbyteries of the churches, that they may communicate it to their Presbyteries and record it in their minutes.

Minutes 1895, pp. 49, 50. Report of committee on applications of Presbyteries on behalf of students, received, its recommendations considered, amended and finally passed, as follows : Whereas the application of catechists and students for leave to rank as special cases, are very numerous ; whereas the increase in the number of regular students is almost sufficient to meet the needs of the Church ; whereas the Church wisely demands that all its ministers should receive a thorough training in arts and theology ; and whereas the increase in special cases is growing to be an injustice to those students who take the regular course ; the Assembly therefore enjoins, that Presbyteries exercise the most anxious oversight over all their students, and earnestly advise every student to take the prescribed course, and specially enquire into the age and fitness of candidates, and, where acquirements and ability are not specially marked, that they seek to prevent applications from being made to the Assembly.

Minutes 1896, p. 71. The following motion was adopted regarding the curriculum to be required of students taking their theological course in foreign countries, and returning to Canada as preachers : " In view of the importance of insuring that the curriculum in arts, prescribed by the Church, shall be completed by all our candidates for the ministry, the General Assembly enacts that no student of the Church who shall take his course in theology in any foreign seminary, without having finished his course in arts, shall, on returning to Canada, be received as a probationer or minister of this Church, until he shall have completed the Church's curriculum in arts, as well as in theology."

PART III.—SCHEMES OF THE CHURCH.

Aged and Infirm Ministers' Fund.

Minutes, 1895, p. 46.—That every minister, on being ordained, be obliged to connect himself with the Aged and Infirm Ministers' Fund, and pay the fixed rate, or lose all benefit in the fund.

REGULATIONS FOR BOTH EASTERN AND WESTERN SECTIONS.
Minutes, 1893, App. No. 14.

1. The fund shall be sustained by annual congregational contributions, ministers' rates, donations and bequests.

2. The invested capital shall not be entrenched upon for the purpose of paying annuities, and all bequests made to the fund shall be added to the capital, unless otherwise ordered by the testator.

3. Settled pastors, ordained missionaries, home and foreign, professors in colleges and church agents, shall, in order to participate in the full benefits of the fund, pay into it an annual rate of : For ages under 30 at date of connection, $4 ; for age 30 and under 35, $5 ; for age 35 and under 40, $6 ; for age 40 and under 45, $7 ; for age 45 and under 50, $9 ; for age 50 and under 55, $12.

4. When a minister resigns his pastoral charge without leave from the General Assembly to retire, but continues in the service of the Church as a preacher, he shall pay into the fund his usual rate, (a) otherwise his annuity shall be only in proportion to the time of his service as pastor.

5. When a minister resigns his pastoral charge, and transfers his services to another Church, or gives himself to another vocation, he shall forfeit all claims to benefit from the fund, beyond the repayment of one-half of the amount paid by him into the fund. The Assembly may, however, grant the application of such minister to retain

---

(*a*) Rule 4 (a) That in the case of the minister *duly* on the Probationers' List, the years of service while on the same be allowed to count for benefit. (b) That the term "his usual rate" be interpreted to mean the age rate. *See Report of Committee, Minutes, 1894, App. No. 14.*

his claim to benefit, corresponding to the number of his years of service in the ministry of this Church, on the following conditions:—
(1) That he shall pay an annual rate of fifteen dollars ($15). (*b*)
(2) That he shall submit to the judgment of the Assembly on any application that he may subsequently make for benefit on the ground of age or infirmity.

6. The rate shall be paid on or before the first of November in each year.

7. Ministers who have not complied with number three of these regulations, and may wish to do so, shall pay the prescribed rate, with interest from the date of their ordination, or their becoming ministers of our Church; provided always that such rates shall not be required further back than the year 1877.

8. The regular procedure, with a view to the retirement of a minister and placing his name on the list of beneficiaries, is as follows:—

(1) When a minister from age or infirmity proposes to retire from the active duties of the Ministry, he makes application in writing to the Presbytery, furnishing whatever information may be necessary and, in case of infirmity, a satisfactory medical certificate. (*c*) The Presbytery thereupon visits his congregation, and summons them to appear by commissioners at a subsequent meeting, that they may be heard for their interests, and that the Presbytery may confer with them anent a retiring allowance to their minister, to take effect on the acceptance of his resignation, and any other matters affected by his proposed retirement, which then considers the whole matter, records its judgment, and sends up the minister's application, its own judgment thereon, and all relative documents to the General Assembly, through the Assembly's standing committee on the Aged and Infirm Ministers' Fund, which shall carefully consider them, and transmit them with its own opinion in reference to the case to the Assembly for final determination. (2) When a minister has obtained permission of the General Assembly to retire from the active duties of the pastorate on account of age or infirmity, he shall be entitled to an annuity only on application of his Presbytery, such application to include all necessary information.

9. When a minister is allowed by the General Assembly to retire after ten year's service, he shall receive an annuity of $100 with

---

(*b*) Rule 5. That in the case of a minister leaving the ministry of our Church, but who has transferred his services to a sister Presbyterian Church, or is engaged in cognate work within the bounds of our Church, the annual rate shall in future be $10.00. *See Report of Committee, Minutes. 1894, App. No. 14.*

(*c*) By the action of the Assembly the medical certificate must be from a doctor named by the committee.

$5 for each additional year of service up to twenty; and for each additional year of service over twenty and up to forty $10, if the state of the fund permit.

10. A minister who has not paid the annual rate into the fund shall receive only one-half the amount to which he would have been otherwise entitled.

11. When a minister is allowed to retire after less than ten years' service in this Church, his case shall be made the subject of special consideration by the Assembly.

12. When a minister's health is impaired, but not so much as to render him wholly unable to discharge the duties of his profession, the committee may grant him half the allowance to which he would be entitled in case of complete disability.

13. When a minister, admitted to the benefits of the fund on account of infirmity, recovers his health sufficiently to engage actively in remunerative employments, the annuity shall be reduced or discontinued.

14. When a minister who has paid rates to the fund attains the age of seventy years, he may claim the privilege of retiring from the active duties of the ministry, and of being placed upon the fund. (*d*)

15. When a minister is mainly dependent upon his annuity from this fund, the committee shall have power, after careful enquiry, to grant such additional allowance as the condition of the fund will permit, such additional allowance in no case to exceed $100.

16. When a minister is removed by orderly translation, from one section of the Church to another, he shall, from the date of his translation, pay the rate into the fund of the section to which he is translated, and he shall have a claim to an interest in it on his retirement by leave of the Assembly to the full extent of the period of his services in both sections.

17. Annuities shall be paid either in quarterly or half yearly instalments.

Minutes 1891, p. 37. The Foreign Mission committee has made the following regulations, providing for aged and infirm missionaries:—When an ordained or medical missionary, either through infirmity or old age, retires with the sanction of the committee, from foreign mission service, he receives from the Foreign Mission Fund, after ten years' service in the field, an allowance of $100 a year, and

---

(*d*) That rule 14 be interpreted to mean that a minister of 70 years of age, or upwards, on being permitted to retire from the active duties of the ministry, shall be entitled to the full benefit of the fund, irrespective of other considerations, save such as affect his ministerial character. *Minutes 1893, p. 31.*

$10 a year for every additional year of service up to forty years, after which is $400 a year. This allowance is made up from the Aged and Infirm Ministers, and the Foreign Mission Funds; and the Foreign Mission committee shall hereafter pay the rates required by the Aged and Infirm Ministers Fund. And the committee hereby requests the General Assembly to instruct the committee on the Aged and Infirm Ministers Fund to receive rates for the medical missionaries appointed by this committee, so that they may be entitled to receive annuities in the same way in which they would be entitled if ordained. The Assembly expressed its approval of the above regulation and instructed the committee of the Aged and Infirm Ministers' Fund as requested.

Augmentation Scheme Regulations.

Eastern Section—1. By whom administered.

The Augmentation Fund shall be administered by a sub-committee of the Home Mission committee, with a secretary appointed by the General Assembly. (*a*)

2. How funds are to be provided.

(1) The funds for home mission work proper and for augmentation of stipends shall be kept distinct, and congregations are instructed to contribute separately to these two objects.

(2) It is hoped also that the fund will be largely increased by generous contributions from individual members of the Church whom God hath prospered.

3. How the list shall be made up.

(1) The list of augmented congregations shall embrace only such charges as have pastors duly called by the people and inducted by the Presbytery, and as in the judgment of the Presbytery are entitled to assistance in support of the ministry.

(2) New congregations formed by the Presbyteries in consultation with the Augmentation committee as hereinafter provided (Sec. 2), and vacant congregations requiring aid when settled.

(*a*) These regulations were prepared for the management of the augmentation scheme in both the eastern and western sections, but in the eastern section the augmentation fund was always administered, not by a sub-committee of the home mission committee, but by a separate committee. Recently new regulations have been prepared for the western section, but these regulations are still followed in the eastern section.

4. GENERAL CONDITIONS IN ORDINARY CASES.

The following general conditions shall be observed with regard to congregations to be placed on the list in ordinary cases, viz.:

(1) Congregations to be placed on the list shall (*a*) contribute towards the minister's stipend at least $400 per annum, and a manse or rented house, or make an allowance of $50 per annum towards house rent; (*b*) they shall also contribute at the rate of not less than $4.50 per member in full communion for ministerial support, and (*c*) they shall, in addition thereto, contribute to the schemes of the Church.

NOTE.—(*a*) In the case of congregations in which the families reported are more numerous than the members in full communion, the contributions shall be at the rate of not less than $4.50 per family. (*b*) In calculating the contribution per communicant or per family, congregations which provide a manse or rented house shall be credited with $50 per annum, in addition to the amount of salary paid.

(2) Congregations having settled pastors (at 1st Oct., 1883) and so situated as to forbid the application of the rule requiring a minimum contribution of $400 and a manse or rented house, or an allowance of $50 per annum for the same, and a minimum rate of $4.50 per communicant (or family), shall be admitted to a place on the list on a lower scale of payment to be afterwards determined; the committee, acting in conjunction with Presbyteries, to prepare a list of such congregations and to submit it to the General Assembly for approval

5. (This regulation was applicable only to Manitoba and the North-West.)

6. GENERAL CONDITIONS IN CASES OF TOWNS AND CITIES.

The following general conditions shall be observed with regard to congregations in cities, and in towns where the cost of living is exceptionally high, viz:

Congregations to be placed on the list (*a*) shall contribute to the minister's stipend at least $500 per annum and a manse or rented house, or an allowance of $100 per annum for the same; (*b*) they shall also contribute at the rate of $4.50 per communicant, or at the rate of $4.50 per family, if the number of families exceeds that of communicants, and (*c*) they shall in addition contribute to the schemes of the Church.

7. SPECIAL CONDITIONS TO BE OBSERVED BY PRESBYTERIES AND COMMITTEE.

The following special conditions shall be observed by Presbyteries and the committee, before admitting a congregation to a place on the list, viz:

(1) In view of exceptional circumstances in certain cases, for instance, where there is not full work for a minister on account of the small number of families in a locality, or on account of the proximity of another congregation, or where there might be a re-arrangement of congregations, so as to secure greater economy and efficiency in carrying on the work, the committee, after correspondence with Presbyteries, shall have discretionary power to withhold aid or to grant less than the full amount required to make the stipend $750 and a manse, and Presbyteries are instructed, where in their judgment the circumstances require it, to make application for a reduced grant.

(2) The committee is empowered to withold until next General Assembly supplement in cases where mission stations have been erected into pastoral charges, or where existing congregations have been divided, if, in the judgment of the committee, it be undesirable to make such grant.

(3) Before settlement shall take place in any congregation requiring aid the congregation shall be visited by the Presbytery, with a view to increase the contributions of the people, and the result of the visitation shall be reported to the committee, who may withhold grants, if they are not satisfied, till the General Assembly has given judgment in the case.

(4) All congregations requiring aid shall be visited by Presbyteries annually between October and March, with a view to secure increased contributions, and the result of the visitation (with the Presbytery's judgment thereon) shall be reported to the committee.

(5) No grant shall be made to any congregation for the year succeeding the March meeting of committee, where arrears of stipend are reported as due on the 31st December preceding, until such arrears of stipend have been paid.

8. PRINCIPLES OF DISTRIBUTION IN ORDINARY CASES.

The principles of distribution of the fund in ordinary cases shall be as follows :

(1) Provision shall be made for ministers of congregations on the ordinary list, so that they shall receive a stipend of $750 per annum, and a manse or rented house, or an allowance of $50 per annum for the same ; but beyond that amount the committee shall be empowered to recognize exceptional liberality on the part of any augmented congregation.

(2) No minister of a congregation on the ordinary list shall receive more than $300 per annum by way of supplement, save where there is exceptional liberality on the part of the congregation interested,

and such liberality shall be first recognized in the case of congregations where under the regulations the stipend would be only $700 and a manse, so that their ministers may receive $750 and a manse.

(3) The general principle above stated shall be limited by the special condition recited in Sec. 7, r. 1.

(Regulations 9 to 11 applied only to Manitoba and the North-West.)

Minutes 1894, p. 44.—The following recommendation of the committee was adopted by the General Assembly: That the minimum stipend in aid receiving congregations be : (1) $700 in the case of an unmarried man, not requiring a house ; (2) $750 and a manse, or an allowance of $50 where there is no manse, in the case of a man requiring a house ; (3) $850 and a manse, or an allowance of $50 where there is no manse in Manitoba and the North-West ; (4) In cases where the cost of living is exceptionally high, the Augmentation committee shall have power to make a larger grant ; (5) The Augmentation committee shall have power to recognize exceptional liberality on the part of aid-receiving congregations by making an increased grant.

WESTERN SECTION. 1.—BY WHOM ADMINISTERED.

(1) The Augmentation scheme is administered by committees (Eastern and Western) appointed annually by the General Assembly.

(2) The Western committee consists of the convener and secretary, together with fourteen other members, four of whom shall be the conveners of the Augmentation committees of the Synods of (*a*) Montreal and Ottawa, (*b*) Toronto and Kingston, (*c*) Hamilton and London, and (*d*) Manitoba and the North-West.

(3) The Synods of the Western Section shall annually appoint Synodical Augmentation committees, consisting of the conveners of Augmentation committees of Presbyteries within the bounds, together with such a limited number of other members as the respective Synods may deem advisable.

2.—HOW FUNDS ARE TO BE PROVIDED.

(1) All congregations are instructed to contribute to the fund.

(2) It is hoped that the fund will be largely increased by generous contributions from individual members of the Church, as also by donations from Young People's Societies, Sabbath Schools, etc., and by bequests.

3.—HOW THE LIST SHALL BE MADE UP.

(1) The list of augmented charges shall embrace only such charges as have pastors duly called by the people and inducted by the Presbytery, and as, in the judgment of the Presbytery and the Assembly's committee, are entitled to assistance in the support of the ministry. Such charges, when vacant, may be retained on the list, and, at the discretion of the committee, may be accorded a grant for supply until settled.

(2) The congregations formed by Presbyteries and other congregations, in their judgment, in circumstances requiring aid, may, on consultation with the committee or its executive, be added to the list from time to time.

(3) Congregations shall not be placed or continued on the list (unless by permission of Assembly) except on the following conditions : (*a*) They shall contribute towards minister's stipend at least $450 per annum ($500 per annum in Manitoba, North-West and cities) and a manse or rented house, or make an allowance of $50 per annum towards house rent ($100 in cities). (*b*) They shall contribute at not less than the rate of $4.50 per member (or $8.00 per family in cases where the ratio of members to families is exceptionally large or small) towards stipend. (*c*) They shall contribute towards the Augmentation and other schemes of the Church.

4.—SPECIAL CONDITIONS AS TO A PLACE ON THE LIST.

The following special conditions shall be observed by Presbyteries and the committee, before admitting a congregation to a place on the list, viz :

(1) In view of exceptional circumstances in certain cases, as for instance where there is not full work for a minister on account of the small number of families in a locality, or on account of the proximity of another congregation, or where there might be a rearrangement of congregations so as to secure greater economy and efficiency in carrying on the work, the committee, after correspondence with Presbyteries, shall have discretionary power to withhold aid or to grant less than the full amount required to make the stipend $750 and a manse, and Presbyteries are instructed, where in their judgment the circumstances require it, to make application for a reduced grant.

(2) The committee is empowered to withhold until next General Assembly supplement in cases where mission stations have been erected into pastoral charges, or where existing congregations have been divided, if, in the judgment of the committee, it be undesirable to make such grant.

(3) Before a settlement shall take place in any congregation requiring aid, the congregation shall be visited by the Presbytery with a view to increase the contributions of the people, and the result of the visitation shall be reported to the committee, who may withhold grants, if they are not satisfied, till the General Assembly has given judgment in the case.

(4) All congregations requiring aid shall be visited by Presbyteries annually, between May and October, with a view to secure increased contributions, and the result of the visitation (with the Presbytery's judgment thereon) shall be reported to the committee through the Synodical committee.

(5) No grant shall be made to any congregation for the year succeeding the October meeting of committee, where arrears of stipend are reported as due on the 30th June preceding, until such arrears of stipend have been paid.

5.—PRINCIPLES OF DISTRIBUTION.

The minimum stipend in aid-receiving congregations shall be : (1) $700 in the case of an unmarried man, not requiring a house; (2) $750 and a manse, or an allowance of $50 where there is no manse, in the case of a man requiring a house ; (3) $850 and a manse, or an allowance of $50 where there is no manse, in Manitoba and the North-West. (In the case of an unmarried man, not requiring a house, in Manitoba and the North-West, the committee fixed the minimum stipend at $800.) (4) In cases where the cost of living is exceptionally high, the Augmentation committee shall have power to make a larger grant. (5) The Augmentation committee shall have power to recognize exceptional liberality on the part of aid-receiving congregations by making an increased grant. All subject to conditions of Sec. 4.

6.—DUTIES OF SYNODICAL COMMITTEES.

(1) To co-operate with the General Assembly's committee in the general supervision of the field and the work within the bounds of the respective Synods.

(2) To hold an annual meeting before the fall meeting of the Assembly's committee, these meetings to be so arranged that the convener and secretary of the Assembly's committee may be present to consult and advise with each Synodical committee. Presbyteries shall prepare schedules and extract minutes for their meetings as they prepare them for the meetings of the Assembly's committee.

The business at these meetings shall be :—(*a*) To revise the list of Augmented congregations as sent up by Presbyteries ; to give judgment as to grants asked, and to report to the Assembly's committee. (*b*) To arrange, as occasion may require, for co-operation with Presbyteries in the visitation (1) of particular districts in which re-arrangements seem desirable in the interests of the fund, and (2) of congregations in which special dealing may be necessary for reducing grants. (*c*) To make arrangements for stirring up interest, especially in aid-giving congregations, and so securing liberal contributions to the fund.

Minutes 1893, p. 52. The Assembly enjoins Presbyteries to take the greatest care in sending up applications to the committee, so that no congregation may receive aid from the fund which it is not fairly entitled to receive, and to act with great caution in erecting new congregations which may become a burden on the fund.

Minutes 1894, p. 27. The General Assembly, feeling the great importance of the Augmentation scheme, and believing that the progress of our Church is largely dependent on its successful working, regrets exceedingly to hear that many of our strong congregations have failed to contribute to it. The Assembly assured that our people will always respond to the appeals of the Church when faithfully presented to them, enjoins upon all our ministers the duty of explaining this scheme to their congregations, and urging upon them their duty regarding it. The Assembly also enjoins each minister to report to his Presbytery what has been done in this matter during the year, and what amount has been contributed by his congregation to the fund ; while at the same time not overlooking the increasing demands of our great mission fields in the North-West and British Columbia.

The Church and Manse Building Fund.

46 Vict. cap. 97 (D.)—An Act to incorporate the Board of Management of the Church and Manse Building Fund of the Presbyterian Church in Canada, for Manitoba and the North-West. (*Assented to 25th May, 1883.*)

Whereas, the persons hereinafter named at present constitute, under the general regulations adopted by the General Assembly of the Presbyterian Church in Canada, in June, 1882, the board to administer the Church and Manse Building Fund for Manitoba and the North-West; and whereas the said board find great inconvenience arising from the want of corporate powers, and having been empowered by the said General Assembly of the said "The Presbyterian Church in Canada" to petition the Parliament of Canada for incorporation, have so done; and whereas it is expedient to grant the prayer of the said petition; Therefore, Her Majesty, &c., enacts as follows:—

1. The Rev. Charles Bruce Pitblado, of Winnipeg, the Rev. James Robertson, of Winnipeg, (*and others, naming them*) and their successors to be appointed in manner hereinafter mentioned, are hereby constituted and declared to be a body corporate and politic under the name of "The Board of Management of the Church and Manse Building Fund of the Presbyterian Church in Canada for Manitoba and the North-West," hereinafter called the corporation.

2. The object of the said incorporation is to enable the said board to hold and possess funds that may be acquired by them by subscription or otherwise for the purchasing and holding of real estate, and for the purchase and erection of churches and manses and buildings, and for the maintenance of the same, for the uses and purposes of the Presbyterian Church in Canada, in Manitoba and the North-West; and also for the purpose of loaning moneys held by them on the security of real estate or otherwise as to them may seem best; and also for the purpose of acquiring, holding and receiving property for the use or uses of any particular congregation or congregations, or mission station or stations in connection with the said Church.

3. The General Assembly of the Presbyterian Church in Canada shall have the power at any time to vary the constitution of the corporation and shall have power to alter, vary, add to or repeal the provisions of its constitution, provided such alteration, variation or addition shall not be inconsistent with the limitations comprised in this Act and the laws in force in the Dominion of

Canada ; and a certified copy of such constitution under the seal of the corporation, and signed by the secretary thereof, shall be received in all courts as *prima facie* evidence of such constitution ; and the said General Assembly shall further have power to appoint successors to the members of the corporation hereby constituted, and to fill all vacancies in the board according to its general rules and regulations.

4. The corporation and their successors may, by the name of the Board of Management of the Church and Manse Building Fund of the Presbyterian Church in Canada for Manitoba and the North-West, have, acquire and hold moneys, promissory notes, bank stocks and public securities, and lend the moneys now held by the board or which may hereafter be acquired, on the security of real estate, or otherwise, as to them may seem best, and at such rate of interest as they may deem advisable, and may also purchase or erect churches, manses and buildings in the Province of Manitoba and the North-West, and may maintain the same for the uses and purposes of the Presbyterian Church in Canada ; and also for the purpose of acquiring, holding and receiving property for the use or uses of any particular congregation or congregations, or mission station or stations in connection with the said church ; and may make, sign, seal and deliver any deed or deeds, mortgage or mortgages under their corporate seal for the purpose of securing the titles thereto, or may sell and dispose of such land, churches, manses and buildings so acquired by them : provided that the corporation shall, within ten years after acquisition of any real estate, dispose of such real estate as is not required for the use and occupation, or other like purposes of the corporation.

5. The corporation shall have power to pass by-laws for the transaction of business, and to provide for such other matters as may be necessary or expedient in the interests of the corporation, subject to the aforesaid limitations.

6. The ordinary place of meeting of the corporation shall be at the City of Winnipeg, in the Province of

Manitoba. Every meeting to be called by the secretary appointed by the corporation.

51 Vict., cap. 107 (D.)—An Act to amend the Act to incorporate the Board of Management of the Church and Manse Building Fund of the Presbyterian Church in Canada, for Manitoba and the North-West. (*Assented to 22nd May, 1888.*)

Whereas the Board of Management of the Church and Manse Building Fund of the Presbyterian Church in Canada, for Manitoba and the North-West, have prayed that the Act passed in the 46th year of Her Majesty's reign, chaptered 97, incorporating the said board, may be amended, and it is expedient to grant their prayer: Therefore, Her Majesty, &c., enacts as follows:—

1. Notwithstanding anything contained in the said Act, the objects for which the corporation thereby created was incorporated, as expressed in the 2nd section of the said Act, and all the powers conferred upon the said corporation, as expressed in the 4th section of the said Act, shall not be limited to the Province of Manitoba and the North-West, but shall extend to and may be exercised throughout all that part of the Dominion of Canada which is, at the time of the passing of this Act, included within the limits or bounds of the Synod of the Presbyterian Church in Canada known as and styled "The Synod of Manitoba and the North-West Territories." (*a*).

REGULATIONS.

Minutes 1887, page 63.—1. The fund shall be called The Church and Manse Building Fund of the Presbyterian Church in Canada for Manitoba and the North-West.

2. The amount to be aimed at in the first place shall be one hundred thousand dollars ($100,000); the fund shall be raised by subscriptions and bequests.

(*a*) The limits or bounds of the Synod extended from Lake Superior to the Pacific Ocean, covering all of Ontario lying west of and including Port Arthur, Manitoba, the North-West Territories and British Columbia.

3. The management of the fund shall be entrusted to a board of fifteen members, twelve of these to be appointed annually by the General Assembly. The other three of the board shall be the superintendent of missions for Manitoba and North-West, the convener of the Home Mission committee of the General Assembly, western section, and one member to be appointed by the said committee. The board shall have power to fill any vacancies made by death or resignation until the meeting of the next General Assembly thereafter. The usual place of meeting of the board shall be at Winnipeg.

4. All applications for aid in the erection of churches or manses shall be made to this board through the Presbytery within whose bounds the congregation is situated, and before being considered by the board must be recommended by the Presbytery, but the board shall be sole judge as to the merits of the application, and the nature and amount of aid to be given.

5. The money constituting the fund shall be, at the discretion of the board, either invested, and the revenue accruing therefrom given in the form of grants to congregations to assist in the erection of churches or manses, or the capital shall be employed to make loans or grants to such congregations.

6. Such loans shall be for a limited number of years, and at a moderate rate of interest. For good reasons the board may remit the interest.

7. The assistance given, when in a form of a grant, shall not exceed one-fifth of the total cost of the building, and when in the form of a loan shall not exceed fifty per cent. of the cost, unless in either case the circumstances are by the board deemed exceptional. The money shall be payable only when the building can be used for service, in the case of grants. In the case of loans the money voted may be paid in instalments as the work of construction advances. No grant, however, is to be made or loan effected until the board is satisfied that a valid title to the property, or a bond to that effect, has been secured by the congregation, and that the deed is in the form approved by the General Assembly.

8. It shall be competent for the board, with the approval of the General Assembly, to make changes in these regulations, but such changes shall have due regard to the proper preservation of the capital entrusted to the board.

9. The board shall report its transactions annually to the General Assembly.

Report of Church and Manse Building Fund Board, Minutes 1890, App. No. 19. The board has adopted a regulation making $700 its maximum loan, and $200 its maximum grant.

Minutes 1890, p. 24. That the report be received and adopted, with the recommendation as to the maximum amount of loan and grant.

Foreign Missions.

Minutes 1891, p. 36. That the question of appointing an agent for the western division of the Church, to act as secretary of the Foreign Mission work of the Church—such agent to represent the Foreign Mission work among the congregations of the Church, as well as to keep the minutes and conduct the correspondence of the committee—be sent down to Presbyteries for consideration, with instructions to nominate a suitable person for the office should they approve of such an appointment, and to report to next Assembly.

Minutes 1892, p. 42. The report of the committee on the Foreign Mission secretaryship was received and the following recommendations adopted: (1) In the judgment of your committee, the qualifications for this position, and which should be looked for in the person elected for the office, should be (*a*) Good business ability, including tact and promptness, in the management of correspondence, and the preparation of information for the press; (*b*) Knowledge of the countries in which our missions are situated, together with the power of effective presentation or address at designation services and other important gatherings. (2) Salary $2,000 a year, and travelling expenses. (3) That it be remitted to the Foreign Mission committee to define more in detail the duties to be performed. (4) That the secretary be *ex officio* a member of the Foreign Mission committee, in addition to the number fixed by the vote of the Assembly.

Page 44. After nominations had been received and ballots cast, it was unanimously agreed, that Rev. R. P. McKay be appointed Foreign Mission secretary.

1.—General Regulations.

1. THE FOREIGN MISSION COMMITTEE AND ITS WORK. (*a*)

1. The Foreign Mission committee of the Presbyterian Church in Canada is appointed annually by the General Assembly to have control of the foreign mission operations of the Church, and of all moneys contributed to the Foreign Mission fund.

(*a*) The following regulations are printed from a copy furnished by Rev. Mr. McKay, the foreign mission secretary.

2. It prepares annually for the Assembly a report of the work under its care, and an estimate of the amount required to carry on that work for the ensuing year,

3. The committee is divided into two parts, and to these is entrusted the direction of the work during the year, the eastern division having the oversight of all the missionary operations of the Church in the New Hebrides and the West Indies, and the western division a similar oversight in China, India, Manitoba, the Western Territories of Canada and British Columbia.

4. These divisions, subject to the approval of the committee and the Assembly, open up, or if necessary withdraw from, fields of labor, appoint, or if necessary recall, missionaries and teachers, determine salaries and other expenditure, make arrangements for the visitation of the churches by missionaries or others, and have supervision of all matters pertaining to the work of their respective fields. All local general regulations for the management of the work in these fields require their sanction.

2. APPOINTMENT OF MISSIONARIES.

1. Applicants for appointment to the foreign field should state in writing their age, education training, ability to acquire languages, religious experience, the work in which they have been engaged, the motives leading them to offer themselves for mission work, and any other facts concerning themselves which may affect their character or work as missionaries.

2. Applicants should furnish testimonials from their pastor and others, as to their history, character, fitness for the work, and any other facts known to them which may have a bearing upon their appointment.

3. When a new language has to be acquired, applicants should, as a rule, be under thirty years of age.

4. Previous to appointment, a medical certificate, testifying to general health and adaptation to the climate of the country where they are expected to labor, is required of all missionaries and missionaries' wives.

5. When the missionary elect is a licentiate, he is ordained by such Presbytery as may be agreed upon by the division of the committee appointing him.

6. A medical practitioner or a licentiate in medicine, seeking appointment as a missionary of the Church, is required: (*a*) To appear in person before the Foreign Mission committee. (*b*) To

furnish evidence to the committee of his having received the degree of M.D., C.M., or its equivalent, from some approved university, medical school or board authorized to grant such. (*c*) To present a certificate or extract minute, recommending his appointment, from the Presbytery within whose bounds he resides. (*d*) To satisfy the committee as to his missionary zeal, Biblical knowledge, aptitude in teaching, and ability to acquire the language of the people to whom he may be sent. (*e*) To answer satisfactorily the first four questions to be put to ministers at ordination or induction. (*f*) The medical missionary is expected to teach the Word of God and to seek the salvation of men, devoting his time and energies to this work as far as compatible with the discharge of strictly professional duties. (*g*) In every field where an ordained minister is stationed, the medical missionary shall co-operate with him, and all work carried on by them jointly shall be so reported by the minister, and the medical missionary shall make a separate report of his distinctly professional services and matters connected with them. Any amounts received for professional services rendered by medical missionaries are placed by them to the credit of the funds of the mission.

These regulations apply to all medical missionaries, male and female.

7. In connection with the sending forth of a missionary a public religious service is held, at which the Foreign Mission committee should be represented by one or more of its members.

3. DUTIES OF MISSIONARIES.

1. Missionaries, when appointed, are expected, unless God in His providence directs otherwise, to devote themselves to this department of labor as their life work.

2. As long as a missionary is under appointment, whether laboring in the foreign field or at home on furlough, he is required to conform to the regulations of the committee and to the directions of the division of the committee appointing him.

3. When a Presbytery exists in the field to which an ordained missionary has been appointed, he reports himself to it on his arrival, presenting his credentials, that he may be enrolled as a member and be subject to its jurisdiction. If there be no Presbytery in the field his name is retained on the roll of the Presbytery to which he belonged at the time of his appointment, or in the case of a licentiate, on the roll of the Presbytery by which he was ordained.

4. In those mission fields in which the committee shall think it desirable, a mission council shall be constituted, to have the control and oversight, subject to the committee's approval or direction, of

the expenditure of all moneys sent out by the Church or raised by the missionary in the field, especially by seeing to the careful preparation of the yearly estimates, and that the expenditure shall not exceed the amounts sanctioned by the committee; allowing nevertheless, as far as possible, liberty to the individual missionary in the expenditure of money within the limits sanctioned by the committee, provided in every case all moneys expended are for schemes of work approved of by the committee— full statements of receipts and expenditures to be sent to the committee each quarter, except when otherwise ordered by the division of the committee under which the council is placed, and the whole to be audited by the council at the end of each year; to see that suitable arrangements are made for the examination from time to time of all missionaries, male and female, touching their acquisition of the native language; and generally to act for the committee in such other matters as may at any time be entrusted to it.

It shall also be the duty of the council to see that no part of the mission funds is paid to any native agent of whose qualifications the council has not fully satisfied itself, except in cases in which the committee has given or may hereafter give specific directions.

5. The mission council in any field shall be composed of all the male missionaries under commission from the committee to that field.

The lady missionaries appointed by the committee to that field shall be entitled to take part in all the deliberations of the council and to vote only upon all matters affecting their own work.

No missionary, whether male or female, shall be entitled to vote in council until such missionary has been at least one year in the field and has passed the first examination in the language prescribed by the council.

6. The missionary, on his first arrival at his field of labor, is expected to devote himself to the acquisition of the language of the people, and one year after his arrival, wherever practicable, he undergoes a written and oral examination, testing his ability to understand, speak and write the language. The result of this examination is reported to the committee. At the end of the second year the missionary, where necessary, is required to undergo a second examination in the language. If at that time he is not able to use that language effectively, his further service in the mission may be discontinued.

7. When new missionaries arrive at a field which has been for some years occupied, it is the duty of the Presbytery, mission council, Synod, or whatever body has the general oversight of the work, or, in the ab-

sence of such a body, of the senior missionary or missionaries, to arrange for the examination of the new missionaries as prescribed. At the end of their second year's residence, the new missionaries undergo a second examination. These examinations may be conducted by the senior missionaries, but where able and impartial examiners not connected with the staff of that particular mission are available, their selection for the duty is recommended. The result of these examinations is reported carefully and fully to the division of the committee making the appointments for the mission, in order that they may be guided in reference to the propriety of continuing the new missionaries longer in the service of the mission. These reports should give definite information in respect to the ability of the missionary examined to speak the language of the people effectively.

8. Each missionary, catechist and teacher appointed by the committee prepares, at the close of each year, a personal narrative of work done during the year, to be forwarded to the committee through the mission council, Presbytery, or Synod.

9. The mission council, Presbytery, or Synod, or whatever body is entrusted with the oversight of each mission, or, in the absence of such a body, the ordained missionary or missionaries, prepares at the close of each year, a general report of the work under its charge, and forwards it, together with the reports of the missionaries, catechists and teachers, to the committee as early as possible after the first week in January.

10. The mission council, Presbytery, or Synod, or whatever body is entrusted with the oversight of the mission, prepares annually for the committee careful and detailed estimates of the probable expense of the work of all its stations for the following year, to be forwarded as early as possible after the first week in January.

11. These estimates should be so complete as to preclude the necessity of special appeals, either to the committee, or to congregations, Sabbath schools, associations, or individuals, for matters not specified in them. Such appeals should not be made without the sanction of the committee. When the mission estimates have undergone the revision which the committee may consider necessary, and have been approved, they govern the expenditure for the year, and must not be exceeded. When special cases arise, they are made a matter of correspondence with the committee, except when funds are provided from local sources, which should be reported to the committee.

12. A missionary, after his first arrival at a mission which has been established for some years, except by the special direction of the

committee, takes no part in the practical administration of the affairs of the mission, until he has undergone successfully his first examination in the language.

13. All communications from missionaries to the committee, of the nature of complaints, or proposals requiring immediate action, or involving charges or expenditure of any kind in their field of labour, must be transmitted through the mission council, Presbytery, or Synod, and should be accompanied by the written opinion of the mission council, Presbytery, or Synod regarding them.

14. Wherever it is deemed necessary by either division of the committee, a treasurer is nominated by the missionaries on the field in such manner as the division concerned may direct. The treasurer carefully preserves all deeds of mission property and other legal papers not transmitted to the committee; receives moneys from the treasurer or agent of the Church, and from other sources for missionary purposes; pays the salaries of the missionaries at the end of each month, or at such other stated period as the missionaries may, through their council, Presbytery, or Synod, as the case may be, decide; and defrays the expenses authorized by the committee, and in no case exceeding them without its approval. He keeps, in books procured at the expense of the mission, clear and correct accounts of all receipts and payments, and has vouchers for the latter; his books must be open for inspection by other members of the mission, or by any of them; his accounts must be audited each year by two members of the mission staff, appointed annually by the ordained missionaries; and a report is made of all receipts and payments to the treasurer or agent of the Church annually, or more frequently if desired, with a balance-sheet clearly exhibiting the condition of the mission treasury. Neither the treasurer nor any member of the mission staff may draw on the agent or treasurer of the Church for funds without first receiving permission, formally expressed.

4. PROVISION FOR MISSIONARIES: OUTFITS, TRAVELLING EXPENSES, SALARY AND FURLOUGH.

1. The provision which the Church makes for her missionaries is fixed upon the principle of giving only what is necessary for their comfort and health.

2. All provision made by these regulations for the children or orphans of missionaries, whether as annual allowance or for travelling expenses, shall apply to children under eighteen years of age, and to these only.

3. Ordained missionaries, under appointment, receive at the rate of $750 per annum, and their necessary travelling expenses, while

engaged in the service of the committee, visiting the churches, prior to their departure, but all contributions obtained by them from the congregations visited, are paid into the Foreign Mission fund, unless the committee has sanctioned collections for some special object.

4. The outfits given to missionaries vary according to the circumstances of the field to which they are appointed. See special regulations.

5. Medical missionaries may receive in addition to the ordinary outfit such a sum for the purchase of books, medicines and surgical instruments as the division appointing them may consider necessary. The articles so purchased are the property of the mission and remain in its possession.

6. When an ordained missionary who has received a medical training is called to practice medicine in his field, he may receive a similar grant upon similar conditions.

7. Missionaries receive all their necessary travelling expenses to their field of labor.

8. The salaries of missionaries vary in different countries according to the expense of living. They may be increased or diminished, but no reduction shall take effect until at least six months' notice has been sent to the missionaries affected thereby. The salary of a missionary begins when he reaches his field of labor and ceases when he leaves it. For the salaries presently paid in the different fields, see special regulations.

9. In addition to the salary, a house is usually provided for a missionary, or house rent paid, and such allowance is made as may be necessary for a teacher of the language.

10. The furloughs allowed to missionaries, to rest and recruit, vary with the distance and circumstances of the field. See special regulations.

11. Missionaries returning on furlough with the sanction of the division of the committee appointing them, receive all their necessary travelling expenses, both in coming home and returning to the field.

12. An ordained missionary or a medical missionary coming home on furlough with the sanction of the division of the committee appointing him, receives furlough allowance at the rate of $750 a year. An additional allowance may be made for house rent, at the discretion of the committee.

13. Furlough allowance begins when missionaries arrive in Canada and ceases when they leave for their field of labor.

14. Missionaries coming home without the sanction of the division of the committee appointing them forfeit all right to travelling expenses and furlough allowance unless reasons are given which are satisfactory to the committee.

15. Missionaries on furlough, when fulfilling appointments by the committee, receive their travelling expenses, but all the contributions obtained by them from congregations visited are paid into the Foreign Mission fund, unless the committee has sanctioned collections for some special object.

5. PROVISION FOR AGED AND INFIRM MISSIONARIES.

1. When an ordained or medical missionary, either through infirmity or old age, retires, with the sanction of the committee, from foreign mission service, he receives from the Foreign Mission fund—after ten years' service in the field, an allowance of $100 a year, and ten dollars a year for every additional year of service up to forty years, after which the allowance is $400 a year. This allowance is made up from the Aged and Infirm Ministers' and the Foreign Mission funds, and the Foreign Mission committee shall hereafter pay the rates required by the Aged and Infirm Ministers' fund.

2. When a lady missionary, appointed by the committee, whether a medical practitioner, nurse, or teacher, either through infirmity or old age retires, with the sanction of the committee, from foreign mission services, she receives from the Foreign Mission fund—after ten years' service in the field, an allowance of $50 a year, and five dollars a year for every additional year of service up to forty years, after which the allowance is $200 a year. In the event of marriage her allowance is discontinued.

3. Missionaries thus retiring receive all their necessary travelling expenses to the country where they wish to reside.

4. Missionaries retiring from foreign mission service without the sanction of the committee, forfeit all right to travelling expenses and retiring allowance.

5. Furloughs taken with the sanction of the committee are reckoned as service in the foreign field.

6. If missionaries retiring through ill health should so far recover as to be able to follow some remunerative occupation, the allowance may be reduced or withheld at the discretion of the committee.

6. PROVISIONS FOR THE WIDOWS AND ORPHANS OF MISSIONARIES IN CHINA, INDIA AND THE NEW HEBRIDES.

1. The committee pays for ordained missionaries the annual rates required of them to place them in connection with the Ministers' Widows' and Orphans' fund, and to retain that connection.

2. In the case of a widow who has spent at least twenty-five years in the foreign field, the committee pays her such a sum as, along with her allowance from the Ministers' Widows' and Orphans' fund, makes her income from Church funds, apart from that of her children, $200 a year.

3. The widows and children, or orphan children of ordained missionaries have all the expenses involved in their removal from the mission field to the country where they are to reside paid.

4. The orphan children of ordained missionaries receive annually in addition to the amounts secured to them from the Ministers' Widows' and Orphans' fund, the following sums: For one child, $50, and for each additional child, $25.

5. The committee makes allowances to the widows and orphans of medical missionaries, securing to them the same income as is provided by the Ministers' Widows' and Orphans' fund, and by these regulations, for the widows and orphans of ordained missionaries. It provides also in the same manner for the expense of the removal of the widow and the orphan children of a medical missionary from the mission field to the country where they are to reside.

II.—SPECIAL REGULATIONS.

1. THE NEW HEBRIDES.

(1). A missionary under appointment receives £30 sterling, for outfit, and if married, he receives an equal amount for his wife. (2). The salary of a missionary is £175 sterling a year, with £10 sterling a year additional for each child when at home, and £20 sterling for each when the children are away from their parents at school. (3). Missionaries may take a furlough of six months in Australia at the expiration of every five years. (4). During this furlough, their salaries, together with allowance for children, shall be paid in full, as when in the field. (5). After two such furloughs, they may, with the sanction of the mission Synod and the eastern division of the committee, take their third furlough for one year to Canada, under the conditions of the general regulations with regard to travelling expenses and furlough allowance. (6). In the event of a missionary wishing to return to Canada for his second furlough, after one furlough in Australia, and obtaining the sanction of the mission Synod and the eastern division of the committee, he may do so, on condition of paying one-half of his travelling expenses.

2. TRINIDAD.

(1). The salary of an ordained missionary is £300 per annum. (2). The salary of a lady teacher is £85 sterling per annum. (3). All missionaries and teachers sent from Canada are entitled, after five years of service, to a furlough of six months. (4). Lady teachers re-receive furlough allowance at the rate of £42 10s. per annum. (5). Each missionary, while having a large share of discretion in working his own field, is subject, in the general management of the work, to the mission council. (6). Missionaries have power to appoint teachers in their respective fields, but agents to be engaged in evangelistic work require to be examined and sanctioned by the mission council.

3. FORMOSA.

(1). A missionary under appointment receives $250 for outfit, and if married, he receives an equal amount for his wife. (2). The salary of an ordained or a medical missionary, if married, is $1,400 a year; with $40 a year additional for each child; if unmarried, he receives at the rate of $1,000 a year. (3). After six years' service, missionaries are allowed a furlough of twelve months to Canada.

4. HONAN.

(1). A missionary under appointment receives $250 for outfit. The wives of missionaries and unmarried women sent out as missionaries receive for outfit a similar amount. (2). The salary of an ordained or medical missionary, if married, is $1,200 a year; if unmarried, $800 a year. (3). Unmarried women, sent from Canada, receive $500 a year. (4). After six years' service missionaries may take a furlough of twelve months to Canada. (5). Unmarried women on furlough are allowed at the rate of $300 a year.

5. CENTRAL INDIA.

(1). A missionary under appointment receives $250 for outfit. The wives of missionaries and unmarried women sent out as missionaries receive for outfit a similar amount. (2). The salary of an ordained or medical missionary, if married, is $1,200 a year, with $100 a year additional for each child, and $140 for medical or hill expenses; if unmarried, $800 a year, with $90 additional for medical or hill expenses. (3). Unmarried women sent from Canada receive $730 a year. (4). After six years' service missionaries may take a furlough of twelve months to Canada. (6). Unmarried women on furlough are allowed at the rate of $300 a year.

6. MANITOBA AND THE NORTHWEST.

The salary is in each instance determined by the western division of the committee, when the appointment is made.

The foregoing regulations shall be binding in all cases, except those in which the division entrusted with the care of the mission may determine otherwise.

PROPOSED REGULATIONS FOR CENTRAL INDIA MISSION.

Approved by the Committee, for submission to the Mission Council, on 25th Sept., 1895.

1. The mission council shall consist of all the missionaries appointed by the Foreign Mission committee, who have been one year in India, and have passed the first examination in the language; and they shall all have equal right to speak, vote or hold office, except that the president shall always be a male missionary. In the absence of the president another male missionary shall be chosen to occupy the chair.

2. The mission council shall hold one meeting each year for receiving the report of their executive, for the election of officers—a president and secretary—for the appointment of an executive, for the receiving and forwarding, with any necessary remarks, to the Foreign Mission committee, of the annual estimates of the different stations, and also the report of the auditor or auditors, and for other business hereinafter specified.

3. The mission council shall appoint annually an executive consisting of six persons, in addition to the president of the mission council, three of whom shall be men and three women. The executive shall attend to business hereinafter specified and to all matters requiring action which may emerge between the annual meetings of the council. Both mission council and the executive shall forward copies of their minutes to the Foreign Mission committee as soon as convenient after each meeting. It is recommended that the mission council should ordinarily appoint part of its executive by rotation. The president of the mission council shall be ex-officio chairman of the executive and he shall have only a casting vote. In the absence of the president the executive shall elect their own chairman.

4. The mission council shall make the necessary arrangements for the examination of the missionaries in the language they are expected to use, and shall, where practicable, appoint examiners who are not members of the mission staff.

5. The mission council shall nominate a treasurer for the approval of the Foreign Mission committee, who shall hold office until a successor is appointed. It shall be the duty of the treasurer to preserve carefully all deeds of mission property and other legal papers not transmitted to the committee (where this cannot be done

with due regard to the safety of the documents the mission council may assign this duty to a station treasurer), to keep in official books, procured at the committee's expense, and to be the property of the committee, clear and correct accounts of all receipts and payments, and to have vouchers for the latter, and to keep files of all official correspondence properly belonging to his department. His books must be open to the inspection of any member of the mission at all reasonable times.

The mission treasurer is the agent of the committee for the distribution of the amount appropriated for the mission, and is responsible for all funds received by him for the purposes of the mission. These funds shall be kept in a bank or other safe depository approved by the mission council.

The home treasurer is directed to remit to the mission treasurer the amount appropriated to the mission for the financial year of the committee, and only that amount; and this is to be forwarded regularly at stated intervals. He shall, however, forward to the mission treasurer special donations sent for the work of individual missionaries; and the mission treasurer shall also forward to the station treasurer such special donations when they come to hand in order that they may, as soon as possible, reach their destination. The receipt of all remittances is to be officially acknowledged by the mission treasurer, and for all such funds he must return an annual report to the committee through the mission council, duly audited by the auditor of the mission.

The home treasurer may require, from time to time, concise statements of the condition of the mission treasury, with summary of receipts and disbursements in Canadian currency, but the full detailed statement of the mission must be rendered once each year. All funds transmitted to the mission treasurer must, except in very special emergencies, be used in substantial accordance with the appropriations as made, and the expenditures must in no case exceed the amount appropriated without special authority being obtained.

6. The mission council shall appoint annually an auditor not connected with the mission staff, to whom all the accounts of the missionaries, and the books and vouchers of the mission and station treasurers and estimates shall be submitted, and the auditor is expected not only to examine the footings and vouchers for the payments, but also to report whether the money has been expended on the objects for which it was granted as set forth in the estimates.

7. At each station where there are three or more members of the mission council they shall constitute a station council. The station council shall annually elect a chairman, secretary and treasurer, and

each station council shall prepare estimates for the ensuing year, to be submitted to the mission council at its annual meeting. The estimates of each station shall include all salaries, children's allowances, medical and hill expenses, native helpers, touring expenses, medical supplies, all outlay for buildings and repairs, etc. The estimates shall also include probable receipts from medical or school fees, from native congregations and from all other sources.

These estimates, after examination by the mission council, shall be forwarded to the committee for final action, with such remarks as they may consider necessary. When these estimates have been returned to India with the approval of the committee, they shall form the basis on which all payments shall be made by the mission and the station treasurers. Members of the mission council living at stations where there is no station council shall be members of such neighboring station council as the executive may think best.

8. Station treasurers are the financial agents of the mission council for their several stations, with powers and responsibilities in their respective spheres similar to those of the mission treasurer. They must submit statements to the mission treasurer as he does to the home treasurer, such statements shall be open to the inspection of the members of the station, and the annual statement shall be duly audited by the mission council's auditor. Station treasurers are agents of the committee to enforce any rules governing the use of revenue derived from such sources as tuition fees, medical fees, press earnings, etc. Such funds must be accounted for to them, and reported by them to the mission treasurer. The station treasurer's books must be open to the inspection of any member of the station at all reasonable times.

9. Station councils are expected to meet frequently for conference and consultation in reference to the interests of the work under their care, and to make such arrangements as may be found practicable for the comfortable and successful prosecution of their work. Should matters arise on which there is serious difference of opinion among the members of the station council at any station, they shall at the request of two or more members be referred to the executive of the mission council for advice, or to the Foreign Mission committee for decision.

10. It shall be the duty of the executive of the mission council, when new buildings are necessary at any station, or extensive repairs are required in existing buildings, to see that plans are prepared and estimates secured by the station council. When these have been approved by the executive they shall be forwarded to the Foreign Mission committee for its sanction; and when the committee has

authorized the erection of the buildings or the making of the repairs, the superintendence of the work shall be under the care of the station council of the station, who may procure assistance from others as they may desire and be able to obtain it. In the erection of buildings in new fields the executive shall make such arrangements as they consider necessary.

11. The mission council shall each year, in connection with their annual meeting, hold a conference for united prayer, the reading of papers and the discussion of topics bearing upon their work, or fitted to deepen the religious life of the members, and where it is considered desirable, to engage in evangelistic services along with the native laborers.

12. It shall be the duty of the executive to make arrangements for this conference, and prepare the programme. The executive shall also do what is necessary in determining the fields where missionaries are to labor when no field has been specially assigned by the committee. When emergent circumstances call for it, they may also transfer laborers from one field to another, but appointments and transfers so made shall not be regarded as permanent until reported to the committee and confirmed by them. The executive are also authorized to determine the qualifications and salaries of native assistants.

Tuesday, 19th May, 1896.

The following resolution was moved and agreed : The committee regret that the council, though fully aware of the anxious thought given by the committee to the preparation and consideration of the proposed regulations for Central India mission, and though they had full opportunity to do so, have failed to express their opinion of the proposed regulations as requested by the committee, in the only way that would aid the committee in coming to a decision in reference to their adoption, and the committee being still of the opinion that the proposed regulations afford the most satisfactory system and code of rules for the regulation of the affairs of the Central India Mission, resolve—That said regulations be, and they are hereby adopted, and that they go into force on and after the first day of October next, and that the missionaries be and they are hereby directed to act in conformity with them.

French Evangelization.

The following regulations have been tentatively adopted by the board :—

1. The operations of the board of French Evangelization shall have respect :

(1). To colportage in any district of the Dominion where the population is wholly or partially French.

(2). To mission schools in any district where there is no efficient public school open to French Protestants, and where a sufficient number of scholars can be secured to warrant their establishment; also the mission schools at Pointe-aux-Trembles, or at such other places as may be deemed desirable.

(3). To mission stations wholly or partly French, which, having been recommended by Presbyteries and approved by the board, have been placed on the list of aid-receiving stations; provided always that no application for aid shall be entertained by the board on behalf of any station unless the Presbytery of the bounds shall have made arrangements with the people for contributing according to their ability, to the salary of the missionary, and the Presbytery shall see to the implementing of such engagements.

(4). To congregations wholly or partly French, not self-sustaining, but prepared to contribute at least $200 per annum, at the rate of at least $2.25 per communicant, and in which, in the judgment of the Presbytery, a pastor is desirable—such congregations having made application to the Presbytery of the bounds, and furnished satisfactory information in regard to their statistics, financial position and prospects, and having received the approval of the Presbytery (which application and information shall also be laid before the board) may be placed on the list of congregations receiving grants.

Cases in which the application of this rule appears to affect injuriously congregations now on the list, or seeking to be placed on it, shall be reported to the General Assembly and grants made only when its sanction has been given.

(5). To mission stations and congregations, wholly or partly French, reported by Presbyteries, but not receiving aid.

2. The list of aid receiving mission stations and congregations shall be revised annually, at a meeting of the board, held in........ previous to which applications must be made by Presbyteries for grants for all fields within their bounds.

3. The list of laborers shall consist of colporteurs, teachers, students, licentiates, and ordained ministers of this Church, speaking the French language. Each of these must be recommended to the board by some Presbytery, except in the case of teachers.

4. The board shall prepare and send to missionaries blank forms, for their reports, so as to ascertain the peculiar circumstances, necessities and general state of the mission stations and congregations throughout the church.

5. The executive shall consider the reports thus rendered and distribute the missionaries among the Presbyteries, as in view of the detailed information before them, may be deemed advisable.

6. Missionaries in fields receiving aid from the funds of the board shall be paid at the following rates:

(1). Colporteurs, a minimum of $30 per month, including travelling expenses.

(2). Students, at the rate of $35 per month for the summer, with travelling expenses to the field. In cases where the field is upwards of 150 miles from the place of departure, a portion of the travelling expenses from the field may also be paid.

(3). Licentiates or ordained ministers, not inducted into the pastoral charge, at a minimum rate of $8 per Sabbath.

(4). Ministers ordained and regularly inducted into the pastoral charge, hereafter at the rate of $750 per annum, with manse, except in cities or large towns, when on application duly made by the Presbytery, it may be increased to $1,000, with an allowance for house rent.

(5). That the salaries of ordained missionaries, appointed by the board to a field, for a term of not less than one year, be fixed after consultation with the Presbytery of the bounds.

7. The board shall not be responsible for the salary of missionaries beyond the amount of aid promised by it to the stations or congregations, and for the time during which they may have labored in said stations or congregations.

8. The board shall prepare a full annual report of its operations, to be submitted to the General Assembly, and shall publish from time to time such information as may serve to call forth the interest and liberality of the church.

Minutes 1890, p. 36. That the Rev. S. J. Taylor, B.A., be appointed the secretary of the board of French Evangelization, in terms of the recommendation of the board (*a*), at a salary of $1,600 per annum.

Minutes 1896, p. 43. (2) That the secretary of the board who has all along discharged the duty of a superintendent of French missions, be hereafter known by that title. (3) That the balance of the Ross bequest (*b*), amounting to $25,000, be invested as a permanent endowment, the revenue of which shall be for the support of the super

---

(*a*) For the report of the board, *See Minutes 1890, App. No. 11*

(*b*) As to this bequest, *See Minutes 1896, App. No. 12.*

intendent of French missions, and that the board be authorized to secure such additional amount as will yield the entire salary. This latter recommendation was referred to the board for further consideration.

Home Missions.

Regulations (a).

Minutes 1876, pages 47, 48, 49. 1. There shall be a central committee for the Home Missions, dividing itself into two sections, the one embracing the Maritime Provinces and the other the rest of the Church.

2. The Assembly shall appoint annually a Home Mission committee, consisting of forty-five members, of whom one third shall be from the Maritime Provinces and two-thirds from the rest of the Church. Each of these committees shall constitute a sub-committee for the carrying on of mission work within its own territory.

Each section shall be empowered to act separately in conducting operations within its own territory.

3. The operations of the committee shall have respect to—

(1) Mission stations which have been recommended by Presbyteries and approved by the committee, shall be placed on the list of aid receiving stations, and mission stations directly under the care of the Home Mission committee; provided always that no application for aid shall be entertained by the committee on behalf of any station, unless the Presbytery of the bounds shall have made arrangements with the people for contributing, according to their ability, to the salary of the missionary; and the Presbytery shall see to the implementing af such engagements. The committee shall make like arrangements in the case of stations directly under its care.

(2) Mission stations reported by Presbyteries, but not receiving aid.

(3) Congregations not self-sustaining, but prepared to contribute at least $400 per annum, at the rate of at least $4.50 per communicant, and $7 per family, and in which, in the judgment of the Presbytery,

---

(a) These regulations were enacted by the General Assembly in 1876, and seem still in force, though from time to time resolutions have been passed which modify some of them. Following these regulations are given the regulations and rules of procedure adopted by the Eastern and Western sections of the committee respectively for their own guidance.

a pastor is desirable. Such congregations, having made application to the Presbytery of the bounds, and furnished satisfactory information in regard to their statistics, financial position and prospects, and having received the approval of the Presbytery (which application and information shall also be laid before the sub-committee), may be placed on the list of congregations receiving supplement. Cases in which the application of this rule appears to affect injuriously congregations now upon the list, or seeking to be placed on it, shall be reported to the General Assembly, and supplements granted to them only when its sanction has been given (*b*).

4. The system adopted hitherto in the different sections of the Church—in the Maritime Provinces, of two funds, one for Home Missions proper, and another for supplementing the stipends of ministers in weak congregations, administered by two committees; and in the western section of the Church, of one fund for both objects, administered by one committee—shall be continued for the present year; and shall be sent down to Presbyteries to consider the subject and report to the next General Assembly.

5. The list of missionaries shall consist of licentiates and ordained ministers of this Church, also students of divinity and catechists, duly approved as the Assembly may direct. Each of these missionaries shall be recommended to the committee by some Presbytery.

6. The committee shall prepare and send down to Presbyteries and through Presbyteries to missionaries blank forms for their reports, so as to ascertain the peculiar circumstances, necessities and general state of the mission stations and supplemented congregations throughout the Church.

7. The sub-committees shall consider the reports thus rendered by Presbyteries and distribute the missionaries among the Presbyteries, as, in view of the detailed information before them, may be deemed advisable.

8. The sub-committees shall give to mission stations and supplemented congregations in paying their missionaries and ministers such aid, as in view of the detailed information before them, may be deemed advisable.

9. The general committee shall prepare a full annual report of all the Home Mission and supplemental operations of the Church, to be submitted to the Assembly, and shall publish from time to time, such information as may seem to call forth the interest and liberality of the Church.

(*b*) These congregations are now under the care of the Augmentation Fund committee, and reference must be made to their regulations respecting that fund, *ante*.

10. The sub-committees shall be empowered to establish mission stations and conduct missionary operations directly in those parts of the Dominion which are not within the bounds of any Presbytery.

11. In mission fields placed directly under the Home Mission committee, and in new and destitute fields of wide extent, within the bounds of Presbyteries, the sub-committees shall be empowered —in the latter case acting in concert with the Presbytery of the bounds—to secure the services of suitable missionaries who may be willing to occupy them for a number of years, and to pay them in excess of the ordinary salaries paid to missionaries.

12. The committee shall not be responsible for the salary of missionaries beyond the amount of aid promised by it to the stations or congregations, and for the time during which they may have labored in said stations or congregations

13. The amount of salary to be paid by each congregation, station or group of stations, shall be determined by the Presbytery of the bounds, and specified to the sub-committee, and there shall be paid by the Presbytery and sub-committee conjointly for a licentiate or ordained minister, a minimum of $8 per Sabbath, with board ; for a student of divinity, during the summer, at the rate of $6 per Sabbath, with board and travelling expenses to the field of labour ; and for a catechist, of $5 per Sabbath, with board. (*c*).

14. The amount of aid granted to any congregation receiving supplement shall in no case exceed the amount necessary to make the salary of the minister from all sources $700. But the sub-committees are empowered to supplement, beyond that amount, the salaries of ordained ministers engaged in mission work in towns and cities. (*d*).

15. The supplement of all aid-receiving congregations shall be calculated from the first day of the ecclesiastical year, and Presbyteries are instructed to make their reports accordingly—supplements being payable half-yearly.

16. Presbyteries are instructed, at an ordinary meeting, previous to the first day of October in each year, to revise the list of mission stations and supplemented congregations, and make such changes as they may deem necessary, reporting the amended list to the sub-committees. The list, thus amended, shall form the basis of the operations of the committee for the then current year.

17. Presbyteries are enjoined to furnish information to the sub-committees, in accordance with the requirements of the above scheme and to co-operate with the committee.

(*c*). For the amounts now paid to missionaries, students and catechists, see the regulations adopted by the Eastern and Western sections, respectively, *post*.

(*d*). See the regulations respecting augmentation, *ante*.

18. All congregations and mission stations are enjoined to make an annual contribution in the western section of the Church to the Home Mission fund; and in the maritime provinces to the Home Mission fund and Supplemental fund.

19. The travelling expenses of members of committee shall be borne equally by the two funds, and the cost of all exploring and aggressive missionary work, undertaken and sanctioned by Presbyteries, shall be defrayed out of the Home Mission fund.

20. In regard to arrears due by supplemented congregations to their ministers, the congregation shall be required to report to the committee, through the Presbytery, in the form provided, before the beginning of each ecclesiastical year, the amounts paid by them as stipends during the previous twelve months ; and in cases where the amount falls short of the stipend promised by them, power shall be given to suspend the payment of the supplements until the arrearages are liquidated.

Eastern Section—Regulations.

The roll of laborers is made up of two classes : (*a*). Ministers and probationers ; (*b*). Students and other laymen, designated catechists.

1.—(1). The first class must satisfy the committee of good standing as licentiates or ministers without charge, in connection with some Presbytery of the Church.

(2). When their names are entered on the roll they shall receive appointments by the committee to Presbyteries for such a term as may be agreed upon. The committee can only appoint to Presbyteries. Presbyteries alone have the right of appointing to congregations or mission stations. The committee can only make appointments for such a number as the Presbyteries apply for from time to time. It is not bound to keep all its men in constant employment.

(3). The committee is at liberty to notify a man at any time that it has no more work for him, if Presbyteries intimate that they do not want him.

(4). When the committee, or its sub-committee, which usually meets once a month, makes an appointment, it is the duty of the secretary of the committee to inform the person appointed, and the Presbytery to which he is sent, of the same ; but the committee throws upon the appointee the responsibility of seeking information from the secretary of the committee, as to what Presbytery he is sent; and from the clerk of such Presbytery as to what congregations he is to serve during the period of his appointment.

(5). It is the duty of each licentiate and minister on the roll to report to the Presbytery in which he has labored, such information concerning the field and his work, and the amount paid him by the people, as will enable the Presbytery to give full information to the committee, and the committee to determine the amount to be paid out of the Home Mission fund for his services.

(6). Presbyteries may appoint an ordained missionary to a field for a year, provided the people raise at least $400. In this case, his name goes off the Home Mission roll, and on to the roll of the Presbytery. His salary is usually $700 per annum. Of this sum, the committee pays whatever amount is agreed upon by it and the Presbytery, never, however, exceeding $300 per annum. He is required to report, at the close of his year, through the Presbytery to the committee.

(7). The remuneration to laborers of the first class, is ten dollars per week and board. It is expected that places supplied will pay the greater portion of this amount. Laborers, in conjunction with Presbyteries, should take steps to have the people do their duty in this regard, so that the Home Mission fund may not be unduly burdened.

2.—(1) Laborers of the second class must present certificates showing that they are students in theology in good standing in some approved institution, or a certificate, from some Presbytery, showing that such Presbytery believe them qualified for the work, and willing to receive them into its own territory for service.

(2) When the committee agrees to enter their names on the roll, they must accept appointments at the hands of the Presbytery to which they are sent, and it is their duty, so soon as they are appointed, to obtain instructions from the clerk of the Presbytery in whose bounds they are to labor. At the close of their term of service they must report to the Presbytery on forms furnished by the committee, giving full statistics and such other information as may aid the Presbytery in dealing with the field.

(3) The remuneration of catechists is $7.00 per week and board. It is expected that the mission fields will raise all they can of this amount, and catechists are required to perfect such organization for collecting money as will secure as much as possible for self support, and for the funds of the Church.

(4) Catechists' bills cannot be paid till approved and recommended by Presbyteries, and ordered by the Home Mission committee.

(5) The committee holds semi-annual meetings in April and November. Catechists are, as a general rule, appointed at the April meeting, and their reports considered and bills settled at the November.

WESTERN SECTION—REGULATIONS.

1. There is a central committee for the western section of the Church annually appointed by the General Assembly.

2. The operations of the committee have respect to (a) mission stations, which having been recommended by Presbyteries and approved by the committee, shall be placed on the list of aid receiving stations, provided always that no application for aid shall be entertained by the committee on behalf of any station, unless the Presbytery of the bounds shall have made arrangements with the people for contributing, according to their ability, to the salary of the missionary, and the Presbytery shall see to the implementing of such engagements. (b) Mission stations reported by Presbyteries, but not receiving aid.

3. The list of missionaries shall consist of licentiates and ordained ministers of this Church, also students of divinity and catechists, duly approved as the Assembly may direct. Each of these missionaries shall be certified to the committee by some Presbytery of the Church.

4. The committee shall prepare and send down to Presbyteries, and through Presbyteries to missionaries, blank forms for their reports, so as to ascertain the peculiar circumstances, necessities, and general state of the mission stations throughout the Church. The committee shall consider the reports thus rendered by Presbyteries, and distribute the missionaries among the Presbyteries, as in view of the detailed information before them may be deemed advisable. The committee shall give to mission stations, in the payment of their missionaries. such aid as, in view of the detailed information before them, may be deemed advisable. The committee shall prepare a full annual report of all the Home Mission operations of the Church, to be submitted to the General Assembly, and shall publish from time to time such information as may serve to call forth the interest and liberality of the Church. The committee shall not be responsible for the salaries of missionaries, beyond the amount of aid promised by it to the field, and for the time during which they may have labored in the field. The amount of salary to be paid by each station, or group of stations, shall be determined by the Presbytery of the bounds, and specified to the committee. The salaries of missionaries, employed under the Home Mission committee, are as follows :

Ordained missionaries—(1) Synod of British Columbia ; a minimum of $850, with power to the Synod's Home Mission committee to increase this, at their discretion, up to $1,000. (2) Synod of

Manitoba and North-West : $800 for married men where there is no manse ; $750 for married men where there is a manse ; $700 for unmarried men. (3) Province of Ontario and Quebec ; $750 for married men where there is no manse ; $700 for married men where there is a manse ; $600 for unmarried men.

Student missionaries—$5.50 per Sabbath and board and expenses to the field, for summer half year ; $6.50 per Sabbath and board and expenses to the field, when engaged for the whole winter half year.

Catechists—$5.00 per Sabbath and board for summer half year ; $5.50 per Sabbath and board for winter half year; $500 per annum for approved catechists engaged for a term of at least one year.

The General Assembly has modified these regulations, so far as they refer to Manitoba, the North-west and British Columbia, as follows :—1. That for the year beginning 1st April, 1896, a sum not exceeding $16,750 be granted to the Synod of Manitoba and the North-West, and a sum not exceeding $15,000 to the Synod of British Columbia—these sums to cover the entire expenditure from the funds of the committee, excepting the salary and expenses of Dr. Robertson, and the travelling expenses of missionaries to and from their fields of labor. 2. That these Synods, through their Home Mission committees, be required to submit to this committee, at its semi-annual meetings in March and October, a financial statement for the six months then ending ; and accompanying this a report, on the schedules prepared by this committee, of the work done during the half-year in the respective mission fields, with the names of the missionaries, the amounts contributed by the people, and the appropriations made by the Synod's committees to the several fields. 3. That these Synods, through their Home Mission committees, be instructed to submit to this committee, on or before the 25th day of April annually, a financial statement of the receipts and expenditure for the year ending 31st March, together with an annual report of the several fields, on the schedules furnished by this committee.—*Home Mission Report, Minutes, 1896, App. No. 1, p. 63.*

SUPERINTENDENT OF NORTH-WEST MISSIONS.

Minutes, 1881, p. 49.—The General Assembly ordered : (*a*). That the superintendent of missions shall be known as the superintendent of missions for the Synod of Manitoba and the North-West Territories. (*b*). That the superintendent shall be a member of the Presbytery of Brandon, and shall have a right to sit and deliberate with each of the other Presbyteries of the Synod; and that he shall be a member of the Assembly's Home Mission committee. (*c*). That the superintendent, in conjunction with the Synod's Home Mission committee, shall prepare for the General Assembly an annual report of mission work in Manitoba and the North-West, containing full statistics of the membership, families and adherents in each mission station, and supplemented congregation within the bounds of the Synod, which report shall be forwarded through the Assembly's Home Mission committee to the General Assembly.

DUTIES OF THE SUPERINTENDENT OF MISSIONS.

Minutes, 1881, p. 49.—The General Assembly order as follows: 1. That the duties of the superintendent of missions shall include the visitation of all the mission stations and supplemented congregations within the bounds of the Synod of Manitoba and the North-West Territories, the organization of new stations, the adjusting of the amounts to be paid by the different stations or congregations for the support of ordinances, and the amounts to be asked from the Home Mission committee, and, in general, the furtherance of the entire mission work of the Church in Manitoba and the North-West. 2. That in the prosecution of this work he shall consult and co-operate with the Synod's Home Mission committee, and especially in reference to the distribution of his time, the allocation of laborers, and the apportionment of the funds to the several Presbyteries or fields. 3. That in reference to the visiting and organizing of stations and congregations, and the adjusting of the amounts to be paid by the fields and by the Home Mission committee, and any other work properly coming within the jurisdiction of Presbyteries he shall consult with and report to the Presbytery of the bounds. 4. That the Home Mission committee of the Synod of Manitoba and the North-West shall furnish to the General Assembly's Home Mission committee, a detailed estimate of the probable amount of money required for the year, in prosecuting the work of the Church in the mission stations within the bounds of the Synod, and furnish, twice a year, a detailed account of the expenditure in the various fields during the preceding six months. 5. That the money apportioned by the Home Mission committee shall be disbursed by the authority of the Synod, and payments made to the fields quarterly. (*a*). 6. That the money for supplements (*b*) be transmitted from the Assembly's Home Mission committee, through the Home Mission committee of the Synod of Manitoba and the North-West Territories, and, in the meantime, payments to be made quarterly, as heretofore.

Home Mission Report, Minutes 1885, App. p. 13. In October, 1884, the Home Mission committee appointed an ordained missionary to labor in and supervise the mission fields in Algoma, Muskoka and

---

(*a*). The payments are now made half-yearly, instead of quarterly.

(*b*). The expression now used is "grants," instead of supplements.

Parry Sound districts, and along the line of the Canadian Pacific railway to North Bay, and to discharge his duties under the direction of the executive of the Home Mission committee, being subject to the jurisdiction respectively of the Presbyteries of Bruce and Barrie while within their bounds.

RULES FOR APPOINTMENT OF MISSIONARIES.

Home Mission Report, Minutes 1885, App. p. 47. 1. The Home Mission committee has the right of appointment through the respective Presbyteries in the following cases: (1) To all mission districts and mission stations, whether these be self-sustaining or requiring aid. (2) To any vacant charge seeking continuous supply such as is provided by the committee.

*Note—*Presbyteries shall forward to the secretary, one week before each meeting, a full list of their fields, and indicate those in which supply is required.

2. The list of missionaries is made up for the regular meetings of the committee, and at the March meeting the list is printed and distributed to the members of committee. The list is made up as follows: (1) The names of all students desiring work and whose names are forwarded by some Presbytery of the Church. (2) The names of all catechists recommended by Presbyteries. (3) The names of ministers and licentiates in good standing in the Church and seeking work under the committee.

Note.—The printed list shall indicate the names of students or others willing to labor in the mission field for the term of one year or more.

3. In allocating missionaries the committee has the following procedure: (1) Appointments are made to Presbyteries, first for fields requiring ordained missionaries for a term of years, and then for the field at large. (2) The Presbyteries have a choice in rotation, beginning at the east and west in alternate years. (3) The Presbytery first choosing any laborer has a claim upon him which shall stand, unless in the judgment of the committee the said laborer should be allocated to another Presbytery. (4) Each Presbytery requiring ten missionaries or over has an extra choice after both first and second rounds, and each Presbytery requiring six missionaries or over has an extra choice after the first round.

4. If any missionary refuses to go to the Presbytery to which he has been allocated, he shall not be employed in any field under the care of this committee until next half yearly meeting, unless with the consent of the Presbytery first choosing him.

5. It is distinctly understood that the practice of making private arrangements shall not be countenanced, except in the case of a settled minister who desires to secure a student to assist him in his own congregation, in which case the name of the missionary shall be reported to this committee to be placed upon the list.

Minutes 1894, p. 62. There was read an overture from the Presbytery of Toronto, asking that the Assembly ordain that in giving appointments to students the Home Mission committee give the preference to students in the order of seniority in their college course, and that the Assembly enjoin all home mission stations to procure their supply through the Home Mission committee. The Assembly adopted the overture and instructed the Home Mission committee to carry out the decision of the Assembly.

Home Mission Report, Minutes 1896, App. No. 1, p. 66. At the March meeting of the committee the following resolution was adopted : That, in the judgment of the committee, the time has come when only those students who have already entered upon the study of theology, and have attended at least one session in the theological classes of one of the colleges of the Church, should receive appointments from this committee for the summer months, and that hereafter the committee will only give employment to such, unless under exceptional circumstances; further, that preference will be given to such theological students as offer their services for twelve or eighteen months' continuous work in the mission field.

Temporalities Board.

22 Vict., cap. 66 (C).—An Act to incorporate the Board for the management of the Temporalities Fund of the Presbyterian Church of Canada in connection with the Church of Scotland. (*Assented to 24th July, 1858.*)

Whereas it hath been represented to the Legislature of this Province, that it is desirable that provision should be made for the management and holding of certain funds of the Presbyterian Church of Canada in connection with the Church of Scotland, now held in trust by certain commissioners, hereinafter named, on behalf of the said Church and for the benefit thereof, and also of such other funds as may from time to time be granted, given, bequeathed, or contributed in addition thereto; and whereas the said funds are so held in trust, and the revenues thereof are to be appropriated for the encouragement and support of ministers and missionaries of the said Church, and for the augmentation of their stipends, and towards making a provision for those who may be incapacitated by age or infirmity; and whereas, secondly, when and if it shall so please the said Church, and so soon as other funds hereafter shall be contributed, subscribed, or paid in from any source for the purpose to the corporation hereby erected, it is desired that such other funds shall be appropriated for granting aid towards the erection and maintenance and endowment of churches and manses in connection with the said Church, and the aiding of young men to study for the ministry; and whereas the erection of a corporation will best promote the purposes aforesaid: Therefore, Her Majesty, &c., enacts as follows:—

1. The Rev. Alexander Mathieson, of Montreal, D.D.; the Rev. John Cook, of Quebec, D. D.; (*and others, naming them*) with four additional members, and their successors, to be elected in the manner hereinafter provided, shall be and they are hereby declared to be a body politic and corporate, in name and in deed, by the name of the "Board for the management of the Tem-"poralities' Fund of the Presbyterian Church of Canada, "in connection with the Church of Scotland," and for the purposes herein aforesaid recited, by that name shall have perpetual succession and a common seal, and they and their successors, by the name aforesaid, may sue and be sued, implead and be impleaded, answer and be answered unto, in any court of record or place of judicature in this Province; and they and their successors shall be able, in law, to take, have and hold and enjoy, possess and retain, and shall henceforth have, hold, enjoy and possess, in trust for the said Church, and for the aforesaid firstly hereinabove specified uses, all moneys, debentures, bonds, bank or other stocks and

securities, which are now held by the said hereinbefore named parties as trustees or commissioners of the said Church, in trust for the said Church; but such holding is subject always to the special condition that the annual interest and revenues of the said moneys and fund now in their hands shall be and remain charged and subject, as well as regards the character as the extent and duration thereof, to the several annual charges in favour of the several ministers and parties severally entitled thereto, of the several amounts and respective characters and durations as the same were constituted and declared at the formation of the said funds, and the joining of the same into one fund; and the said board shall also have power without license of mortmain, or *lettres d'amortissement*, to have, hold, receive, take, enjoy and possess, by gift, voluntary conveyance, devise, bequest, or otherwise, to them and their successors, any real or personal estate, to and for the use of the said board for any or either of the purposes aforesaid; provided always, that any real estate which may be so acquired, by the said board, shall be sold within two years from the date of such acquisition thereof by the said corporation, and the proceeds thereof invested in the public securities of the Province, municipal debentures, stock of the chartered banks, or other securities, for the uses aforesaid; and provided further that any such real estate which shall not be sold and alienated within two years from the time when the same is received by the corporation, shall revert to the party from whom the same came to the corporation, or to his or her heirs, devisees or other representatives; and provided also, that no will shall be valid and sufficient to pass any real or personal estate to the said corporation, unless such will shall have been executed by the testator six calendar months prior to his decease; and such board and their successors shall, moreover, have power to sell, dispose of, exchange, alter, vary, or renew any of the investments heretofore made by them, or hereafter to be made of the said funds, or such other funds, or any of them, and to re-invest any moneys arising therefrom, and acquittances, conveyances, transfers, releases, receipts and discharges to make and give as occasion may demand.

2. At the first meeting of the Synod of the said Church hereafter, there shall be elected by the said Synod seven members of the said board, of whom four shall be laymen and three ministers, all members of the Presbyterian Church of Canada in connection with the Church of Scotland, in place of two laymen and one minister, members of the said board who shall then retire, but who shall be eligible, as shall all other retiring members, for re-election; and thereafter, two ministers and two laymen shall retire from the said board annually in rotation, on the third day of the annual meeting of the Synod or other court of highest jurisdiction of the said Church, and their places shall be supplied by two ministers and two laymen, then elected by the said Synod; and the mode in which the said trustees hereby named shall retire, shall be defined by by-law of the said corporation, or in default thereof by the Synod, but the members of the board who shall from time to time be elected in the stead of the afore-named members shall, after all the said eight members of the board named in this Act, have gone out, retire from office in the proportions aforesaid in rotation according to the seniority of their election: In the event of the death, resignation, removal from the Province, or leaving the communion of the said Church of any member of the said board, the remaining members, or a majority of them present at any general meeting duly convened for that purpose, shall choose a minister or layman to fill such vacancy, subject, however, to the approval of the said Synod or other court at its next meeting, so that the said board shall always consist of twelve members, of whom five shall be ministers and seven shall be laymen, all being ministers or members in full communion of the said Church: provided always, that until such first annual meeting of the Synod as aforesaid and the election of the said seven members thereat, all the powers, rights and duties conferred upon the said board by this Act, shall be exercised by the said eight persons

named in this Act, as fully and effectually as if the said board consisted of twelve members as aforesaid.

3. The said Rev. John Cook, D. D., or in his default any other of the said eight persons named in this Act, shall call a meeting of the said board, within six months after the passing of this Act, at the City of Montreal, at which meeting the members of the said corporation then present, or a majority of them, shall then choose and elect from among the members of the said board, a chairman, holding office during the pleasure of the said corporation, and such corporation shall elect successors to him as often as occasion may require or the by-laws of the said corporation shall prescribe; and at such meeting, and at all other meetings of the said board, seven shall constitute a quorum: the said corporation shall further have power, if they see fit, to appoint an executive committee of three members, defining their duties and powers by by-law or by by-laws, and shall also have power and authority to appoint on such terms as they may deem suitable, a secretary, who shall not be a member of the board, and such subordinate officers as may be necessary, and the same to dismiss or remove as they shall see fit, and shall further have power and authority to make and defray all necessary expenditure for and on behalf of the said corporation.

4. The said corporation or the majority thereof present at any meeting of the said corporation duly convened, shall have power and authority to frame and make statutes, by-laws, rules and orders, touching and concerning the good government of the said corporation, and the collection, administration, investment, application, appropriation and management of the funds aforesaid, and any other matter or thing which to them shall seem fit or expedient for the effectual attainment of the objects of the said corporation and the administration of its concerns and for fixing, ascertaining and establishing the scale or rate of stipend from the said funds to the ministers or others entitled thereto under the pro-

visions of this Act, subject, however, to the aforesaid original annual or other charges, and the scale or rate of annuities payable to superannuated or disabled ministers, and the same to vary, alter, repeal or make anew: provided always, that all such by-laws shall be submitted to the first meeting of the Synod, or other supreme court thereafter, for confirmation, amendment or rejection, but in the meantime shall till then be operative, as *interim* by-laws.

5. The said board shall prepare and submit annually to the said Synod or other Supreme Court of the said Church, on the first day of the annual session thereof, a balance-sheet of the financial affairs of the fund, exhibiting the receipts and disbursements of the said corporation during the financial year next preceding such meeting, and also a report of their proceedings during such period.

6. The said corporation shall hold their meetings at such place or places within this Province as they shall from time to time direct and appoint.

---

32 Vict., cap. 76 (Q.)—An Act to amend the Act of the late Parliament of Canada, intituled: "An Act to incorporate the Board for the management of the Temporalities Fund of the Presbyterian Church of Canada in connection with the Church of Scotland. (*Assented to 5th April, 1869.*)

Whereas, by petition, it hath been represented that the Act of the late Parliament of the Province of Canada, passed in the 22nd year of Her Majesty's reign, and intituled: "An Act to incorporate the board for the management of the Temporalities Fund of the Presbyterian Church of Canada in connection with the Church of Scotland," requires to be amended in such wise as to define the classes of security in which the said board may invest their funds; and it is expedient so to amend the same; Therefore, Her Majesty, &c., enacts as follows:

1. The board for the management of the Temporalities Fund of the Presbyterian Church of Canada in connection with the Church of Scotland, may invest their funds in any stock or bonds of the Province of Quebec, or Ontario, or of the Dominion of Canada, or in the stock or bonds of any city or municipal or other corporation in the said Provinces of Quebec or Ontario, and may also invest their funds on the security of hypothecs on real estate in the Province of Quebec, and the said board shall have power, from time to time, to vary, alter or renew, any of the investments made, or to be made by them, in manner aforesaid.

2. Any real estate within the Province of Quebec, which having been hypothecated to the board may become the property of the board by purchase at sheriff's sale or otherwise, in order to the protection of the interest therein of the said board, shall be sold within five years from the time when the same becomes the property of the said corporation, and if sold within the said period of five years, shall not revert to the party from whom the same came to the corporation, or to his or her heirs, devisees or other representatives, anything in the said Act to the contrary notwithstanding.

---

38 Vict., cap. 34 (Q.)—An Act to amend the Act intituled "An Act to incorporate the Board for the management of the Temporalities Fund of the Presbyterian Church of Canada in connection with the Church of Scotland."

In the case of *Dobie* v. *Temporalities Board*, 7 Appeal Cases, 136, the Judicial Committee of the Privy Council decided that this Act was *ultra vires*, and accordingly the Act which immediately follows was got from the Dominion Parliament.

---

45 Vict., cap. 124 (D)—An Act to amend the Act of the late Province of Canada, entitled "An Act to incorporate the Board for the Management of the Temporalities Fund of the Presbyterian Church of Canada, in connection with the Church of Scotland," and the Act amending the same. (*Assented to 17th May, 1882*).

Whereas, by petition, it hath been represented that the Synods of the Presbyterian Church of Canada, in connection with the Church of Scotland; of the Church of the Maritime Provinces, in connection with the Church of Scotland; of the Presbyterian Church of the Lower Provinces, and the General Assembly of the Canada Presbyterian Church, have united together and have formed one body or denomination of Christians, under the name of "The Presbyterian Church in Canada," and that an Act of the Province of Quebec, 38th Victoria, chapter 64, was passed on the 23rd day of February, 1875, containing provisions similar to those contained in this Act, but which Act of the Quebec Legislature has been declared to be unconstitutional by Her Majesty's privy council; and whereas, the present acting members of the hereinafter mentioned board have since the passing of the said last-mentioned Act, been acting under the provisions thereof; and whereas, the Act of the late Province of Canada, intituled "An Act to incorporate the board for the management of the Temporalities Fund of the Presbyterian Church in Canada, in connection with the Church of Scotland," and amendments thereto, require to be amended, in consequence of such union, and in order to the carrying into effect of certain resolutions passed by the Synod of the Presbyterian Church of Canada, in connection with the Church of Scotland, with reference to the said Temporalities fund, and for the protection of those interested in the same: Therefore Her Majesty &c. enacts as follows:—

1. Notwithstanding anything in the said Act of the late Province of Canada, relating to the said Temporalities fund, or amendments thereto, all the acts and do-

ings of the said board and of the acting members thereof, from and since the passing of the said Act of the Province of Quebec, 38th Victoria, chapter 64, had thereunder, are hereby ratified and confirmed, and the present acting members of the said board are hereby authorized to hold office and administer the said fund according to the terms of this Act, until replaced by others elected hereunder; until all the present vested rights of all ministers and probationers shall have ceased or lapsed, the said Temporalities fund shall remain, as at present, in the hands of a board, the membership of which shall be continued in the manner hereafter provided, and the administration of the fund shall continue on the same principles and for the same purposes as at present, until the vested rights of all ministers and probationers shall have lapsed; and these rights shall be held to be the following: (1). The annual receipt by ministers now receiving $450, $400, or $200, of the same amount during their life time, and good standing in the Church; (2). The annual receipt of $2,000 in perpetuity, by the Treasurer of Queen's College, for the use and benefit of the said college; (3). The annual receipt of $200 by all the ministers who shall be on the Synod roll and by all recognized probationers and licentiates engaged in active service at the time of the union, during the lifetime, and good standing in the Church of such ministers, probationers and licentiates; all salaries of $200 to be increased to $400 each, when the recipients of them shall have retired, or who have already retired in the Province of Quebec, with the consent of the Church, from the active duties of the ministry; the Temporalities board shall, if necessary, draw upon the capital of the fund in order to meet the aforesaid requirements; so soon as any part of the revenue accruing from said fund is not required to meet the payments of said incomes and other vested rights in the fund, and expenses therewith, the same shall pass to and be subject to the disposal of said united Church; and as soon as the fund, or any part of it, shall no longer be required for these purposes, it shall, with the exception of the aforesaid annual payment to Queen's College of $2,000, or the same capitalized (and the board shall have power at any time after the passing of this act to capitalize the same and pay it over to the treasurer of Queen's College, for the use and benefit of the said college), be appropriated to a Home Mission fund for aiding weak charges in the united Church.

2. Provided always, that all ministers and probationers interested or possessing rights in or to the said Temporalities fund at the time when such union was carried into effect, who decline to become parties to such union, or to enter into the said proposed united Church, shall be entitled to all the pecuniary rights and claims upon the said fund they would have enjoyed had they entered into such union, that is to say, so long as they shall continue to be Presbyterian ministers in good standing within the Dominion of Canada, whether in active service or retired; and the said board shall administer the said fund so as to protect their rights until their said rights shall have respectively lapsed and been extinguished; provided also, that nothing contained in this Act shall be so construed as to deprive any professor in Queen's College of any right to participate in the said Temporalities fund to which, as a minister of the Presbyterian Church of Canada, in connection with the Church of Scotland, he would have been entitled had he continued in the active duties of the ministry of the said Church.

3. As often as any vacancy in the board for the management of the said Temporalities Fund occurs, by death, resignation or otherwise, the beneficiaries entitled to the benefit of the said fund may each nominate a person, being a minister or member of the said united Church; or in the event of there being more than one vacancy, then one person for each vacancy, and the remanent members of the said board shall thereupon from among the persons so nominated as aforesaid, elect the person or number of persons necessary to fill such vacancy or vacancies, selecting the person or persons

who may be nominated by the largest number of beneficiaries, but in the event of failure on the part of the beneficiaries to nominate as aforesaid, the remanent members of the board shall fill up the vacancy or vacancies from among the ministers or members of the said united Church.

4. The said board of management shall, within twelve months after the passing of this Act, call a meeting of the said beneficiaries at such time and place as may be found most convenient, and at such meeting the said beneficiaries shall have power to make by-laws regulating all matters relating to the mode in which notice of vacancies occurring as aforesaid shall be given to them, the time within which such notice shall be given, the form of nomination papers, the time after receiving notice of a vacancy within which the same are to be sent in, the person or persons to whom the same shall be sent and by whom the same shall be opened, the recording the result of such nominations and of the elections consequent thereon, and all other matters relating to or affecting such nominations and elections.

(2) After the first and third classes of payments named in section one shall have been extinguished and provision shall have been made for the annual receipt in perpetuity of the sum provided for in the second class of payments, each congregation which declined to become a party to the union, and which shall not have entered the union before the time of the extinction of such payments shall be entitled to a share of the residue, such share to be in the proportion of one to the whole number of congregations on the Synod roll on the 14th day of June, 1875, the date of the union.

5. The board of management of the said Temporalities Fund shall, once in each year transmit by post to each beneficiary a printed statement of the affairs of the said fund, and a report of the proceedings of the board for the preceding year, containing such information as may be required by the by-laws to be passed, as hereinafter provided.

6. The books and affairs of the said board shall be audited once in each year by auditors appointed by the beneficiaries, in manner hereinafter provided.

7. At the meeting to be called and held pursuant to section 4, the beneficiaries may make by-laws regulating the appointment of auditors, and all matters relating to the audit of the affairs of the fund, and to the annual statement and report to be made under section 5.

8. The third section of this Act shall continue in force until the number of beneficiaries is reduced below fifteen ; and so soon as the number is reduced below fifteen, the said board shall be continued by the remanent members filling up any vacancy or vacancies from among the ministers or members of the united Church, and the auditors shall in like manner be appointed by the said board.

BY-LAWS FOR THE MANAGEMENT OF THE TEMPORALITIES' FUND.
(*Passed 23rd May, 1860*).

Whereas the board for the management of the Temporalities' fund of the Presbyterian Church of Canada, in connection with the Church of Scotland, are authorized to frame and make statutes and by-laws for the purposes specified in the Act incorporating said board, and intituled, "An Act to incorporate the board for the management of the Temporalities' fund of the Presbyterian Church of Canada, in connection with the Church of Scotland."

At a meeting of the said corporation, duly convened and holden at the City of Montreal, on the 23rd day of May, in the year of our Lord 1860, at which meeting there were present: Thomas Paton, Esq., Rev. Dr. Cook (*and others, naming them*) members thereof, and in pursuance of the aforesaid powers ;

Be it therefore enacted by the board for the management of the Temporalities' fund of the Presbyterian Church of Canada, in connection with the Church of Scotland, by virtue of and under the authority of the said Act of the Parliament of Canada, 22 Vict., cap. 66, and it is hereby enacted by authority of the same :

1. That the remaining trustees named in the second clause of the said Act shall retire from the said board and cease to hold office therein, in the following order, that is to say : Messrs. J. Cameron and

Hugh Allan, laymen, and the Rev. Drs. Mathieson and Cook, ministers, shall retire on the third day of the meeting of the Synod.

2. The chairman of the said board shall be elected annually by the members present at the first meeting of the said corporation, duly convened and holden after the annual election of members of the said corporation by the said Synod, but if still a member, shall hold office until his successor shall be elected. He shall countersign all cheques, and shall be and is authorized to receive all dividends and interest accruing to the board from any of its stocks or securities, and to grant receipts and discharges therefor.

3. That an executive committee, consisting of three members, of whom the chairman shall be *ex officio* a member, be appointed annually by the said board, at the said first meeting, which shall be duly convened and holden after the rising of the said Synod, but shall hold office until their successors are appointed, the members thereof being eligible to re-election. That such committee shall have power and authority to carry out the instructions of the board in relation to the collection, investment, administration and management of the funds of the said corporation. Such committee shall alone have power to receive, accept and execute transfers of bank or other stocks or debentures, or to execute acts, deeds and discharges on behalf, and in the name of the board; but every such transfer, acceptance or other instrument must be signed and executed by the chairman and the other two members of the said committee. Such committee shall in the first instance consist of Thomas Paton, Esq., Rev. Alexander Mathieson, D.D., and Hugh Allan, Esq. But in the absence or death of any member, the board shall nominate a substitute or successor,

4. Meetings of the board shall be held on the second Tuesday of the months of May and November in each year for the transaction of business; and adjourned meetings may be held at such times as a quorum of the corporation shall direct.

5. The chairman, or in his absence the secretary, shall have power to call special meetings of the board when necessary, at such time and place, giving three day's notice thereof, exclusive of the day on which such notice shall be dated and posted, as he shall appoint, and it shall be his duty to call such special meetings when any three members of the board shall request him in writing to do so, stating the object of such meeting.

6. In the absence of the chairman a quorum of the members of the board present may appoint one of themselves as chairman to preside at the meeting, and as such chairman shall, for the purpose of such meeting, be invested with the powers and authority of the

chairman. The chairman, or member of the board so presiding, shall vote as a member of the board, and shall also, in case of an equality of votes, have a casting vote.

7. No business shall be transacted or entered upon, at any ordinary meeting of the board, until the minutes of the preceding meeting have been read and approved of.

8. No change of the investments of the board, nor sale of any part thereof, shall be made until the same be specifically authorized by a resolution of the board entered upon the minutes, and the board shall, from time to time, as occasion may arise, decide upon the alteration, exchange, or renewal of any of the investments of the board, and upon the description of bonds, stocks, or securities in which any re-investment thereof shall be made.

9. The officers of the board shall consist of a treasurer and secretary, and such number of clerks and subordinary officers as may, from time to time, be deemed necessary by the board, provided that the offices of secretary and treasurer may be united if deemed desirable by the board, and such officers shall and may, from time to time, be appointed or removed by the resolution of the board; and their salaries shall be determined by the board.

10. The executive committee shall have authority to direct the secretary and other officers of the board, in all matters necessary for the interest of the board, in the intervals between the meetings of the board, subject to the approval of the board at the next meeting.

11. The treasurer shall give security, to the satisfaction of the board, to such an amount and with such sureties, as to the board may seem fit, for the faithful discharge of the trust and duties of his office. He shall receive all moneys accruing to the board from ordinary annual congregational or other collections, and shall deposit the same to the credit of the board, and in their name, in such bank or banks as the board shall, from time to time, determine by resolution. He shall sign cheques against the bank account of the board for the payment of the stipends of ministers, and other expenses of the board (which shall be countersigned by the chairman), and shall take receipts from all persons to whom he shall deliver cheques. He shall keep a regular set of books, containing the accounts of the board and of all its funds, which may pass through and come into his hands, and whenever required by the board, shall furnish a detailed statement of all such accounts, and he shall make and deliver for the use of the board a complete settlement and balance of the books, and accounts of the board made up to such period in each year as the board may require.

12. The secretary shall carry on the correspondence of the board, and keep a minute book, and register of its proceedings. He shall lay before the board, at its semi-annual or other meetings, all communications received by him subsequent to each preceding meeting, and he shall in like manner submit a statement of all matters passing in his office during such period. He shall summon all meetings of the board, whenever requested to do so by the chairman, and in his absence, at the request of three members, and generally he shall discharge all such other duties as shall be imposed on him from time to time by resolution of the board.

13. It shall be the duty of the chairman and secretary-treasurer on receiving from Presbytery clerks, lists of ministers of their respective Presbyteries, with the dates of their ordination and induction, to pay to the ministers who commuted £112 10s. per annum, to the ministers on the roll of the Synod at the time of the secularization of the clergy reserves, but who were not allowed to commute £100 per annum, and to all others until such time as this board shall otherwise determine a minimum stipend of £50 a year, the whole in half-yearly payments, and also £500 a year to the treasurer for the time being of Queen's College, to be employed, as heretofore, in the payment of professors, being ministers of the Church.

14. That any ministers now entitled to the guaranteed stipend of £112 10s. per annum, or £100, or other allowance, and who from age or infirmity now are or shall from time to time, be released from their respective charges by their respective Presbyteries, with the sanction of the Synod, duly signified by the clerk of Synod to this board, shall be entitled to receive the same, or such other allowance as shall be agreed upon with the Synod for life.

15. That the original funds arising from the said commutation, and which were constituted into one fund and amount to the sum of £127,000, shall be kept separate and distinct from any other funds which may come into the possession of the board, and a separate account shall be kept thereof until it shall otherwise be ordered by the board by a by-law to that effect; and further, that separate accounts be opened, first for congregational collections and secondly for annual or other subscriptions for the sustentation of the Church, the former to be designated as the "contingent fund," and the latter as the "Home Mission fund of the Church," which last mentioned fund shall be invested as a permanent fund.

16. That a list by name, residence and Presbytery of the several ministers who commuted their allowance and joined the same into one fund, and also a list in like manner of the ten surviving non-commuting ministers shall be prepared by the board, engrossed in

one of the books of the board, and authenticated by the signatures of the chairman and secretary, as of record.

17. That in the event of any minister departing this life who shall then be a beneficiary of the board, the widow of such deceased (or should he leave no widow, his child or children, if of full age, or their tutor or guardian) shall be entitled to receive from the said board the current half-year's stipend, to which such minister would or might have become entitled as such beneficiary as aforesaid, and the receipt of such widow, child or children, tutor or guardian, shall be a sufficient discharge therefor.

18. Travelling expenses of members of the board shall be paid by the board.

At a meeting of the Temporalities' board held in Montreal on the eighteenth day of November, 1863, it was unanimously resolved that the following be added to the by-laws of the board, and that it come into force this day :—

That it shall be a condition of any minister other than those privileged by, or at the time of commutation, receiving £50 per annum from the fund at the disposal of the board, that he shall obtain from his congregation or otherwise, a subscription to the fund of $50 per annum, and that in any case in which such subscription has not been sent, the chairman and secretary be authorized to retain $25 of the allowance half-yearly.

EXTRACTS FROM RESOLUTIONS OF THE BOARD.

14th November, 1865, Resolved.—(1) That ministers resigning their charges and employed by a Presbytery as ordained missionaries shall not lose their place on the list of recipients from the board. (2) That ministers or ordained missionaries while receiving £100 and over a year from the colonial committee shall not receive stipend from the board.

The case of the application of Queen's college was taken up when the board agreed to record their understanding :

1. That the commutation of stipend, whether made by ministers having charges, or being professors, having been personal, the stipend derived from it should continue to be enjoyed by those who commuted while they continue in the service of the Church, whether in charges or in the college.

2. In the event of there being commuting ministers in Queen's college whose stipends together amount to £500 per annum, no additional payment shall be made to the college by the board.

3. In the event of there not being commuting ministers in the college receiving salary from the board to the amount of £500 per annum, the board shall make up the deficiency.

8th May, 1866, Resolved.—That no money be paid out of the fund at the disposal of the board to any minister who teaches a school. In reference to this resolution the Synod agreed in June, 1866, that "it is one which should be carried into effect subject to the Synod's determination in each case."

BY-LAWS. (PASSED 2ND FEB., 1876.)

At a meeting of the beneficiaries of the Temporalities board, duly convened and held in St. Paul's Church, Montreal, on Wednesday, the 2nd day of February, 1876, in conformity with the provisions of the Act of the Province of Quebec, 38 Vic. cap, 64, intituled an Act to amend the Act intituled "An Act to incorporate the board for the management of the Temporalities Fund of the Presbyterian Church of Canada in connection with the Church of Scotland."

The following by-laws were, under the authority of the said Act, agreed to unanimously and passed :

1. Within 10 days after the occurrence of a vacancy in the board of management of the Temporalities fund shall have come to the knowledge of the secretary to the board, he shall cause to be mailed to each beneficiary an intimation of the same, duly registered, and shall enclose therewith a paper for the nomination of a person to fill the vacancy, which paper shall be returnable to the secretary of the board not later than 40 days from the date of his intimation. Unless the nomination paper, duly dated and signed, be in possession of the secretary of the Temporalities board within 40 days from the time of issuing his intimation of said vacancy, such nomination shall not be taken into account.

2. The intimation by the secretary may be in the following terms :

To the Rev. —————, Sir, A vacancy having occurred in the board of management of the Temporalities fund by the death [or resignation, removed or otherwise] of the Rev. —————, [or Mr. —————], I enclose a paper for the nomination of a minister [or other member as the case may be] of the Presbyterian Church in Canada to fill the said vacancy. You will please insert in the blank left for the purpose the name of the person you wish to nominate, and take notice that your nomination will be of no account unless the nomination paper now enclosed, after being duly dated and signed by you, be in my office within forty days after the date of issuing this intimation. Dated —————, Signed —————,
Secretary-Treasurer, Temporalities Board.

3. The nomination paper to be enclosed with the secretary's intimation may be in the following form :

I hereby nominate——————, to fill the vacancy in the board of management of the Temporalities fund caused by the death [or resignation, removal or otherwise] of——————. Dated at——— ——in the Province of ———— this———day of—————18—. Signature—————.

4. In the event of there being two or more vacancies at the time, the secretary to the Temporalities board shall issue a separate intimation and nomination paper for each such vacancy.

5. The secretary to the Temporalities board shall open the nomination papers addressed to him, and in a book prepared and kept for the purpose, shall enter in the order in which the papers shall be opened, the names and residences of the beneficiaries returning them, the dates of receipt, and the persons nominated.

6. The secretary shall, within 10 days from the expiry of the 40 days within which said nomination papers must be filed, call a meeting of the executive committee of the board of management of the Temporalities fund, and such meeting shall examine and verify the nomination papers received by the secretary and the record of the same as made by him, and shall by resolution determine and elect the persons entitled to fill such vacancy, selecting the person or persons nominated by the largest number of beneficiaries, and such person or persons shall forthwith, and from the time of said resolution, become a member or members of said board ; always provided that, in the event of a tie occuring between two or more persons nominated, the said executive committee shall report the fact, and all details connected therewith, to the board of management, who shall determine by resolution which of said two or more persons shall be chosen and elected members of said board.

7. At the first meeting of the board of management after the time for receiving nomination papers from the beneficiaries shall have expired, the secretary to the board shall report the result of the nominations, and the same, together with the election or elections by the board consequent thereon, shall form part of the minutes of the meeting.

8. The secretary to the board of management of the Temporalities fund shall each year, and within 20 days after the meeting of the board in May, transmit by post to each beneficiary a statement of the financial affairs of the board, a schedule of the investments, an account of the revenue and expenditure, and of the payments to ministers during the then past year, together with the report of the proceedings of the board for the year, similar to the statements and re-

ports heretofore annually rendered by the board, and, specially, making mention of any changes that may have occurred in the membership of the board during the year preceding.

9. Messrs. James Mitchell and Alexander McPherson, both of the City of Montreal, are hereby appointed auditors of the books and affairs of the board for the management of the Temporalities fund.

10. In the event of a vacancy in the auditorship occurring from any cause, the vacancy shall be filled in the same manner as a vacancy occurring in the board of management for the Temporalities fund.

11. The chairman of the Temporalities board shall call a meeting of the beneficiaries, when requested to do so by a requisition signed by not less than ten of their number—which meeting shall be held not less than 30 nor more than 40 days from the time of issuing notice of such meeting, and at such meeting and all other meetings of the beneficiaries, fifteen shall constitute a quorum.

Widows' and Orphans' Fund—Presbyterian Church in Connection with Church of Scotland.

10 & 11 Vict., cap. 103 (C.)—An Act to incorporate the Managers of the Ministers' Widows' and Orphans' Fund of the Synod of the Presbyterian Church of Canada in connection with the Church of Scotland. (*Assented to 28th July, 1847.*)

Whereas it hath been represented to the Legislature of this Province, that it is highly expedient and desirable that provision should be made for the establishment of a fund for the support of the widows and orphans of ministers of the Presbyterian Church of Canada in connection with the Church of Scotland; and whereas the due and proper collection, administration, investment, application and management of such a fund will be best secured by the erection of a corporation for that purpose, composed of members of the said Church: Be it therefore enacted, &c. :—

1. That the Rev. Alex. Mathieson, D. D., the Rev. John Cook, D.D., (*and others, naming them*) and their successors, to be elected in the manner hereinafter provided, shall be, and they are hereby declared to be a body corporate and politic in name and in deed, by the name of The Managers of the Ministers' Widows' and Orphans' Fund of the Synod of the Presbyterian Church of Canada in connection with the Church of Scotland, and by that name shall have perpetual succession and a common seal, with power to change, alter, break, or make new the same as often as they shall judge expedient; and that they and their successors by the same name may sue and be sued, implead and be impleaded, answer and be answered unto, in any court of record or place of judicature in this Province; and that they and their successors, by the name aforesaid, shall be able and capable in law to purchase, take, have, hold, receive, enjoy, possess and retain, without license in mortmain, or *lettres d'amortissement*, all messuages, lands, tenements and immoveable property, money, goods, chattels, and moveable property which have been, or hereafter shall be paid, given, granted, purchased, appropriated, devised or bequeathed in any manner or way whatsoever to, for, and in favour of the said The Managers of the Ministers' Widows' and Orphans' Fund of the Synod of the Presbyterian Church of Canada in connection with the Church of Scotland, to and for the use and purpose aforesaid, provided the same shall not exceed at any time in yearly value the sum of £1500 currency.

2. And be it enacted, that one minister and two laymen shall retire from the said corporation annually, in rotation, on the second day of the annual meeting of the said Synod, and their places shall be supplied by one minister and two laymen, who shall be then and there chosen for that purpose by the said Synod, the retiring members being eligible for re-election; and whenever a vacancy shall occur by the death, removal, resignation or secession from said Church of any member of the said corporation, his place shall be supplied by a minis-

ter or layman as the case may be, chosen by the rest of the members thereof, or the major part of them, who shall be present at a general meeting duly convened for that purpose (subject, however, to the approval of said Synod at its then next meeting), so that the said corporation shall always consist of twelve members, of whom four shall be ministers and eight shall be laymen, all being members of the said Presbyterian Church of Canada in connection with the Church of Scotland.

3. And be it enacted, that the retirement of the first members of the said corporation shall take place in the inverse order to that in which they are named in this Act, so that the minister and the two laymen who are last above named shall be the first to retire, and the minister and the two laymen who are first above named shall be the last to retire; and when there shall no longer be one of the ministers above named in the said corporation who shall not have once retired in annual rotation, that minister shall retire therefrom each year as above directed, who shall have been longest a member thereof without having been re-elected; and in like manner when there shall no longer be any of the laymen above named in the said corporation, who shall not have once retired in annual rotation, those two laymen shall retire therefrom each year as above directed, who shall have been longest members thereof without having been re-elected; and if it should happen that there should remain at last, from any cause, but one of the said laymen above named who shall not have once retired in annual rotation, and two or more laymen who shall have been longest members without having been re-elected, shall have so been members during an equal time, or if at any time, for any cause, it shall become a question which of two or more lay members of the said corporation, having been equally long members thereof, without having been re-elected, should retire therefrom in rotation, that one of those two of such members shall so retire who shall have been elected at his or their last election by the fewest votes in the said Synod.

4. And be it enacted, that the said Rev. Alexander Mathieson, may call a meeting of the members of the said corporation at such time within twelve months from the passing of this Act, and at such place as he may see fit to appoint, at which meeting the members of the said corporation, or the major part of such of them as shall be then and there present, shall choose from among the members of the said corporation one chairman, one treasurer, and one secretary, who shall hold their respective offices during the pleasure of the said corporation, and whose places shall be filled by new elections from among the members of the said corporation, as often as occasion shall require.

5. And be it enacted, that the members of the said corporation, or the major part of such of them as shall be present at any general meeting of the said corporation duly convened, shall have power and authority to frame and make statutes, by-laws, rules and orders, touching and concerning the good government of the said corporation, and the income and property thereof, and the collection, administration, investment, application and management of the fund aforesaid, and any other matter or thing which to them may seem fit or expedient for the effectual attainment of the objects of the said corporation, and the administration of its concerns, and for fixing, ascertaining and establishing the scale or rate of contribution to the said fund by the ministers or others entitled to contribute thereto under the provisions of this Act, and the scale or rate of annuities payable to the widows and orphans of such contributors; and also, from time to time, by such new statutes, by-laws, rules and orders as to them shall seem meeet, to alter or repeal those so made as aforesaid; provided always, that no such statutes, by-laws, rules or orders shall be repugnant to the laws of the Province or to this Act.

6. And be it enacted, that the professors of Queen's College at Kingston for the time being, whether ministers or laymen, shall at all times be entitled to the

benefit of the said fund, on the same terms and conditions as any minister of the Synod of the said Presbyterian Church of Canada in connection with the Church of Scotland.

7. And be it enacted, that it shall be the duty of the officers and members of the said corporation for the time being, to prepare annually, and to cause to be laid before the Synod at its yearly meeting, a full account of the receipts and disbursements of the said corporation, during the year next preceding such meeting.

8. And be it enacted, that this Act shall be deemed and taken to be a public Act, and as such shall be judicially noticed by all the courts, judges and justices of the peace, and by all other whom it may concern, without being specially pleaded.

---

38 Vict., cap. 61 (Q.)—An Act to amend "An Act to incorporate the managers of the Ministers' Widows' and Orphans' Fund of the Synod of the Presbyterian Church of Canada in connection with the Church of Scotland," and amendments thereto.

Under the decision of the Judicial Committee of the Privy Council in *Dobie* v. *Temporalities Board*, 7 Appeal Cases, 136, this Act was *ultra vires*, it is therefore not printed here. After the decision of the above case the Act which immediately follows was got from the Dominion Parliament.

---

45 Vict., cap. 125 (D.)—An Act to amend the Act of the late Province of Canada, intituled: "An Act to incorporate the managers of the Ministers' Widows' and Orphans' Fund of the Presbyterian Church of Canada, in connection with the Church of Scotland," and amendments thereto. (*Assented to 17th May, 1882.*)

Whereas by petition it hath been represented that the Synods of the Presbyterian Church of Canada, in connection with the Church of Scotland, of the Church of the Maritime Provinces, in connection with the Church of Scotland, and of the Presbyterian Church of the Lower Provinces, and the General Asembly of the Canada Presbyterian Church, have united together, and have formed one body or denomination of Christians, under the name of "The Presbyterian Church in Canada," and that an Act of the Province of Quebec, 38 Victoria, chapter 61, was passed on the 23rd day of February, 1875, containing provisions similar to those contained in this Act, and that doubts have been raised as to the constitutionality of the Act lastly cited, and that the present acting members of the said corporation of managers have, since the passing of the said last mentioned Act, been acting under the provisions thereof; and that the Act of the late Province of Canada, 10 & 11 Victoria, chapter 103, intituled "An Act to incorporate the managers of the Ministers' Widows' and Orphans' Fund of the Synod of the Presbyterian Church of Canada, in connection with the Church of Scotland," and amendments thereto, require to be amended with a view to such union, and in order to the carrying into effect of certain resolutions passed by the Synod of the Presbyterian Church of Canada, in connection with the Church of Scotland, with reference to the said fund and for the protection of those interested in the same : Therefore Her Majesty, &c., enacts as follows :—

1. Notwithstanding anything in the said Act, and the amendment or amendments thereto contained, the fund presently existing for the benefit of the ministers' widows and orphans of the said Church, shall continue for the benefit of the widows and orphans of those ministers who shall have been members of the Synod of the said Church at the date of union : and all the acts and doings of the said corporation of managers and of the acting members thereof, from and since the passing of the said Act of the Province of Quebec, 38 Victoria, chapter 61, had thereunder, are hereby ratified.

2. Those persons who were the managers of the said fund at the date of union shall continue to be the man-

agers thereof, unless they resign, so long as they shall remain members or adherents of a Presbyterian church in Canada, until they are relieved of their office in the manner hereinafter provided for, that is to say : that one minister and two laymen shall retire from the corporation annually, at the annual meeting of the board, those longest in office retiring first and so on in rotation ; and their places shall be supplied by one minister and two laymen, who shall then and there be chosen for the purpose by the said board, the retiring members being eligible for re-election ; provided, that the person or persons so chosen shall be ministers whose rights in the fund are guaranteed by this Act, or members or adherents of their congregations; and the board so constituted shall have power to hold all moneys, properties and mortgages, and to exercise all the rights appertaining to the present board of managers; and they are hereby authorized to receive such legacies and bequests as may be made for the benefit of such fund.

3. Until such time as an equitable arrangement for the establishment of a ministers' widows' and orphans' fund for the united church shall have been made, the widows and orphans entitled to receive annuities from the said fund at the date of union, or the widows and orphans of those ministers, who, at the date of union were members of the Synod aforesaid, and had contributed personally and through their congregations to the said fund, in terms of the by-laws thereof, shall receive annuities at a rate not lower than the scale fixed by the board previous to the date of union, if the funds permit : provided, that the ministers, whose widows or orphans shall be placed on the list of annuitants on the said board, after the union, shall have continued to contribute to the said fund $6 semi-annually as heretofore, and shall have secured annual contributions from their congregations to the said fund.

4. As soon as an arrangement for the establishment of a fund for the benefit of the ministers' widows and orphans of the united church, satisfactory to the board, as representing the interests of the widows and orphans

of those ministers who had formerly belonged to the Presbyterian Church of Canada in connection with the Church of Scotland, shall have been made by the supreme court of the united church, the board shall be empowered to hand over to such board or committee as may be created for the management of such new fund for the benefit of the widows and orphans of the ministers of the united church, all moneys, properties and mortgages they shall at the time hold : provided always, that no widow or orphan of a minister, who had formerly belonged to the Presbyterian Church of Canada in connection with the Church of Scotland, shall receive less annuities from the fund of the united church than would have pertained to them, in terms of the scale in force by the board, at the date of union, if the said Churches had not united.

5. In the event of any minister or ministers of the Synod of the Presbyterian Church of Canada in connection with the Church of Scotland, who possessed rights in this fund at the date of the said union, declining to enter into the united church, he or they shall be entitled to the same pecuniary rights and claims in and upon the said fund as were possessed by him or them previous to the said union : provided, that those ministers thus declining to enter the said united church continue their ministerial and congregational contributions as heretofore ; but those ministers who only continue to contribute to the fund personally $6 semi-annually, and whose congregations do not contribute, shall be only entitled to claim from that part of the said fund consisting of ministers' contributions and not from that part consisting of congregational contributions, except to the extent that they may have contributed to the congregational funds prior to the 15th day of June, 1875, and in the proportion provided for by the existing by-law.

6. All provisions contained in any previous Act or amendment thereto inconsistent with the provisions of this Act, relating to the said managers of the ministers' widows' and orphans' fund are hereby repealed.

BY-LAWS.

Section 1—Meetings.

1. The quarterly meetings of the board shall be held on the first Wednesday in the months of August, November, February, and May at 10 o'clock in the forenoon. Intermediate meetings may be called by circular on the requisition of the chairman or any two members of the board, but two full days must intervene between the time of calling and of the meeting.

2. That at each quarterly meeting the treasurer shall submit his books of account, and a statement of his receipts and disbursements since the previous meeting. That at the quarterly meeting held in May the treasurer shall submit to the board a full and complete statement of the affairs of the corporation ; and the chairman, or in case of his absence, the secretary, at the same meeting, shall submit the draft of the annual report, that these papers may be duly considered, and, if approved of, transmitted to the Synod.

3. That three members shall form a quorum for the transaction of ordinary business ; but it shall be necessary for five to be present to consider all loans of money applied for to the trust.

4. That, in case of equality of votes, the chairman, or member occupying the chair, shall have an additional or casting vote.

Section 2—Rates and Collections.

5. That the board accept the quota, which the Synod has agreed to furnish to this board, of $12 per annum from each minister, payable by a draft on the Temporalities' board, which, considering the slender pittance of too many of them, evinces the anxiety of the clergy to alleviate the dependent position in which their families may be left by their death.

6. That the depositing by any minister in the hands of the Temporalities' board of a written authority to pay into this fund half-yearly on his account the sum of $6 be, when duly provided for, considered a payment of the contribution so as to entitle his family to benefit.

7. That on the occasion of the collection authorized by the Synod to be made in every congregation for the benefit of this fund, the secretary do issue a circular to every such congregation, urging the claims of this institution on their liberality.

8. That intimation be given through the " Presbyterian " that a circular will be sent to all congregations, which have not sent in their collections to the treasurer previous to the 25th March, calling their attention to the delay.

9. That in such circular each congregation in default, and which may have contributed less than $12 to the funds the last year, be informed of the average of the collections, and how much they have fallen short of the same.

10. That ministers be requested to furnish to the board the number of families in their congregation, so that the board may see what proportion the collections bear to the number of those who ought to contribute.

Section 3—Funds.

11. That the treasurer shall keep the funds of the corporation in three accounts. The first to be composed of the contributions made annually by the clergy themselves. The second, composed of the congregational collections. The third, a legacy account, the interest of the said fund to be applied to the ministers' department of the fund.

Section 4—Annuities.

12. That the corporation shall, from time to time, determine what annuity shall be paid to widows and orphans out of the ministers' department of the funds, which shall in all cases be alike to such widows and orphans. That the payment to be made out of the second of these funds shall be upon a scale determined by the board.

13. That, until otherwise determined, the annuity to be paid to all parties entitled thereto shall be at the rate of $50 per annum from the fund consisting of ministers' contributions, and according to the following scale from the fund consisting of congregational collections, viz:—where the average annual amount collected is under $12, the managers may, in their discretion, allow an annuity not exceeding $60.

Where the average is $12 and does not amount to $18 the annuity shall be $138

Do.	$18	do.	$24	do.	156
Do.	24	do.	30	do.	175
Do.	30	do.	36	do.	188
Do.	36	do.	42	do.	200
Do.	42	do.	48	do.	212
Do.	48	do.	54	do.	231
Do.	54	do.	60	do.	244
Do.	60	do.	72	do.	256
Do.	72	do.	84	do.	281
Do.	84	do.	96	do.	312
Do.	96	do.	108	do.	344
Do.	108	do.	120	do.	375
Do.	120	do.	132	do.	437
Do.	132 and upwards				469

No annuity from the congregational portion of this fund is to exceed the last mentioned sum of $469. All collections averaging less than $12 shall be made a subject of special consideration, but the managers shall in no case grant an annuity in such cases exceeding $100.

14. That, in the case of widows having children, males under 18 years and females under 21 years of age, an addition payable to the mother shall be made to the above scale of annuities at the following rates, viz:—$16 for one child, $28 for two children, $36 for three children, $40 for four children, and $4 for each additional child, as the number may be.

15. That in the event of a child or children coming on the fund, in consequence of the death of both parents, the same annuity as in the case of a widow shall be payable for the benefit of the minor, or minors, until the youngest daughter shall attain the age of 21 years, or the youngest boy shall attain the age of 18 years, unless he is studying with a view to the ministry in the Church of Scotland, or in this Synod, when it shall continue to be paid until he attains the age of 21 years. When the youngest daughter shall have attained the age of 21 years, the managers may allow to each unmarried daughter during the period of her natural life an annuity not exceeding $50. Whenever any daughter is married, her interest in the fund shall cease. In case of boys who, from mental or physicial incapacity, are unable to support themselves, the managers may allow an annuity for a longer time than their attaining the age of 18,—such annuity in no case to exceed half of what would be allowed to a widow.

16. That, whenever an annuity shall become due and payable, in consequence of the death of any minister, any portion of the contribution of $12, remaining unpaid for that year, shall be deducted from the first payment.

17. That, in cases of congregations not contributing at all, or of ministers leaving the province, their widows and orphans shall have no claim for relief, except from the ministers' department of the fund; and then only in the event of such ministers having regularly contributed during their lives the sum of $6 on the 1st of July and on the 1st of January, in each year respectively.

18. That the annuities to widows shall be payable for the full half year in which the decease of the husband occurs, he being a minister on the fund.

19. That, on the death of a widow, the annuity shall be paid to the end of the running half year.

Section 5—Loans and Investments.

20. That the treasurer shall engross in a proper book a list of the mortgages held by the fund, in order that the *Official Gazette* may be carefully examined from time to time, as to those of them affecting Lower Canada real estate, with a view to the due protection of the interests of the board.

21. The board direct all mortgages to be called in as they mature, and the proceeds reloaned at the current rates of interest, unless they continue satisfied with the security, and agree with the borrowers for the renewal of the loans.

22. The board direct that in future where part of the security for loans consists of buildings, the premiums of insurance against fire be paid by the board and charged to the borrower, and that the policies be held by the board.

23. In case of loans, a deposit shall be required to be made, with the title deeds, to cover registry charges and solicitor's fees.

24. That loans be made to the extent of the value of the one half of the property mortgaged.

25. As it is essential to the stability and prosperity of the fund, that every minister of the church should contribute toward its maintenance, it is hereby declared that any minister, refusing or neglecting to pay his annual subscription, shall cease to be entitled to any benefit of the fund for his widow and orphans.

26. Any minister refusing or neglecting to take up the annual collection from his congregation shall cease to be entitled to any benefit of the fund for his widow and orphans.

27. That any minister, who shall fail or cease to become a member, and afterwards desire to participate in the benefits of the fund, shall make application to the board, and, if the board shall favorably receive his application, it shall only be on payment of all arrearages of subscriptions with interest.

28. That upon the voluntary removal of a minister from the Province of Canada he shall thereby forfeit all right or claim to annuity for his widow or orphans from the congregational and legacy funds, unless he shall continue to contribute the annual rate to the minister's department of the fund. But all such cases shall be submitted to, and adjudicated on, as they arise by the board, who shall fix the annuity, which the collections received during the incumbency of such minister would entitle to, taking into calculation the actual number of years of his ministry over a church, whether here or elsewhere, in connection with this or the parent Church, and distributing the collections over such number of years.

29. That any minister, being forty years or upwards at his admission, who shall marry, shall pay to the fund, in order to be entitled to its benefits, a marriage tax equal to three annual subscriptions.

30. That any minister, aged forty years or upwards, coming into the Church, shall be admitted to the benefits of the fund only after a special application to the board to be made a recipient of its benefits, and upon such terms as the board shall upon consideration of the case in its discretion impose.

31. That every widow or the guardian or tutor of any of the orphans of a minister, desiring an annuity from the fund, shall apply by petition to the board, setting forth the date of the decease of said minister, the name of such widow, and the name and age of each of the children, as the case may be, and such memorial shall be presented to the board through the Presbytery of the bounds, and accompanied by their certificate of the authenticity thereof.

32. That every annuitant of the fund shall, before being paid his or her half yearly annuity, make one of the following declarations in the presence of a magistrate, or minister, which declaration shall be attested by the magistrate or minister before whom it is made :

Declaration to be made by a Widow.

I,   , do hereby declare that I am the widow of the late Rev.   , late minister of   , that I am entitled to an annuity from the ministers' widows' and orphans' fund of the Presbyterian Church of Canada in connection with the Church of Scotland, and that I am still a widow—

Signed before me

Name.

Description.

Residence.

Declaration to be made by the Guardian or Tutor of Children.

I,   , do hereby declare that I am duly appointed of the children of the late Rev. whose names are respectively written below : that they are entitled to an annuity from the ministers' widows' and orphan's fund of the Presbyterian Church of Canada in connection with the Church of Scotland, and that they are of the respective ages stated beneath—

Names of children.   Age next birthday.

Signed before me

Name.

Description.

Residence.

33. That the annuities to widows or orphans form no part of the estates of the contributors, and are payable to annuitants free from responsibility for the contributor's debts (except such as they may owe to the fund) and are and shall be free from attachment by any party whomsoever.

34. That annuities payable to widows shall be forthwith forfeited by re-marriage.

35. Should any doubt arise as to the interpretation of any of these by-laws or the construction which should be put upon any of them, such doubts shall be referred to the board, who shall appoint a committee to consider the same and report to the board ; and the decision of the board, after receiving such report, shall be final and conclusive.

WIDOWS' AND ORPHANS' FUND,—MARITIME PROVINCES.

28 Vict., cap. 57, (N. S.)—An Act to incorporate the Trustees of the Presbyterian Ministers' Widows' and Ophans' Fund. (*Passed 18th April, 1865.*)

Whereas the Presbyterian Churches of the Lower Provinces of British North America have recently adopted certain proceedings with the view of raising a fund for the support of the widows and orphans of the ministers of said Church ; and whereas, it is desirable that any funds raised or to be raised for that purpose, shall be vested or managed by trustees : Be it therefore enacted, &c., as follows :

1. The Rev. David Ray and John Stuart, of New Glasgow ; (*and others, naming them*) are hereby incorporated under the name of "the Trustees of the Presbyterian Ministers' Widows' and Orphans' Fund."

2. All moneys raised, or to be raised, for the purposes of said fund, are hereby vested in the corporation.

3. The corporation are authorized to invest moneys on mortgage bonds, debentures or other securities, for the purposes of the said fund.

4. The corporation may, subject to the approbation of the Synod, make by-laws for the regulation of the said fund, prescribe the terms of admission to the benefit thereof, and, generally, for the management, investment, collection, disbursement, appropriation and distribution of the said fund, and of all matters connected therewith, which may be necessary or expedient with a view to carry out the object for which the said fund was organized.

5. It shall be lawful for the Synod, at any regular annual meeting, to appoint any number, not exceeding six, to be additional trustees, and on such appointment being duly made and accepted, by notice to the clerk of Synod, the persons so appointed shall thenceforth be trustees in the same manner as if named in this Act.

6. Vacancies in the trust, by death, resignation, or otherwise, shall be filled by the Synod at its regular annual meeting.

7. The trustees may hold real estate by devise, gift, purchase or otherwise, for the purposes of this Act.

---

46 Vict., cap. 98 (D.)—An Act to amalgamate the Presbyterian Ministers' Widows' and Orphans' Fund in connection with the Presbyterian Church of the Lower Provinces, and the Widows' and Orphans' Fund of the Presbyterian Church in the Maritime Provinces, in connection with the Church of Scotland, and to create a corporation to administer such funds. (*Assented to 25th May, 1883.*)

Whereas by petition it hath been represented that by chapter 57 of the Acts of the Province of Nova Scotia, passed in the 28th year of Her Majesty' reign, intituled "An Act to incorporate the Trustees of the Presbyterian Ministers' Widows' and Orphans' Fund," certain persons were erected a body corporate, for the purposes mentioned in the said Act, which said corporation was by the said Act made subject to the control of the Synod of the Presbyterian Church of the Lower Provinces of British North America, and certain sums of money are now vested in the said trustees for the benefit of the widows and orphans of the ministers of the said Church ; and that in the year of our Lord 1874, the Synod of the Presbyterian Church of the Maritime Provinces in connection with the Church of Scotland, created a fund for the benefit of the widows and orphans of the ministers of the said Church, which fund was designated " The Widows' and Orphans' Fund of the Presbyterian Church of the Maritime Provinces in connection with the Church of Scotland," and the said fund is now vested in and held by James J. Bremner and George Mitchell, of the City of Halifax, merchants, as trustees thereof for the purposes aforesaid ; and that the said two Synods together with the Synod of the Presbyterian Church of Canada in connection with the Church of Scotland, and the General Assembly of the Canada Presbyterian Church, have united together and have formed one body or denomination of Christians, under the name of " The Presbyterian Church in Canada " ; and that by chapter 100 of the Acts of the Province of Nova Scotia passed in the 38th year of Her Majesty's reign, intituled " An Act concerning the Presbyterian Church of the Lower Provinces of British North America," it was among other things enacted that the said Presbyterian Ministers' Widows' and Orphans' Fund should bear the same relation in all respects to the General Assembly of the Presbyterian Church in Canada that it then bore to the Synod of the Presbyterian Church of the Lower Provinces, and until such General Assembly should provide or otherwise direct, the said fund should be managed by the board then having charge thereof, and that such General Assembly should have power to unite the said fund with the fund held by any other of the said uniting churches for similar objects ; and that at a meeting of the Synod of the Presbyterian Church of the Maritime Provinces in connection with the Church of Scotland, held on the 10th day of June in the year of our Lord 1875, and prior to the consummation of the said union, it was (among other things) resolved that the committee having in charge the said Ministers' Widows' and Orphans' Fund in connection with such Synod should hold such fund in charge until the consolidation should take place of such fund with the Widows' and Orphans' Fund of the other negotiating Churches, and that the relation of ministers or congregations of the Presbyterian Church in the Maritime Provinces in connection with the Church of Scotland, who might defer entering or might not enter the united church, should be similar in all respects to that of ministers and congregations who should become members of the united church, it being understood that such ministers and congregations should comply with the terms of the constitution of such fund ; and that a scheme has been arranged and agreed upon by and between the committees or trustees having charge of the said respective funds, by which the same may be amalgamated and hereafter managed by one board, and such scheme, having been submitted to the General Assembly of the Presbyterian Church in Canada, such General Assembly approved of such scheme and authorized all necessary steps to be taken by legislation or otherwise to carry such proposed amalgamation into effect, and nominated the persons hereinafter named as the corporators in any Act of Parliament that might be obtained for that purpose (a). Therefore Her Majesty, &c., enacts as follows :—

1. The Rev. Allan Pollock, D. D., the Rev. George Paterson, D.D., (*and others, naming them*) and their successors to be appointed in the manner hereinafter provided, shall be and they are hereby declared to be a body politic and corporate in name and in deed, by the name of "The Trustees of the Ministers' Widows' and Orphans' Fund of the Synod of the Maritime Provinces of the Presbyteterian Church in Canada," for the purpose of maintaining and administering a fund for the support of the widows and orphans of Presbyterian ministers, and by that name shall have perpetual succession and a common seal, with power to change, alter,

(*a*) *See Minutes, 1882, p. 44*; and for terms of amalgamation, *Ibid, App., p. 155*.

break or make new the same as often as they shall judge expedient; and they and their successors by the same name may sue and be sued, implead and be impleaded, answer and be answered unto, in any court of record or place of judicature in Canada; and they and their successors by the name aforesaid shall be able and capable in law to purchase, take, have, hold, receive, enjoy, possess and retain all messuages, lands, tenements, money, goods, chattels and effects which have been or shall hereafter be paid, given, granted, purchased, appropriated, devised or bequeathed in any manner or way whatsoever, to, for and in favour of the said "The Trustees of the Ministers' Widows' and Orphans' Fund of the Synod in the Maritime Provinces of the Presbyterian Church in Canada," to and for the uses and purposes of such corporation.

2. At the close of the annual meeting of the General Assembly of the Presbyterian Church in Canada, all the members of the said corporation shall retire, their places being supplied at such meeting by twelve persons who shall be then and there chosen by such General Assembly, the retiring members being eligible for re-election; provided, however, that the General Assembly shall not appoint as a member of such corporation, any minister who is not a contributor to the funds thereof, or any person who has not been previously nominated therefor by the Synod in the Maritime Provinces of the Presbyterian Church in Canada, or who is not a member of such Church; and if the said General Assembly should, at any time, fail to appoint the members of the said corporation, the old members shall continue to act until their successors are duly appointed.

3. All the messuages, lands, tenements, moneys, goods, chattels, choses in action and effects now held, possessed, or owned by, on behalf of, or in trust for the said "The Trustees of the Presbyterian Ministers' Widows' and Orphans' Fund," and also all messuages, lands, tenements, moneys, goods, chattels, choses in action and effects now held, possessed, standing in the

name of, or owned by the said James J. Bremner and George Mitchell, as trustees of "The Widows' and Orphans' Fund of the Presbyterian Church of the Maritime Provinces, in connection with the Church of Scotland," or by any other person or persons for, or on behalf of such fund, are hereby transferred to, and vested in the corporation hereby created, subject however, to any lien, charge, incumbrance or obligation that may exist on, or in respect to the same, or any part thereof; and the said corporation are hereby declared to be entitled to ask, demand and receive from any person or persons holding the same, all such property and effects as are hereby vested in, or transferred to such corporation; and the said two funds are hereby amalgamated, and shall continue to be one fund, under the management and control of the corporation created by this Act.

4. Forthwith, after the passing of this Act, any four members of the said corporation may call a meeting of the members thereof, at such time and place as they may see fit to appoint, at which meeting the members of the said corporation, or the major part of such of them as shall be then and there present, shall choose one chairman, one secretary and one treasurer, who shall hold their respective offices during the pleasure of the said corporation. The same individual may be appointed to more than one office in the corporation.

5. The members of the said corporation, or the major part of such of them as shall be present at any general meeting, duly convened, shall, subject to the limitations hereinafter contained, have power and authority to frame and make by-laws, rules and orders touching and concerning the good government of the said corporation and the income and property thereof, and the collection, administration, investment, application and management of the fund aforesaid, and any other matter or thing which, to them, may seem fit or expedient for the attainment of the objects of the said corporation and the administration of its concerns, and for fixing, ascertaining and establishing the scales or rates of contribution

to the said fund, by the ministers or others entitled to contribute thereto under the provisions of this Act, and the scales or rates of annuities payable to the widows and orphans of such contributors; and also from time to time, by such new by-laws, rules and orders as, to them, may seem meet, to alter or repeal those so made as aforesaid, but all such by-laws, rules and orders so made shall be in force only when and after the same shall have been submitted to and approved of by the General Assembly of the Presbyterian Church in Canada and by the Synod of such Church in the Maritime Provinces.

6. All by-laws, rules and orders which may hereafter be made by the said corporation in relation to persons already interested, either as contributors or annuitants, in either of the two funds by this Act amalgamated, shall be subject to the following provisions, that is to say :—(1). Those ministers now contributing to the funds of the Minister's Widows' and Orphans' fund of the late Presbyterian Church of the Lower Provinces shall continue to pay the same amounts per annum as heretofore, that is to say : Those in the first class, $8; those in the second class, $12; and those in the third class, $16. (2). Those ministers now contributing to the said other fund who have been paying the ministerial rate of $12 per annum, with a rate from their congregations, may continue to pay in the same manner, or if they prefer, they may pay at the rate of $16 in lieu of both, and those who have been paying only the ministerial rate of $12 may continue to pay at the same rate, and shall be in the same position as those in the second class of the Presbyterian Ministers' Widows' and Orphans' fund, but it shall be open to them up to the first day of July next to join the higher class, paying thenceforward at the rate of $16 per annum. (3). Widows and orphans now annuitants upon the Presbyterian Ministers' Widows' and Orphans' fund, shall (subject to such diminution as the corporation hereby created may find it necessary hereafter to make) receive the following amounts per annum : (*a*) Widows in the first class, $75; widows in

---

(*a*). The annuities payable to widows and orphans have been increased one-tenth. *See Minutes, 1893, p. 53.*

the second class, $112.50; widows in the third class, $150. If a widow be in the highest class, she shall receive in addition: For one child, $20; for two children, $36; for three children, $50; and $10 for each additional child, and if she be in either of the other classes, in the same proportion. In the event of the decease of both parents, if there be one orphan, the said corporation shall pay for the benefit of such orphan, two-thirds of the amount payable to widows in each class, and for the highest class, if there be two orphans, $25 shall be added to the amount; if there be three, $20 more; if there be four, $17.50 more; and $12.50 for each additional orphan, and the other classes in proportion, to be continued in each case till they reach the age of eighteen years. (4). Widows and orphans now annuitants upon the said other fund, receiving on account of both ministerial rates and congregational contributions, and those who may hereafter be annuitants upon the amalgamated fund, entitled to receive on account of both, shall receive at the highest rate received by the widows and orphans of the other fund, and those only entitled to receive the rate allowed for ministerial contributions alone, shall hereafter receive at the same rate as widows and orphans in the second class of the said other fund. (5). In all other respects, all connected with either fund shall be subject to the rules that may hereafter be adopted for the management of the amalgamated fund.

7. It shall be the duty of the officers and members of the said corporation, for the time being, to prepare annually, and to cause to be laid before the said Synod and General Assembly, at their annual meetings, a full account of the receipts and disbursements of the said corporation during the year next preceding such meetings, and also a general statement of its funds and property.

8. Until by-laws for the management thereof are framed and passed by the said corporation, and approved of by the said General Assembly and Synod, the proposed rules for the management of the said amalgamated

fund, agreed upon by the joint committee appointed to arrange the terms of such amalgamation, shall, so far as the same are not inconsistent with this Act, be the by-laws of such corporation.

9. All provisions contained in any Act of the Legislature of Nova Scotia inconsistent with the provisions of this Act, relating to the said Presbyterian Ministers' Widows' and Orphans' fund, are hereby repealed.

RULES FOR THE MANAGEMENT OF THE FUND.

1. The management of the fund shall be entrusted to a committee of twelve, five of whom shall be a quorum, who shall elect their chairman, secretary and treasurer, and who shall be the trustees of the fund, in whose name all obligations shall be taken; the said committee to be nominated by the Synod of the Maritime Provinces and appointed by the General Assembly annually, the ministerial members of the committee to be contributors to the fund.

2. The trustees shall meet by notice from the chairman, through the post office, to each member, at least one week before the time of meeting, or by regular adjournment from one meeting to a specified date.

3. It shall be the duty of the secretary to keep a regular minute of all the proceedings of the trustees, and also a record book, in which shall be inscribed a correct record from the schedules forwarded to him, of the names and dates of birth of all ministers contributing, the names and dates of birth of their wives and children, the names of widows and orphans in receipt of aid, and such other statistics as may be required, and he shall also prepare an annual statement to be submitted to the Synod and General Assembly, of such changes as may have taken place during the year preceding in the statistics of the ministers contributing and their families, through admissions, marriages, births, deaths, or the like.

4. The treasurer shall every year prepare an account to be laid before the Synod and General Assembly, of the sums of money received and expended since the previous statement, and also a general statement of the funds and effects in the hands of the trustees.

5. Ministers ordained by any Presbytery of the Synod of the Maritime Provinces, or ordained over congregations which did not enter the union, may be admitted to the benefits of the scheme by entering on or previous to the second 1st July following ordination and pay-

ing the regular rates from that date. But should any one neglect doing so at that time, he may join any time within three years after, by paying arrears from that date with interest.

6. Each applicant shall be required to furnish the committee in writing with a statement of the date of his birth, and if married, of the date of his wife's birth, and also a statement of the name and date of the birth of each of his children under 18 years of age.

7. There shall be two classes of beneficiaries, and every person, on becoming a member, shall signify which class he chooses; and the choice being once made, he shall not afterwards have the power of rising to the higher class; but he shall, at any time, have the liberty of taking the lower class, it being understood that no part of the sum already paid or due by him can be returned or abated to him, and that his widow or orphan children will henceforth be entitled only to the annuity of the class then chosen by him.

8. Every person coming on the scheme shall pay annually, on or before the 1st July in each year, at the following rates:—

	Class 1.	Class 2.
Ministers under 35 years of age	$ 7 00	$14 00
Ministers between 35 and 45	8 75	17 50
Ministers between 45 and 50	10 50	21 00

The application of any minister over fifty years of age shall be made the subject of special consideration. In all future cases there shall also be chargeable a marriage equalizing tax for every year exceeding five that the minister's age exceeds that of his wife.

	Class 1.	Class 2.
Under 45	$2 00	$ 4 00
Under 60	4 00	8 00
Over 60	6 00	12 00

The same to be paid on every subsequent marriage, except when he marries a widow already on the fund, with the understanding that the committee shall have power in special cases to remit or reduce the amount. In all cases he shall be bound to furnish a statement of the date of his own birth and of that of his wife.

9. Members not making payment of their annual rates on or before the 1st July in each year, shall be subject to the following fines:—

Class 1.	Class 2.
10 cts.	20 cts.

for each month thereafter, until payment be made; and those who neglect payment for four full years, shall from that period cease to be members, and shall forfeit all privileges connected with the fund, and shall have no claim to the money they have paid into it. Intimation shall, in all cases, be sent to ministers in arrears, before they shall be cut off from the benefits of the fund.

10. As soon as correct tables for the purpose can be prepared, members shall be entitled at any time to redeem their annual rates, payable for life, by the payment of a single sum at once, or to commute them into an increased annual payment, to cease on their completing the 60th or 65th year of their age.

11. The annuities for widows shall be as follows :—

Class 1.	Class 2.
$75 00	$150 00

But, in order to enable the widow to recover an annuity, six payments of annual rates shall be made, such payments, so far as they have not been made, to be deducted yearly from the annuity.

12. Annuities to widows shall be payable half-yearly, on the 1st January and 1st July of each year, commencing at the first of these dates succeeding the husband's death, and ending at the term succeeding the death of the widow, or her subsequent marriage.

13. There shall also be payable to each orphan child of any member the sum of $20, when on the highest class, until such child shall reach the age of 18, and for those on the other class in the same proportion. In the event of the decease of both parents, if there be one orphan, the board shall pay for the benefit of such orphan $100 for those on the highest class, and $20 for each additional orphan, and for those on the other class in proportion, to be continued in each case till they reach the age of eighteen. In the case of orphans over 18 years of age, whose fathers died while paying into the fund, incapacitated either physically or mentally for earning their own living, the committee shall have the power of continuing annuity for such time and to such an amount as they may see fit.

14. The funds, so far as they are not required for immediate application or expenditure, shall be invested in security upon real estate, or in savings banks or government or city securities, or in any of the chartered banks of the Dominion, in the name of the trustees.

15. There shall be an investigation of the funds of the institution every fifth year, and a revision of the rates, when the amount of annuities to widows and orphans may be increased or diminished, as the state of the funds will warrant, or the amount of the annual rates may be altered. But no alteration in these shall take place at other times.

16. No alteration in these rules shall be made until considered by the committee, and the proposed alterations be submitted to a meeting of those in full standing as contributors, and adopted by a majority of those present, and afterwards submitted to Synod and Assembly and approved by them.

17. All differences or disputes that may arise in regard to sums due shall be referred to arbitrators, of whom the trustees shall name and elect one, the other party one, and if necessary, a third to be chosen by these two, being persons not beneficially interested directly or indirectly in the funds of the institution.

18. In the case of any minister, a widower or unmarried, having made 40 payments and having reached the age of 70 years, on his agreeing to relinquish all claim upon the fund, he shall be entitled to receive the sum of $300 when on the highest class, and $150 when on the lowest.

19. In the event of any minister or professor ceasing to be a minister or professor of the Church, by resignation, deprivation, or in any other way, it shall, nevertheless, be in his power to uphold and continue the right and interest of his widow and children to participate in the benefits of the fund, by making regular payment of all sums payable under these regulations.

20. Every minister on the fund shall be required to furnish annually to the secretary a notice of the changes in his family, by birth, death, or marriage, which shall be duly entered on the record book.

21. The annuities payable to widows and orphans being intended as alimentary provisions, form no part of the estate of the contributor, and shall not be assignable or subject to arrestment or other legal proceedings at the instance of creditors, but shall be paid only to the widows and the tutors and guardians of the children, and in case the widow shall be under any legal or natural disability, or in case the children shall have no tutors or guardians, it shall be competent for the trustees of the Widows' fund to name two or more persons as trustees, to manage and apply the annuities in such a manner as shall appear to them to be most for the benefit of such widows or children.

22. Ministers ordained elsewhere and being inducted in congregations of the Synod of the Maritime Provinces, or in congregations of the late Synod of the Maritime Provinces, in connection with the Church of Scotland, which did not enter the union, or entering the service of either Church as missionaries or professors, shall have the privilege of joining the scheme on the terms laid down for ministers at present inducted, but not now upon the fund. See Nos. 7 and 8 of

terms of amalgamation. Provided that application be made on or before the second 1st July after their induction in this part of the Church.

Report Ministers' Widows and Orphans Fund, Maritime Provinces, Minutes 1893, App. No. 15. This being the period of the quinquennial revision of our rates, the committee have carefully considered the subject and have agreed to recommend the following alterations in the terms of the fund : (1) That the annuities payable to widows and orphans be increased one tenth ; (2) That rule 5 be amended by substituting for the words "second first July following" the words "first of July two years after." These proposals, according to by-laws 15 and 16, having been submitted to a meeting of ministers beneficially interested in the fund, and also to the Synod of the Maritime Provinces, and approved by them, are now submitted to the General Assembly for adoption.

Minutes 1893, p. 53. The Assembly approves of the alteration in the rules, recommended by the committee and adopted by the ministers beneficially interested in the fund.

Widows and Orphans Fund—Western Division.

REGULATIONS.

1. That in addition to the revenue derived from capital, the fund shall be maintained by the annual rates of ministers connected with it, by congregational contributions, and such donations and bequests as shall be received from time to time.

2. That the rate of ministerial contributions shall be as follows :
Ministers of this Church at present not connected with any fund, and any ministers, who after this date shall be admitted to participate in the benefits of this fund, under thirty-five years of age, shall pay into the fund annually eight dollars ($8) ; such as are between thirty-five and forty years of age, ten dollars ($10) ; those who are between forty and fifty years of age, shall pay twelve dollars ($12) per annum. The application of any minister, over fifty years of age, to be admitted to the benefits of the fund, shall be made the subject of special consideration.

3. That the following be the scale of annuities payable to widows and orphans : Each widow shall receive one hundred and fifty

dollars ($150) per annum. If a widow have children, she shall receive, in addition to her own annuity, for one child, twenty dollars ($20) per annum; for two children, thirty-six dollars ($36) per annum; for three children, fifty dollars ($50) per annum; and ten dollars ($10) per annum for each additional child; but she shall not receive anything from the fund for children over eighteen years of age. The claim of the widow shall date from the beginning of the half-year in which the death of her husband occurred, and the annuity shall cease at the end of the half-year following her death or re-marriage. In the event of her re-marriage the children's claims shall continue.

In the event of the decease of both parents, if there be only one orphan the board shall pay for the benefit of such orphan one hundred and fifty dollars ($150); if there are two orphans, twenty dollars ($20) shall be added to the allowance made for one; if there are three orphans, sixteen dollars ($16) more shall be paid on their behalf; and if there are four orphans, fourteen dollars ($14) shall be added to the allowance; and ten dollars ($10) shall be given for each additional orphan; but no allowance shall be made for children over eighteen years of age.

4. That on behalf of professors, foreign missionaries, missionaries under the French Evangelization committee, ministers on the Aged and Infirm Ministers' fund, and the agents of the Church, the sum of $8 shall, in addition to the personal rate, after the amalgamation of the funds of the several branches of the now united Church, be paid to this fund by the boards or committees with which they are respectively connected. Ministers who have retired from active duty with permission of the Church, and for whom no aid is sought from the fund for Aged and Infirm Ministers, shall pay the sum of $8 annually, in addition to the rate previously paid by them.

5. Any minister withdrawing from the Church shall continue to enjoy his rights in this fund, on condition of his paying annually into the fund $12 in addition to the rates previously paid by him.

6. That it be an instruction to Presbyteries to use their utmost endeavors to secure that every minister, when he is inducted into a charge, shall become connected with the fund.

7. That any minister who may, at the time of his induction, decline to join the fund, may be allowed to do so within four years from the date of his induction, on condition of his contributing a sum equivalent to the total payments he should have made, provided he had connected himself with the fund at his induction, together with an

addition of $1 a year for each year he has declined to contribute to the fund after his induction. (*a*).

8 The rates of ministers are payable in advance, on the 1st of November annually, for the year then beginning.

(*a*) By action of the General Assembly of 1896, this regulation was modified as follows : That with a view to having as many ministers as possible connect themselves with the fund, discretionary power be given to the committee to admit to connection with the fund, prior to 1st January, 1897, all ministers desiring this, even though more than four years have elapsed from the date of their induction, upon their contributing a sum equivalent to the total payments they should have made, provided they had connected themselves with the fund at induction, together with at least $1.00 per year additional for each year since induction.—*See Report Widow's and Orphan's Fund Committee. Minutes 1896, App. No. 16.*

PART IV.—CONGREGATIONAL PROPERTY.

Ontario.

Rev. Stat. Ont., 1887, cap. 237.—An Act respecting the property of Religious Institutions.

Her Majesty, &c., enacts as follows :—

1. Where any religious society or congregation of Christians in Ontario desire to take a conveyance of land for the site of a church, chapel, meeting-house, burial-ground, residence for a minister, book-store, printing or publishing-office, or for any other religious or congregational purpose whatever, such society or congregation may appoint trustees, to whom and their successors, to be appointed in such manner as may be specified in the deed of conveyance, the land requisite for all or any of the purposes aforesaid may be conveyed; and such trustees and their successors in perpetual succession, by the name expressed in the deed, may take, hold and possess the land, and maintain and defend actions in law or equity for the protection thereof, and of their property therein. (a)

2. Any congregation or society of Christians entitled to the benefit of any land held under the provisions of this Act, or otherwise, may, from time to time, by a resolution passed by a two-thirds vote of the persons entitled to vote in respect of the appointment of trustees, increase or decrease the number of trustees by the deed or otherwise to be appointed for the purpose of holding such lands; or may, in like manner, fix the number of trustees in case the deed makes no provision as to their number.

3. No such resolution shall be passed unless the said meeting has been duly notified in the same manner as a meeting for the election of trustees for such lands is required to be notified, or unless notice has been given at the time of such notification that a proposal for increasing (or decreasing or determining, as the case may be) the number of the trustees, will be considered at such meeting.

4. In case the resolution passed provides for the appointment of more trustees than are authorised by the deed, or more than there are in fact if the number is not limited by the deed, the same shall take effect forthwith; and the additional trustees to be appointed may be elected at the meeting at which the resolution is passed, or at

---

(a) Every place of worship, and land used in connection therewith, churchyard or burying-ground is exempt from municipal taxation. But land on which a place of worship is erected, and land used in connection with a place of worship is liable to be assessed in the same way and to the same extent as other land for local improvements. 55 Vict., c. 48, sec. 7 sub-sec. 3. (O.)

a subsequent meeting. If the resolution provides for a smaller number of trustees than the deed provides for, then such resolution shall not take effect until vacancies occur, by death or otherwise, reducing the number of trustees to the number provided for by such resolution; and no other trustees shall be appointed under the authority of this Act, until the number of trustees has been reduced as aforesaid below the number authorized by the resolution.

5. A record of the proceedings of such meeting shall be made out in writing, and entered and transcribed in the minute book or other official register of the acts and proceedings of such congregation or society, and shall be signed by the chairman and secretary thereof, and shall thereafter be deposited of record among the archives of the congregation or society, and a copy of such record, certified to be a true copy by the chairman or secretary, on oath (or affirmation) before a justice of the peace, may be recorded in the registry office of the county or other registration division in which the property is situate.

6. A copy of such proceedings taken from the minute book or other official register of the congregation, and certified by the clerk or custodian of the records of the congregation or a copy certified by the registrar of the registration division wherein the same has been registered according to the preceding section, shall be *prima facie* evidence of the contents thereof.

7. The provisions contained in the preceding five sections in this Act shall not be construed so as in any way to repeal, alter, affect, or vary any of the provisions in any special Act contained with reference to any religious body or congregation of Christians in this Province.

8. (1) Where a debt has heretofore been or is hereafter contracted for the building, repairing, extending or improving of a church, meeting-house, chapel, book-store, printing-office or other building, on land held by trustees for the benefit of any religious society in Ontario, or for the purchase of the land on which the same has been or is intended to be erected, the trustees, or a majority of them, may from time to time secure the debt or any part thereof by a mortgage upon the land, church, meeting-house, chapel, book store, printing-office or other building; or may borrow money to pay the debt or part thereof, and may secure the repayment of the loan and interest by a like mortgage upon such terms as may be agreed upon.

(2) The authority conferred by this section to mortgage land as security for a debt, contracted for the building, repairing, extending, or improving of a church, meeting-house, chapel, book-store, printing-office or other building on land held for the benefit of the society, shall extend to any land so held, although the church or other building in respect of which the debt is contracted, is not erected on the said land.

9. The grantees in trust named in any Letters Patent from the Crown, or the survivors or survivor of them, or the trustees for the time being appointed in manner prescribed in the Letters Patent, whereby lands are granted for the use of a congregation or religious body, and any other of the trustees for the time being entitled by law to hold lands in trust for the use of a congregation or a religious body,

may lease, for any term not exceeding 21 years, lands so held by them for the use of a congregation or religious body, at such rents and upon such terms as the trustees, or a majority of them, deem reasonable.

10. In such lease the trustees may covenant or agree for the renewal thereof at the expiration of any or every term of 21 years, for a further term of 21 years or a less period, at such rent and on such terms as may then by the trustees for the time being be agreed upon with the lessee, his heirs, executors, administrators or assigns, or may consent or agree for the payment to the lessee, his executors, administrators or assigns, of the value of any buildings or other improvements which may at the expiration of any term be on the demised premises; and the mode of ascertaining the amount of such rents or the value of such improvements may also be specified in the original lease.

11. The trustees shall not so lease without the consent of the congregation or religious body for whose use they hold the land in trust, and such consent shall be signified by the votes of a majority of the members present at a meeting of the congregation or body, duly called for the purpose; nor shall the trustees lease any land which, at the time of making the lease, is necessary for the purpose of erecting a church or place of worship or other building thereon, or for a burial-ground for the congregation for whose use the land is held.

12. The trustees for the time being entitled by law to hold land in trust for a congregation or religious body, may, in their own names, or by any name by which they hold the land, sue or distrain for rent in arrear, and may take all such means for the recovery thereof as landlords in other cases are entitled to take.

13. (1) When land held by trustees for the use of a congregation or religious body becomes unnecessary to be retained for such use, and it is deemed advantageous to sell the land, the trustees for the time being may give public notice of an intended sale, specifying the premises to be sold and the time and terms of sale; and after publication of the notice for four successive weeks in a weekly paper published in or near the place where the lands are situated, they may sell the land at public auction according to the notice; but the trustees shall not be obliged to complete or carry a sale into effect, if in their judgment an adequate price is not offered for the land: but this provision shall not affect or vary any special powers or trusts for sale contained in any deed or instrument, and inconsistent herewith.

(2) The trustees may thereafter sell the land either by public or private sale; but a less sum shall not be accepted at private sale than was offered at public sale.

14. (1) Before any conveyance is executed in pursuance of a public or private sale, the congregation or religious body for whose use the lands are held shall be duly notified thereof, and its assent obtained to the execution of the said deed, and such assent shall be signified by the votes of a majority of the members present at a meeting of the congregation or body duly called for the purpose.

(2) Such assent shall be held in favour of the grantee and his assigns to be conclusively testified by the execution of said deed by the

chairman at such meeting, or by the official head of such religious body, or by some person appointed at such meeting for the purpose; and the person assuming to execute said deed as chairman, official head or appointee, shall be presumed to be such chairman, official head or appointee, as the case may be.

(3) Instead of such assent of the congregation or religious body aforesaid, it shall be sufficient for the validity of any such deed of conveyance, that the sale be sanctioned and the deed approved of by the judge of the county court of the county in which the land sold is situate. (*a*).

15. It shall be lawful for any congregation or society of Christians of any denomination, on whose behalf lands in this Province are now, have been, or hereafter may be held by a trustee or trustees, without the manner of appointing successors being set forth in the deed of grant, conveyance, will or devise of such lands, or who may be entitled to any lands without being a body corporate, at any time hereafter to assemble in a public meeting duly convened by notice in writing, signed by at least five members of such congregation or society, and affixed to the door of their place of worship, at least eight days previous to the day appointed for holding such meeting; and at such meeting, by the votes of a majority of the members of such congregation or society then and there present, to determine in what manner the successors to such trustee or trustees shall be appointed out of the members of the religious denomination on whose behalf such lands were originally granted, conveyed or conceded, or to appoint a trustee or trustees of any lands to which the said congregation or society is entitled, and their successors in the trust. (*b*).

16. (1) A record of the proceedings of the meeting shall be made out in writing, and entered and transcribed in the minute book or other official register of the acts and proceedings of such congregation or society, and shall be signed by the chairman and secretary thereof, and shall thereafter be deposited of record among the archives of the congregation or society, and a copy of such record, certified to be a true copy by the chairman or secretary, on oath (or affirmation) before a justice of the peace, shall be recorded in the registry office of the county or other registration division in which the property is situate.

(2) A copy of such proceedings taken from the minute book or other official register of the congregation, and certified by the clerk or custodian of the records of the congregation, or a copy certified by the registrar of the registration division wherein the same shall have been registered, according to this section, shall be *prima facie* evidence of the contents thereof.

17. Such determination shall, in every such case, have the same effect as a clause in the grant, concession or conveyance of the lands

---

(*a*) The sanction of the sale and the approval of the deed by the county court judge under this subsection, is sufficient in lieu of all that is required by the two preceding subsections. *Re Wansley & Brown*, 21 Ontario Rep. 34.

(*b*) It is not necessary that the mode of appointment be determined on at one meeting, and the appointment itself made at another; both things may be done at one meeting. *Dorland* v. *Jones*, 7 Ontario Rep. 17. This and the two next succeeding sections authorize only the appointment of successors to trustees dead or legally removed, and do not empower a congregation to remove trustees competent and willing to act. *Lage* v. *Mackenson*, 40 Upper Canada Rep. 388.

to which it relates, setting forth the manner of appointing successors to the trustee or trustees named, would have ; and any lands to which any religious congregation or society, not being incorporated, is entitled, shall from time to time vest in and be held by the trustee or trustees to be appointed as hereinbefore mentioned, and in the successors in the trust, immediately upon the registration of the proceedings in the last preceding section mentioned, and without any or further conveyance or instrument whatsoever.

18. Where members or adherents in any locality of two or more religious societies desire to build a house for public worship, it shall be lawful for each of the societies respectively to appoint from time to time one trustee in the manner and form prescribed in this Act, and the trustees of the religious bodies so united shall have the like powers as conferred on trustees under this Act, and no others ; and as to any act, deed or thing to be done or made by trustees under this Act which requires the sanction or assent of the congregation or religious body, the trustees under this section shall obtain the sanction or assent of each and every of the congregations or religious bodies so united, to be ascertained and signified in the manner hereinbefore mentioned.

19. (1) All deeds of conveyance executed before the 29th day of March, 1873, for any of the uses, interests or purposes enumerated therein, if the same were registered before the 30th of March, 1874, shall be as valid and effectual as if registered within twelve months after the execution thereof respectively, except in so far as the same may be affected by the prior registration of other deeds or instruments relating to the same lands respectively,

(2) But in all cases where any such religious bodies had not erected any buildings or made improvements, and any person claiming to hold or to be entitled to any real estate or property included in any such deed on account of the omission to register the same, had, in virtue of such claim, taken possession of such real estate before the said 29th day of March, 1873, and also in all cases where the persons claiming to hold or to be entitled to such real property, on account of such omission as aforesaid, had actually sold or departed with, or had actually contracted to sell or depart with such real estate before the said date, the provisions of this section shall not extend to render invalid any right or title to such estate, but such right or title shall be taken and adjudged to be as if this Act had not been passed.

20. The trustees of any lands to which the provisions of this Act apply, shall, within twelve months after the execution of the deed of conveyance, cause the deed to be registered in the office of the registrar of the county or other registration division in which the land is situate, or otherwise the same shall be void ; and further, such deed shall be subject to the law affecting priority of registration in the same manner as if made between private parties.

21. Trustees selling or leasing land under the authority of this Act shall, on the first Monday in July in every year, have ready and open for the inspection of the congregation or religious body which they represent, or of any member thereof, a detailed statement showing the rents which accrued during the preceding year, and all sums

of money whatever in their hands, for the use and benefit of the congregation or religious body, which were in any manner derived from the lands under their control or subject to their management, and also showing the application of any portion of the money which has been expended on behalf of the congregation or body.

22. This Act shall not be construed so as in anywise to repeal, alter, affect or vary any of the provisions in any special Act contained with reference to any religious body or congregation of Christians in this Province, but, on the contrary, any of the said provisions, while differing from or inconsistent with any of the provisions of this Act, shall prevail, and where any additional rights or privileges are conferred by this Act, they shall be construed as supplementary to the provisions contained in any such special Act ; and in every case the special trusts or powers of trustees contained in any deed, conveyance, or other instrument, shall not be affected or varied by any of the provisions of this Act.

23. Any religious society or congregation of Christians in Ontario may, by the name thereof, or in that of trustees, from time to time take or hold, by gift, devise or bequest, any lands or tenements, or interests therein, if such gift, devise or bequest is made at least six months before the death of the person making the same, but the said religious society or congregation shall at no time take or hold by any gift, devise or bequest, so that the annual value of any lands or tenements, or interests therein, so to be taken or held by gift, devise, or bequest, at any one time exceeds in the whole the sum of $1,000; and no lands or tenements, or interests therein, acquired by gift, devise, or bequest, shall be held by the said religious society or congregation for a longer period than seven years after the acquisition thereof; and within such period they shall respectively be absolutely disposed of by the said religious society or congregation, which shall have power in the name thereof, or in that of the trustees for said society or congregation, to grant and convey the said lands to any purchaser, so that it no longer retains any interest therein ; and the proceeds on such disposition shall be invested in public securities, municipal debentures, or other approved securities, not including mortgages, for the use of the said society or congregation ; and such lands, tenements, or interests therein, or such thereof as have not, within the said period, been so disposed of, shall revert to the person from whom the same were acquired, his heirs, executors, administrators or assigns.

24. Whenever two or more different parcels of land adjoining each other, or in the same neighborhood, are held as sites for burial grounds by different bodies of trustees, whether of the same denomination, society, or congregation, or of different denominations, societies, or congregations of Christians, and such trustees think it desirable that, for purposes of economic management, or any other reason, such parcels should be vested in one body of trustees, such two or more bodies of trustees, or the majority of each of such bodies may, by deed under their hands, appoint trustees to whom, and their successors, to be appointed in such manner as may be specified in such deed, all or any of the lands vested in such appointing bodies of trustees as sites for burial grounds may be conveyed, and such trustees so, by such deed, appointed, and their successors in perpetual succes-

sion by the name expressed in the deed, may take, hold and possess the lands thereby or thereafter conveyed to them as a site or sites for a burial ground, and maintain and defend actions for the protection thereof, and of their property therein, and the said several appointing bodies of trustees may, in or by the same deed of appointment, or by any other deed or deeds, convey and assure all or any of the parcels of land so, as aforesaid, vested in them respectively to such trustees so appointed and their successors upon, with and subject to such trusts, powers, limitations and provisions not inconsistent with the purposes of a burial ground, as shall by the parties thereto be deemed proper.

25.—(1). No such deed of appointment of trustees, and no such conveyance or assurance shall be made or executed by any body, or the majority of any body of trustees, unless or until the congregation or religious body for whose use the lands are held shall be duly notified thereof, and its assent obtained, for the execution of such deed of appointment, or of such conveyance or assurance, and such assent shall be signified by the votes of a majority of the members present at a meeting of the congregation, or body, duly called for the purpose.

(2). Such assent shall be held in favor of such new trustees and their successors, to be testified by the execution of said deed by the chairman at such meeting, or by the official head of such religious body, or by some person appointed at such meeting for the purpose; and the person assuming to execute such deed as chairman, official head, or appointee, shall be presumed to be such chairman, official head or appointee, as the case may be.

52 Vict., Cap. 54 (O).—An Act to make further provision respecting the property of Religious Institutions. (*Assented to 23rd March, 1889*).

Her Majesty, &c., enacts as follows :—

1. Conveyances made to the trustees of any religious society, or congregation, for any of the purposes authorized by the Act respecting the property of religious institutions, being Chapter 237 of the Revised Statutes of Ontario, 1887, may be made to such trustees under a collective name, and it shall not be necessary to set out the individual names of the trustees in such deed as parties thereto, or as grantees therein, provided such names be set out, or appear by recital or otherwise, in the said deed. This section shall apply to conveyances heretofore made, as well as to those hereafter to be made to such trustees.

2. In case the name by which any religious society or congregation as aforesaid, or trustees therefor, have heretofore held, or shall hereafter hold lands under and pursuant to the powers of the said Act, has been, or shall be changed by such religious society or congregation, by by-law or resolution, such change of name shall not prejudice or affect the title of the society or congregation, or their trustees to the said lands.

3. In the case of separate, but contiguous parcels of land held under separate conveyances by trustees for the same religious society

or congregation under the said Act, if such parcels of land be so used, occupied, or built upon as to become indivisable except by the removal, alteration, or destruction, in whole or in part, of such user, occupation, or building, the trustees of such parcels may join in any mortgage authorized by section 8 of the said Act.

QUEBEC.

REV. STAT. QUEBEC, Title 9, cap. 3.—Religious Congregations.

SECTION 1.—Lands held by Religious Congregations.

3443 (Lands in possession of religious congregations on 19th March, 1839, to be deemed to be held in mortmain forever.)

3444. (Provided that the titles thereto and descriptions thereof have been registered.)

3445. Whenever any parish mission, congregation or society of Christians, of any denomination whatsoever, not being a parish recognized by the civil law of the Province, is desirous of acquiring lands for the site of the churches, chapels, meeting houses, burial grounds, dwelling houses for their priests, ministers, ecclesiastics, or religious teachers, and school houses, and the appurtenances thereunto necessary for the said several purposes, such parish, mission, congregation or society of Christians, may appoint one or more trustees to whom and to whose successors (to be appointed in the manner set forth in the deed of grant, concession or conveyance), the lands necessary for each and every of the purposes aforesaid may be conveyed; and such trustees and their successors for ever, by the name by which they and the congregation on whose behalf they act, are designated in such deed or grant, concession or conveyance, may acquire by purchase, donation, exchange, or as a legacy, and hold and possess, the lands so acquired, and may institute and defend all actions at law, for the conservation of such lands and of their rights therein.

3446. The successors of such trustees appointed in the manner provided in such deed or grant, concession or conveyance as aforesaid, or in the manner provided at a meeting of the congregation or society held in the manner and within the period prescribed by the Act 19 and 20 Victoria, chapter 103, shall have the same rights and powers as if appointed in such deed of grant, concession or conveyance.

3447. A copy of the record of the proceedings of such meeting, certified by the notary in whose office a copy of such record certified by the chairman and secretary of the meeting, was deposited by *acte de depot*, in the manner prescribed by the Act last mentioned, shall be *prima facie* evidence of the contents of such record.

3449. Where any congregation or society of Christians have held property, as aforesaid, within any parish established by law on the said 19th day of March, 1839, the property so held by such congregation or society of Christians, shall not be vested in such parish, but the administration and control thereof shall remain with the said trustees of such congregation or society of Christians, to be held in mortmain for ever, for the benefit of such congregation or society of Christians as aforesaid.

3450. Such trustees, or such rectors and church wardens, shall within two years after they have acquired such lands, conform to the provisions of the second paragraph of the first section of this Act, concerning the registrations to be made with regard to such lands at the office of the prothonotary, such registration being made in the office of the prothonotory of the Superior Court, in the district in which the lands lie, and for which enregistration the prothonotaries of the several districts respectively, shall be entitled to a fee not exceeding five cents for every 100 words.

The quantity of land so acquired for the purposes aforesaid, within the walls of the cities of Quebec and Montreal, respectively, shall not, on the whole, exceed one arpent (whereof no part shall be used as a burial ground, excepting for ecclesiatics and religious persons of either sex, or for private vaults for the donors of the ground) and out of the walls but within the limits of the said cities, shall not exceed eight arpents in superficies; and the quantity of land so held in any other place for the use of each parish, mission, congregation or religious society, shall not exceed 200 English acres.

SECTION 2.--Cemeteries held by Religious Congregations.

3453. Any parish, mission, congregation or society of Christians, not being a parish recognized by law, may acquire in any of the ways indicated by the preceding section, and hold and possess as thereby provided, any lands for cemeteries, subject to any trust express or implied touching the same, in favour of any persons or classes of persons, not being of such parish, mission, congregation or society; and all trusts created or indicated so to be, by any deed, grant, concession or conveyance of such lands for cemeteries to any such parish, mission, congregation or society shall be held validly to affect the same, and shall have due effect given to the same accordingly.

SECTION 3.—Appointment of successors to trustees of lands held in the name of Religious Congregations.

3455. It shall be lawful for any congregation or society of Christians, of any denomination, on whose behalf lands in this Province, are now, have been, or hereafter shall be held by a trustee or trustees, without the manner of appointing successors being set forth in the deed of grant, concession or conveyance of such lands, at any time to assemble in a public meeting duly convened by notice in writing, signed by at least five members of such congregation or society, and affixed to the door of their place of worship, at least eight days previous to the day appointed for holding such meeting, at such meeting by the votes of a majority of the members of such congregation or society then and there present to determine in what manner the successors to such trustee or trustees shall be appointed from among the members of the religious denomination on whose behalf such lands were originally granted, conveyed or conceded.

3456. A record of the proceedings of the meeting shall be made out in writing, and entered and transcribed in the minute book or other official register of the acts and proceedings of such society or congregation, and shall be signed by the chairman and secretary thereof, and shall thereafter be deposited of record among the archives of the congregation or society, and a copy of such record, certified to be a true copy by the chairman or secretary, on oath or affirmation, before a justice of the peace, shall be recorded in the registry office of the county or registration division in which the property is situated, and a copy of such proceedings taken from the minute book or other official register of the congregation, and certified by the clerk or custodian of the records of the congregation, or a copy certified by the registrar of the registration division wherein the same shall have been registered, according to this section shall be *prima facie* evidence of the contents thereof.

3457. Such determination shall, in every such case, have the same effect as a clause in the deed of grant, concession or conveyance of the lands to which it relates, setting forth the manner of appointing successors to the trustees named, would have and no more.

Nova Scotia.

Rev. Stat., Nova Scotia, (5th Series), cap. 22.—Of Religious Congregations and Societies.

1. When any number of persons not less than twenty, capable of contracting, desire to form themselves into a congregation of Christians for the public worship of God according to their peculiar rites and ceremonies, they may, by deed by them executed in the presence of two or more witnesses, which shall be recorded in a book kept for that purpose, constitute themselves such congregation, and adopt a suitable name therefor, and declare the place where the same is established and the particular denomination of Christians with whose doctrines such congregation is connected ; and they may name two or more persons of the congregation to be trustees thereof and give them a name of office, and describe in such deed by bounds the particular situation of all lands conveyed to or in trust for the congregation for all purposes connected therewith ; and they may also set forth in such deed the constitution of the congregation, the mode of admission of future members, by whom the right of voting at meetings shall be enjoyed, how the votes shall be ascertained and given, the manner in which vacancies in the trust shall be supplied, and such other particulars as they may think proper.

2. The deed shall be duly registered in the office of the registrar of deeds for the county or district where the congregation is established ; and, after its registry, all the lands described therein and all real and personal estate granted to the congregation or to their use shall be vested in the trustees named in the deed for the use of the congregation, and after the death or removal of any trustee or his becoming incapable to act, shall vest in the succeeding trustees sub-

ject to the same trusts without any assignment or conveyance except the transfer of stock and securities in the public funds: and shall also in any suit at law or in equity or in any criminal prosecution be deemed the property of the trustees.

3. Such trustees in all cases concerning the real and personal estate of the congregation may sue and be sued by their name of office; and no action shall abate by the removal or death of the trustees or any of them, but shall be proceeded in by or against the succeeding trustees, who shall pay or receive the like moneys and costs as if the action had been prosecuted in their names, for the benefit of or to be reimbursed from the funds of the congregation.

4. Every congregation established under these provisions may hold, in the name of their trustees, real estate not exceeding the yearly value of $8,000, and personal property not exceeding in the whole at any one time $40,000; and may use and dispose of such real and personal estate as the congregation shall deem expedient.

5. The members of every such congregation may meet when they shall think proper, and at such meetings by the votes of the majority of the members present may make and put in execution such regulations, not being contrary to the laws of this Province nor to any rule or regulation embodied in the deed under which the congregation or society may be constituted, as the majority shall deem necessary for the government of the congregation and may change such regulations as they may think proper; and such majority may also choose trustees to supply any vacancy in the trust, and may remove from office any of the trustees for the time being, and manage and superintend the affairs of the congregation; the time and place of meeting shall be duly notified as prescribed by rules therefor; and some fit person shall be chosen chairman at every meeting, and all proceedings thereat shall be entered in the books of the congregation, and signed by the chairman and clerk of the meeting, and proof of such entry so signed shall be deemed sufficient evidence of such proceedings, and of the regularity of the meeting.

6. Every person admitted a member of the congregation after the registry of the deed, shall execute the same in the presence of two witnesses before he shall be deemed a member.

7. All real estate which at the formation of any congregation under this chapter shall be held therefor by any trustees not appointed under any Act or deed of incorporation, shall, by such trustees or their survivors, or by such of them as then remain in this Province, be conveyed to the new trustees named in the deed by their name of office; and. upon the conveyance being made and registered, all the estate and interest of the original trustees, or the survivors of them and their heirs, shall be vested in the new trustees to the use of the congregation as effectually as if all the original trustees had joined in the conveyance.

8. Any religious society or congregation incorporated by special Act of incorporation, or by deed under the provisions of the Act heretofore in force for such purpose, may avail themselves of the provisions of this chapter; provided the parties executing the deed comprise two-thirds at least of the members of the former corporation

who at the time form part of the congregation, and also two-thirds at least of the persons actually exercising the functions of trustees by their individual names as such trustees; and, upon the new deed being registered, the former Act or deed of incorporation shall from thenceforth cease to be in operation, and the property held thereunder shall vest in the new trustees in accordance with the terms of the deed; but nothing herein contained shall affect the legality of any proceedings regularly had under the former Act or deed of incorporation.

9. By the vote of the majority of members of any congregation present at any regular meeting of the congregation, the trustees for the time being shall sell, mortgage, lease, or convey any real estate of the congregation for such estate, or on such terms as the meeting shall direct; and every conveyance thereof executed by the trustees for the time being, and signed by the chairman of the meeting which shall order such disposal, shall be valid in law to convey such estate in the lands therein described.

10. Whenever the congregation using any building for the purpose of public worship, may wish to dispose thereof, on account of the same having become dilapidated or otherwise, and shall not have legal power to do so, the proprietors of such building at a meeting held for the purpose, after public notice thereof given in at least three of the most public places within the settlement wherein the building is situate, at least ten days previously, may by a vote of three-fifths of the proprietors present at such meeting appoint a committee of three of their number to make sale of such building; and the committee shall sell the same conformably to the instructions given at the meeting, and cause the removal thereof, and shall apply the proceeds of the sale as directed by the meeting; but no meeting shall be valid for such purpose, unless a majority of the proprietors are present.

11. In case the building shall be vested in trustees who shall not have legal power to sell the building, the same may be disposed of by a meeting of the persons for whose benefit such building is held, called and constituted as directed in the preceding section, and a majority of three-fifths of the persons so interested present at the meeting, may empower the trustees or a committee to sell the building and apply the proceeds.

12. Nothing herein shall authorize the sale of the land on which any building so to be disposed of shall be situated.

13. Under the order of any such meeting, or of a meeting of the church members, when by provisions of the deed of constitution, or by the regulations of the congregation, the choice of a minister shall be vested in the church members, the trustees may enter into agreements in writing with any clergyman or minister whom the congregation or church shall appoint to their spiritual charge, for such period and salary as shall be agreed upon.

14. The trustees having agreed with any minister or clergyman, shall without delay cause the agreement to be entered at length in the books of the congregation.

15. The trustees for the time being, by the vote of the majority of the members of the congregation at any such meeting, shall, in cases where the funds at their disposal are inadequate to the discharge of the claims upon them, sue for and recover from members a rateable share, to be fixed according to the rules of the congregation, of such amount or deficiency, by separate suit for their respective rateable proportion of the whole amount against the respective surviving and solvent members of the congregation, or the representatives of deceased members liable to such payment.

16. Any religious society incorporated by Act of this Province, or constituted by deed under the provisions of this chapter, may at any regular meeting held in accordance with their Act of incorporation or deed of constitution, alter or amend their constitution or by-laws; but the constitution shall not be altered unless two-thirds of the members present at any general meeting concur in such alteration.

17. Any religious society or congregation not incorporated or constituted by deed under this chapter, may, at any meeting of the congregation held in pursuance of a notice stating the object of such meeting, given at their usual place of holding public worship, during divine service, either by verbal announcement to the congregation, or by posting the same on the door of such place of worship, for three Sundays preceding such meeting, proceed to appoint a chairman and secretary; and may, upon the vote of two-thirds of the male members of the congregation and of adherents, actually contributing to the funds thereof, above twenty-one years of age actually present, proceed to the adoption of a declaration, by resolution or otherwise, to the effect that they constitute themselves a religious congregation or society; and may, at any such meeting, or any subsequent meeting called in the same manner, proceed by the majority of votes, to the adoption of a permanent constitution and by-laws not inconsistent with the laws of this Province as they shall consider necessary, and may appoint trustees and such other office-bearers as they shall see fit, and define their powers and duties, and may regulate the terms of membership in the society or congregation.

18. The real and personal estate of the society or congregation shall be vested in such persons as shall be duly appointed trustees thereof by resolution of such meeting, recorded in the books of the congregation, during their continuance in office.

19. The officers appointed from time to time by the congregation or society shall be invested with all such powers for the holding and transference of the property and management of the business of the congregation or society as shall be conferred upon them by the constitution.

20. The constitution of the society may be altered by the vote of two-thirds of the members present at any meeting of the congregation or society, duly called, as hereinbefore mentioned. All other business of the society not delegated to the office-bearers thereof shall be transacted by the votes of the majority of the members present at any such regular meeting.

21. Any religious society or congregation of Christians not duly incorporated or constituted under this chapter, or, if so incorporated

or constituted, not having power to dispose of its place of worship for the purpose of erecting a new place of worship, may, at any regular meeting of the society or congregation, by resolution of the majority of two-thirds of the members present, authorize such persons as they may appoint for the purpose to sell or otherwise dispose of the place of worship of the society or congregation in such manner as the meeting shall appoint ; and a sale thereof, under the authority of such resolution, shall be valid and effectual : provided such resolution and authority are duly recorded in the county or district registry of deeds.

22. Any episcopal corporation sole holding real estate in trust for any religious denomination in this Province, may dispose of the same by deed executed by him, and any three ordained clergymen of the denomination to which he belongs, and residing within the diocese.

23. In cases where real estate has been, or shall hereafter be, conveyed in trust for erecting thereon houses for public worship, or dwelling or other houses or buildings intended for the accommodation of ministers of the gospel or clergymen officiating or engaged to officiate for any church or congregation of Christians, and the mode of appointing new or other trustees than the grantees is provided for in the deed of conveyance creating such trust, or otherwise in writing, when a vacancy shall occur by reason of the death, removal, resignation or displacement of any trustee, it shall not be held necessary that the remaining or surviving trustee or trustees, if any, shall make or shall have made any deed or conveyance to the newly appointed trustee, in order to invest him with the estate, functions, trusts and powers of the original trustees under such deed or declaration of trust or instrument in writing creating such trust and directing the appointment of future or succeeding trustees ; but such newly appointed trustee shall thereupon, without deed or other conveyance, be seised in fee or other estate to the uses and trusts created, as fully and completely as were the original grantees; provided that the terms or conditions for such appointment are duly complied with.

24. Nothing herein contained shall affect any of the provisions of the chapter "Of the Church of England," nor shall interfere with the spiritual government and discipline of any Church further than may be provided for in the deed or declaration under which the society or congregation is constituted.

REV. STAT., NOVA SCOTIA (5th Series), cap. 23.—Of Assessments for Repairs of Meeting Houses.

1. When funds are required for repairing, finishing or painting any meeting house or church, the proprietors thereof, at a public meeting, whereof notice shall have been previously given during the time of divine service at such meeting house or church, on three several Sundays, may, by vote of three-fifths of the proprietors present at such meeting, declare what repairs are necessary and the amount required therefor, and may also nominate three or more persons a committee to assess and apportion the sum so voted on the several pews of the meeting house or church, according to the relative size and value of such pews, at an equitable rate; of which as-

essment and apportionment public notice shall be given by posting up the same in some conspicuous place in the meeting house or church, and also on the door thereof for three successive Sundays on which divine service shall be performed thereat, next after the making thereof.

2. If after such notice the persons interested in any of the pews shall not pay the sums assessed on such pews within three months thereafter, the committee, after notice having been given on the previous Sunday immediately after divine service, may proceed to let such pews at auction, for such period, not exceeding ten years, as may be sufficient to pay the sum so assessed thereon respectively ; or they may, on giving the like notice, let such pews from year to year until the rate or assessment be fully paid, so that such letting shall not extend beyond the term of ten years.

3. The persons who shall so lease the pews shall be put in possession thereof by the committee, and shall have the exclusive occupation thereof during the term of their lease ; and the committee may sue for and recover the rent, and shall have power to hold or occupy such pews, and to eject any person illegally in possession thereof.

4. If the money arising from the leasing of the pews shall not amount to the assessment thereon, the committee may make a new assessment in the same way as the original amount is hereby directed to be assessed.

5. Nothing in this chapter shall extend to any church or chapel belonging to or connected with the Church of England, or to any meeting-house belonging solely to the denomination of Christians called Wesleyan Methodists.

MANITOBA.

REV. STAT. MANITOBA, cap. 20.—An Act respecting Church lands vested in trustees. (*As amended by 55 Vict., c. 3, and 56 Vict. c 4*).

Her Majesty, &c. enacts as follows :—

1. This Act may be cited as "The Church Lands Act."

2. When any religious society, church, or congregation of Christians in Manitoba desire to take a conveyance, or transfer, or certificate of title, under the Real Property Act, of land to be used for the support of public worship, the propagation of Christian knowledge, or of not more than twenty acres of land to be used for the purposes of a cemetery, such conveyance, transfer, or certificate may be taken to trustees in the form set forth in the Schedules A. B. and C. respectively, to this Act, and such trustees and their successors in perpetual succession by the name expressed in the deed, transfer, or certificate may take, hold and possess the lands therein described, and maintain and defend actions at law and suits in equity for the protection thereof and of their property therein ; provided that no such society or

congregation shall be capable of taking or holding more than three hundred acres and such other lands as may be alloted to any such society or congregation as commutation under the Manitoba Act for any right of common and of cutting hay, held and enjoyed by such society or congregation. (*a*).

3. Each of the said trustees shall hold office until he shall die or resign, or cease to be a member of such society or congregation, or until he shall be removed in the manner hereinafter provided and no longer.

4. In case any trustee or trustees shall cease to hold office as such, the remaining trustees shall have all the estate and powers originally vested in the whole number, until another trustee or other trustees shall have been appointed in the manner hereinafter provided.

5 A general meeting of such society, church, or congregation may be held on the third Tuesday in January in each and every year, which shall be called by written notice read to the congregation, during or at the close of public worship, and before the congregation shall have been dismissed, on each of the two Sundays next preceding the holding of the said meeting by the officiating minister, and if from any cause such a meeting shall not be held on that day, or if for any reason, after the holding of such a meeting, no successor shall have been appointed to any person who has ceased to be a trustee as aforesaid, either before or since such meeting, then, if the trustees or seven members of the society or congregation in full communion therewith shall, by writing under their hand, request him so to do, the minister or ministers officiating upon any two successive Sundays shall, in like manner, call such a meeting for any day in the week immediately following the second of such Sundays, and any such meeting may be adjourned, as occasion shall require, and at such regular or adjourned meeting, the said society or congregation by the votes of the majority of the members thereof, in full communion there present, may remove any trustee and may elect and appoint any member or members of the said society or congregation to be trustees in the place or stead of any person who has ceased to be a trustee, and thereupon the trustee or trustees so appointed with such of the trustees originally named in the conveyance, transfer, or certificate of title as have not ceased to be trustees, if any, shall have all the estate and powers originally vested in the said original trustees.

6. A minute of every such removal, election, or appointment, or the adoption of the name under the seventh section of this Act, shall be entered in a book to be kept for the purpose, and shall be signed by the person who presides at the meeting, and such minute so signed shall, for all purposes, be sufficient *prima facie* evidence of such removal, election, or appointment, or the adoption of such name, but the omission or neglect to make or sign such minute shall not invalidate such removal, election, or appointment, or the adoption of such name.

(*a*). Buildings used exclusively as places of public worship, and the land used in connection therewith, not exceeding two acres, are free from municipal taxation, but are liable to special assessments for local improvements. R. S. M. c. 101, sec. 3, sub-secs. (*n*) and (*r*).

(2). A certificate by the secretary of the society, or congregation, or other officer in whose custody such book is kept, as to such removal, election or appointment, or the adoption of such name shall be conclusive evidence thereof for the purpose of the district registrar of any land titles district.

7. Any conveyance of lands made before the first day of July, 1883, to any persons described as trustees for any such society or congregation as aforesaid, and purporting to be made to such persons and their successors, shall be deemed to have the same effect as if the same had been a conveyance of the lands described therein under this Act, and where more than one of such conveyances have been made for the benefit of any such society or congregation under different names, such society or congregation may, at a general meeting, duly called, as aforesaid, by a majority vote, as aforesaid, adopt one of such names as the name whereby the trustees for the said society or congregation shall hold the said lands as in the second section of this Act mentioned, and thereupon the name so adopted shall be the name whereby the said trustees shall hold in perpetual succession, as aforesaid.

8. The trustees shall, within twelve months after the execution of the deed of conveyance or transfer, cause the deed or transfer to be registered in the registry office or land titles' office in which the land is situate, otherwise the said deed or transfer shall be void.

9. When a debt has been, or shall be hereafter contracted, for the building, repairing, extending or improving of a church, meeting-house, chapel, manse, parsonage, or residence of the minister, on land held by trustees for the benefit of any religious society in Manitoba, or for the purchase of the lands on which the same has been, or is intended to be erected, the trustees, or a majority of them, may, from time to time, secure the debt, or any part thereof, by a mortgage upon all or any of the land, church, meeting-house, chapel, manse, parsonage, or residence of the minister, held for the benefit of such society or congregation, or may borrow money to pay the debt, or part thereof, and may secure the repayment of the loan and interest by a like mortgage, upon such terms as may be agreed upon.

10. The grantees in trust, named in any letters patent from the crown, or the survivor or survivors of them or their trustees for the time being, appointed in manner prescribed in the letters patent, whereby lands are granted for the use of a congregation or a religious body, and any other trustees for the time being entitled by law to hold lands in trust for the use of a congregation or religious body, may lease, for any term not exceeding 21 years, lands so held by them for the use of a congregation or religious body, at such rent and upon such terms as the trustees, or a majority of them, may deem reasonable.

11. In such lease, they may covenant or agree for the renewal thereof, at the expiration of any or every term of 21 years, for a further term of 21 years, or a less period, at such rent and on such terms as may then, by the trustees for the time being, be agreed upon with the lessee, his heirs, executors, administrators or assigns, or may covenant or agree for the payment to the lessee, his executors, administrators or assigns, of the value of any buildings, or other improvements, which may at the expiration of any term, be on the

demised premises ; and the mode of ascertaining the amount of such rent or the value of such improvements, may also be specified in the original or any subsequent lease.

12. But the trustees shall not so lease without the consent of the congregation or religious body for whose use they hold the land in trust ; and such consent shall be signified by the votes of a majority of the members present at a meeting of the congregation or body duly called for the purpose ; nor shall the trustees lease any land which, at the time of the making of the lease, is necessary for the purpose of erecting a church or place of worship, or other building thereon, or for a burial ground, for the congregation for whose use the land is held.

13. The trustees for the time being entitled by law to hold land in trust for a congregation or a religious body may, in their own names, or by any name by which they hold the land, sue or distrain for rent, or arrears of rent, and may take such means for the recovery thereof as landlords in ordinary cases are entitled to take.

14. When land held by trustees for the use of a congregation or a religious body becomes unnecessary to be retained for such use, and it is deemed advantageous to sell the land, the trustees for the time being may give public notice of an intended sale, specifying the premises to be sold and the time and terms of sale, and after publication of the notice for four successive weeks in a weekly paper published in or near the place where the lands are situated, they may sell the land at public auction, according to notice ; but the trustees shall not be obliged to complete or carry a sale into effect, if in their judgment an adequate price is not offered for the land.

15. The trustees may thereafter sell the land, either by public or private sale, but a less sum shall not be accepted at private sale than was offered at public sale.

16. Before a deed or transfer is executed in pursuance of a public or private sale, the congregation or religious body for whose use the lands are held, shall be duly notified thereof, and the sanction of a Judge of the Court of Queen's Bench obtained for the execution of the deed or transfer (*a*) and after such sanction, the said deed or transfer shall be deemed sufficient for every purpose.

17. Trustees selling or leasing lands under the authority of this Act, shall, on the first Monday in July in every year, have ready and open for the inspection of the congregation or religious body which they represent, or of any member thereof, a detailed statement, showing all rents which accrued during the preceding year, and all sums of money whatever in their hands for the use and benefit of the congregation or religious body, which were in any manner derived from the lands under their control, or subject to their management, and also showing the application of any portion of the money which has been expended on behalf of the congregation or religious body.

(*a*) The congregation or religious body must be notified, not only of the fact that a sale has been made, but also of the time at which the Court will be applied to, to sanction the execution of the deed, *Re Methodist Church, Manitou*, 8 Man. R. 136. The application must be made before the trustees execute the deed or transfer.

18. Any Judge of the Court of Queen's Bench may, in a summary manner, on complaint upon oath of three members of a congregation or religious body of any misfeasance or misconduct on the part of trustees in the performance of their duties under this Act, call upon the trustees to give in an account, and may enforce the rendering of such account, the discharge of any duties and the payment of any money, so that the congregation or religious body may have the benefit thereof, according to the true intent and meaning of this Act: and the Judge may compel the trustees, in case of any misconduct, to pay the expense of the application to be made; or if it be made on grounds which he considers insufficient, frivolous or vexatious he may order the applicant to pay the costs.

19. Nothing in this Act contained, differing from or altering the Act chaptered 50 of the Consolidated Statutes of Manitoba, shall affect directly or indirectly any rights brought in question in any legal proceedings begun on or before the 7th day of October, 1883, upon any cause of action arising before the 7th day of July of the last mentioned year, or before the passing of any private Act affecting any religious body or bodies.

20. The said trustees and their successors in office may, by resolution of the society or congregation at any annual or special meeting, called in pursuance of this Act, be and become a body politic and corporate under the name of the "Trustees of ———— Church, in the ———— of ————, in the Province of Manitoba," and shall have perpetual succession and a common seal, and by such name have all the powers and privileges possessed by or given to trustees under this Act, and under said name may sue and be sued, plead and be impleaded, answer and be answered in all courts and places whatever, and the said corporation shall have all the powers of corporations under The Manitoba Interpretation Act, provided always that a copy of such resolution, signed by the chairman and secretary of the meeting at which it was adopted, and by the said trustees duly verified as to the execution thereof by statutory declaration, shall, within six months after the date of such meeting, be filed in the office of the Provincial Secretary, and the same shall be conclusive evidence of such incorporation, and a copy thereof, under the hand of the Provincial Secretary, shall be received in all cases as *prima facie* proof of the facts and matters therein stated, without proof of the signature of the Provincial Secretary.

21. In all cases where trustees have executed a mortgage or mortgages upon lands held by them for the benefit of any church or religious society in Manitoba, the trustees for the time being or a majority of them shall have, and are hereby declared to have always had, the power to release or convey to the mortgagee or his assigns without any previous formality the equity of redemption in the lands so mortgaged, or in any part thereof in satisfaction of the whole or part of the mortgage debt as may have been or may be agreed upon between the trustees and the mortgagee or his assigns, provided that the mortgage was or shall be in arrear as to either principal or interest at the time of executing such release or conveyance, and provided further the trustees were or are authorized so to release or convey at a meeting of the society or congregation regularly called in pursuance of section 5 of this Act or of any similar provision for which said section has been substituted.

22. When a lot has been sold by the trustees for a burial site, the conveyance shall not be required to be registered for any purpose whatever, and shall not be affected by any registry Act or the Real Property Act, nor shall any judgment, mortgage or encumbrance subsist on any lot so conveyed.

23. The deed from the trustees may be in the following form :—
" Know all men, by these presents, that the (*giving name of trustees*) in consideration of ....dollars, paid to them by..............of ....(the receipt whereof is hereby acknowledged) do grant unto the said.... .... his heirs and assigns,........ lot of land in the cemetery of the said trustees, called............ and situate in the..........of. ....which lot is delineated and laid down on the map of the said cemetery, and is therein designated by .... containing by admeasurement........superficial feet ; to have and to hold the herein above named premises, &c."

24. The provisions of sections 14, 15 and 16 hereof shall not apply to sales of plots of land so held for cemetery purposes or any part thereof, but the majority of said trustees may from time to time, as they may deem advisable, make sale or sales thereof for such price as they deem advisable.

25. The trustees of the land so held for cemetery purposes for any religious society, church or congregation shall not require to be the same persons who hold other land as trustees under section 2 hereof.

26. All lots or plots of ground in the cemetery, when numbered and conveyed by the trustees as burial sites or lots shall be indivisible, but may afterwards be held and owned in undivided shares.

Schedule A.

This Indenture, made (in duplicate) the   day of   in the year of our Lord one thousand eight hundred and   in pursuance of the Act respecting short forms of indentures between   of the first part and   as trustees for the congregation of   church, in   in Manitoba, of the second part, witnesseth that in consideration of   lawful money of Canada, now paid by the said parties of the second part, to the said part   of the first part (the receipt whereof is hereby by acknowledged,)   the said part   of the first part do   grant unto the said parties of the second part, their successors and assigns for ever : All and singular th   certain parcel   or tract   of land and premises, situate, lying and being
To have and to hold unto and to the use of the said parties of the second part, and their successors as trustees for the congregation of   church, in   in Manitoba, for ever. The said part   of the first part covenant   with the said parties of the second part that   ha   the right to convey the said lands to the said part   of the   part, notwithstanding any act of the said part   of the first part. And the said parties of the second part shall have quiet possession of the said lands free from all encumbrances. And the said part   of the first part covenant   with the said parties of the second part that   will execute such

further assurances of the said lands as may be requisite. And the said part   of the first part covenant   with the said parties of the second part that   ha   done no act to encumber the said lands. And the said part   of the first part release   to the said parties of the second part all   claims upon the said lands. In witness whereof, the said parties hereto set their hands and seals. Signed, sealed and delivered in presence of

Schedule B.

MEMORANDUM OF TRANSFER.

I, A. B., being registered owner of an estate (*state nature of estate* subject, however, to such encumbrances, liens and interests as are notified by memorandum under written (*or endorsed hereon*) in all that land containing (*as the case may be*) (*here state the rights of way, privileges, easements, if any, intended to be conveyed along with the land; and if the land dealt with contained all included in the original grant, refer thereto for description of parcels and diagrams, otherwise set forth the boundaries and accompany it by a diagram*) do hereby, in consideration of the sum of $ paid to me by E. F. &c., the trustees of   church in the   of   in the Province of Manitoba, the receipt of which sum I hereby acknowledge, transfer to the said E. F. &c., as such trustees, all my estate and interest in the said piece of land. (*When a lesser estate, then describe such lesser estate.*) In witness whereof I have hereunto subscribed my name this   day of   .

Signed on the day above named ⎫ Signature.
  by the said A.B. in the presence ⎬
of   ⎭

Schedule C.

CERTIFICATE OF TITLE.

A. B. of   as trustee of   church in the   of   in the Province of Manitoba, (*here insert description, and if certificate be issued pursuant to any transfer referred to, insert memorandum of transfer*) is now seised of an estate in fee simple, (*here state whether in fee simple or for life*) subject to such incumbrances, liens and interests as are notified by memorandum underwritten (*or endorsed hereon*) in that piece or parcel of land known or described as follows :

In witness whereof I have hereunto signed my name and affixed my seal this   day of   .

Signed in the presence of   ⎫
             this   day ⎬
of   .   ⎭
                District Registrar for the Lands
                Titles District of

North-West Territories.

N.W.T., 1888, cap. 35.—An ordinance respecting the holding of lands in trust for Religious Societies and Congregations.

The Lieutenant-Governor, &c., enacts as follows:

1. When any religious society or congregation of Christians in the Territories desire to take a conveyance of land for the site of a church, chapel, meeting-house, burial ground or residence or glebe for the minister, or for the support of public worship and the propagation of Christian knowledge, such society or congregation may appoint trustees, to whom, and their successors, to be appointed in such manner as may be specified in the deed of conveyance, or a resolution passed in the manner provided for in the tenth section of this ordinance, the land requisite for all or any of the purposes aforesaid, may be conveyed, and such trustees, and their successors in perpetual succession, by the name expressed in the deed or resolution, may take, hold and possess the land, and maintain and defend all actions or suits for the protection thereof, or of their property therein; provided always that no religious society or congregation shall be capable of holding more than 320 acres of land, under the provisions of this ordinance.

2. Such trustees shall, within twelve months after the execution of the deed of conveyance, cause the deed to be registered in the registry office of the land registration district in which the land is situated, otherwise the said deed shall be void.

3. When a debt has been, or may hereafter be contracted, for the building, repairing, extending, or improving a church, chapel, meeting-house, or residence for the minister, on land held by trustees under the provisions of this ordinance, or for the purchase of the land on which the same has been, or is intended to be erected, the trustees, or a majority of them, may, from time to time, secure payment of the debt, or of any part thereof, with or without interest, by mortgage upon the land, church, chapel, meeting-house, or residence for the minister, or may borrow money to pay the debt, or any part thereof, and may secure the repayment of the loan, with or without interest, by a like mortgage.

4. The trustees may lease, for any length of time not exceeding 21 years, land held by them under this ordinance, or part thereof, at such rent and upon such terms as the trustees, or a majority of them, may deem reasonable, provided always that the trustees shall not lease any land which, at the time of the making of the lease, is necessary for the purpose of erecting a church, chapel, meeting-house, or residence for the minister, or for a burial ground for the religious society or congregation for whose use the land is held, and provided further, that the trustees shall not lease the land so held by them, or any part thereof, for a term exceeding 3 years, without the consent of the religious society or congregation for whose use the land is held, which consent shall be signified by resolution passed by the votes of a majority of those persons who, by the constitution of the said religious society or congregation, or by the practice of the Church with which it is connected, are entitled to vote in respect of church business, pre-

sent at a meeting of the religious society or congregation, duly called for the purpose of considering the proposed lease.

5. In any lease made under the last preceding section, the trustees may covenant or agree for the renewal thereof at the expiration of any or every term of 21 years, for a further term of 21 years, or any less period, at such rent and on such terms as may then, by the trustees for the time being, be agreed upon with the lessee, his executors, administrators or assigns, or may covenant or agree for the payment to the lessee, his executors, administrators or assigns, of the value of any buildings, or other improvements, which may, at the expiration of any term, be on the demised premises; and the mode of ascertaining the amount of such rent, or the value of such improvements, may also be provided for in the original or any subsequent lease.

6. The trustees for the time being holding land under this ordinance, which has been leased under the powers contained in the fourth and fifth sections of this ordinance, may take all such means and proceedings for the recovery of rent, or arrears of rent, which landlords are by law entitled to take.

7. When land held by trustees for the use of a religious society or congregation becomes unnecessary to be retained for such use, and it is deemed advantageous to sell the same, the trustees for the time being may give public notice of an intended sale, specifying the premises to be sold, the terms of payment, and the time of sale, and after publication of the notice, not less than once in each week for four successive weeks, in a weekly newspaper published in or near the place where the land is situated, sell the land at public auction, according to notice, but the trustees shall not be obliged to complete or carry a sale into effect if, in their judgment, an adequate price is not offered for the land; and in such a case, the trustees may, at a subsequent time, sell the land, either by public auction or private sale, but a less sum shall not be accepted at private sale than was offered at public sale.

8. Before a deed is executed in pursuance of a public or private sale, the religious society or congregation, for whose use the land is held, shall be notified and the sanction of a Judge of the Supreme Court usually exercising jurisdiction in the Judicial District in which the land is situated, obtained for the execution of the deed.

9. Trustees selling or leasing land under the authority of this ordinance shall, in the month of January in each year, at a meeting of the religious society or congregation, duly called according to the constitution thereof, or according to the practice of the church with which it is connected, have ready and open for the inspection of the said society or congregation and of any or every member thereof, a statement showing all rents which accrued during the preceding year, and all sums of money in their hands for the use and benefit of the said society or congregation, which were in any manner derived from the land under their control or subject to their management, or from the proceeds of the sale thereof, and also showing the manner in which they may have expended or dealt with the said money or any part thereof.

10. When land is granted or conveyed to trustees for the use of any religious society or congregation, and the grant or deed of con-

veyance of such land does not specify the manner in which the successors to the trustees therein named are to be appointed, the religious society or congregation for whose use such land is held, may, at a meeting of the said society or congregation, duly called according to the constitution thereof, or according to the practice of the Church with which it is connected, by the votes of a majority of those persons who, by the constitution of the said society or congregation, or by the practice of the Church with which it is connected are entitled to vote in respect of church business, then present at said meeting, pass a resolution specifying the manner in which the successors of the trustees for the time then being, are to be appointed, and such resolution endorsed on, or annexed to, the deed or conveyance under which the land is held for the use of the said society or congregation, signed by the chairman and secretary of the meeting at which the resolution is adopted, shall govern and regulate the manner in which the successors of the trustees, named in the original grant or conveyance, shall be appointed, and from and after the passing of such resolution the rovisions of this ordinance shall apply to the said society or congregation and to the trustees thereof.

11. In the case of a congregation connected with the Presbyterian Church in Canada, for the use or benefit of which land is now held, or may hereafter be held, by the Board of Management of the Church and Manse Building Fund of the Presbyterian Church in Canada for Manitoba and the North-West, pursuant to the powers contained in the Act of Parliament of Canada, passed in the 46th year of the reign of Her Majesty, and chaptered 97, incorporating the said Board of Management, or in the case of any congregation of the said Church which has received from the said Board a loan, under the provisions of the said Act, no resolution passed under the last preceding section shall have any force, or be operative, until the same has been submitted to the Board of Management, and the consent thereto of the said Board of Management has been endorsed in writing under their corporate seal.

British Columbia.

Consolidated Acts, 1888, cap. 100.—An Act respecting the property of Religious Institutions.—(*As amended by 54 Vict., c. 38.*)

Her Majesty, &c., enacts as follows :—

1. This Act may be cited as the "Religious Institutions Act."

2. Where a religious society or congregation of Christians in British Columbia desire to take a conveyance of land for the site of a church, chapel, meeting-house, school, belfry, burial-ground, residence for the minister, or for the support of public worship and the propagation of Christian knowledge, such society or congregation may appoint trustees, to whom, and their successors, to be appointed in such manner as may be specified in the deed of conveyance, the land requisite for all or any of the purposes aforesaid may be conveyed ; and such trustees and their successors in perpetual succession,

by the name expressed in the deed, may take, hold and possess the land, and maintain and defend actions for the protection thereof, and of their property therein.

3. All the rights and privileges conferred upon any religious body, society, or congregation by the last preceding section shall extend in every respect to every Church, to be exercised according to the government of the said Church.

4. *Repealed.*

5. When a debt has been, or may hereafter be contracted for the building, repairing, extending or improving of a church, meeting-house, chapel, school or belfry, on land held by trustees for the benefit of any religious society in the Province of British Columbia, or for the purchase of the land on which the same has been or is intended to be erected, the trustees or a majority of them, may from time to time secure the debt or any part thereof by a mortgage upon the land, church, meeting-house, chapel, school or belfry ; or may borrow to pay the debt or part thereof, and may secure the repayment of the loan and interest by a like mortgage upon such terms as may be agreed upon.

6. The grantees in trust named in any letters patent from the Crown, or the survivor or survivors of them, or the trustees for the time being appointed in manner prescribed in the letters patent, or other deed, whereby lands are granted for the use of a congregation or religious body, and any other trustees for the time being entitled by law to hold lands in trust for the use of a congregation or religious body, may let, for any term not exceeding 21 years, lands so held by them for the use of a congregation or religious body, at such rent and upon such terms as the trustees, or a majority of them, deem reasonable ; and in the lease they may covenant or agree for the renewal thereof at the expiration of any or every term of 21 years, for a further term of 21 years, or a less period, at such rent and upon such terms as may then by the trustees for the time being be agreed upon with the lessee, his heirs, executors, administrators or assigns, or may covenant or agree for the payment to the lessee, his executors, administrators or assigns, of the value of any buildings or other improvements which may, at the expiration of any term, be on the demised premises, and the mode of ascertaining the amount of such rent or the value of such improvements, may also be specified in the original lease.

7. But trustees shall not have the power so to let, without the consent of the congregation or religious body for whose use they hold the land in trust, such consent to be signified by the votes of a majority of the members present at a meeting of the congregation or religious body duly called for the purpose ; nor to let any land which at the time of making the lease is necessary for the purpose of erecting a church, place of worship, or other building thereon, or for a burial ground for the congregation for whose use the land is held.

8. *Repealed.*

9 Trustees selling or leasing land under the authority of this Act shall, on the first Monday in July in every year, have ready and

open for the inspection of the congregation or religious body which they represent, and of any minister (*a*) thereof, a detailed statement showing the rents which accrued during the preceding year, and all sums of money whatever in their hands, for the use and benefit of the congregation or religious body, and which were in any manner derived from the lands under their control or subject to their management, and also showing the application of any portion of the money which has been expended on behalf of the congregation or religious body.

10. The trustees for the time being entitled by law to hold lands in trust for a congregation or religious body may, in their own names or by any name by which they hold the land, sue or distrain for rent in arrear, and take all such means for the recovery thereof as landlords in other cases are entitled to take.

11. The Supreme Court may, in a summary manner on complaint upon oath by three members of a congregation or religious body of any misfeasance or misconduct on the part of trustees in the performance of duties authorized by this Act, call upon the trustees to give in an account, and may enforce the rendering of such account, the discharge of any duties, and the payment of any money, so that the congregation or religious body may have the benefit thereof, and the Court may compel the trustees, in case of any misconduct, to pay the expense of the application, or may award costs to the trustees in case the application is made on grounds which the Court considers insufficient, or frivolous, or vexatious.

12. Nothing in this Act shall empower any trustees of any religious body to occupy or use land for burial purposes within the limits of any towns or cities in British Columbia.

54 Vict., cap. 38.—An Act to amend the "Religious Institutions Act."

Her Majesty, &c., enacts as follows :—

[1. and 2. Amend section 1 and repeal sections 4 and 8, of the Religious Institutions Act.]

3. The trustees may from time to time, and at all times hereafter, acquire and hold as purchasers for the general purposes of the congregation or religious body, any lands, tenements, or hereditaments, and personal property in the Province of British Columbia ; and the same or any part thereof, from time to time may sell or exchange, mortgage, lease, let or otherwise dispose of, and with the proceeds arising therefrom, from time to time acquire other lands, tenements, hereditaments, and other property, real or personal, for the use and purposes of the congregation or religious body.

In the Province of New Brunswick there is no general Act which provides for the holding of property by trustees for churches and religious societies ; nor does there seem to be such an Act in the Province of Prince Edward Island.

(*a*) *Sic* in the Act, but no doubt a typographical error. It should read "member."

PART V.—MISCELLANEOUS STATUTES.

ONTARIO.

59 Vict., cap. 39 (O).—An Act to consolidate the Acts respecting the solemnization of Marriage.

Her Majesty, &c enacts as follows :

1. This Act may be cited as "The Marriage Act, 1896."

2. The following persons being men, and resident in Canada, may solemnize the ceremony of marriage between any two persons not under a legal disqualification to contract such marriage : (1). The ministers and clergymen of every Church and religious denomination, duly ordained or appointed according to the rites and ceremonies of the Churches or denominations to which they respectively belong. (*a*).

4.—(1). No minister, clergyman, or other person shall celebrate the ceremony of marriage between any two persons, unless duly authorized so to do by license, under the hand and seal of the Lieutenant-Governor or his deputy duly authorized in that behalf, or by a certificate under this Act, or unless the intention of the two persons to intermarry has been proclaimed once openly, and in an audible voice, either in the church, chapel, or meeting-house in which one of the parties has been in the habit of attending worship, or in some church, chapel, or meeting-house, or place of public worship of the congregation or religious community with which the minister or clergyman who performs the ceremony is connected, in the local municipality, parish, circuit, or pastoral charge, where one of the parties has, for the space of 15 days immediately preceding, had his or her usual place of abode; nor, where both parties live in the same local municipality, parish, circuit, or pastoral charge, unless there is delivered to the person proposing to celebrate the marriage a certificate (Sched. A) showing that a similar proclamation has been made in the local municipality, parish, circuit, or pastoral charge (being within Canada, where the other of the contracting parties has for the space of 15 days immediately preceding had his or her usual place of abode. (2). Every such proclamation shall be made on a Sunday, immediately before the service begins or immediately after it ends, or at some intermediate part of the service. (3). The said certificate of proclamation of intention shall be signed by the clergyman, minister, clerk, secretary, or other person who actually proclaimed the same, and shall show the official position of the person who signs it.

(*a*). Only those portions of the Act which may be of importance to Presbyterian ministers are given.

5.—(1). No marriage shall be solemnized under the authority of any proclamation of intention to inter-marry, unless such proclamation has been made at least one week previously, nor unless the marriage takes place within three months after the Sunday upon which the proclamation was made ; nor shall a marriage be solemnized under the authority of any license or certificate unless within three months after the date thereof. (2). No clergyman, minister, or other person shall solemnize a marriage between the hours of 10 p.m. and 6 a m., unless he is satisfied, from evidence adduced to him, that the proposed marriage is legal, and that exceptional circumstances exist which render its solemnization between the said hours advisable. (3). No clergyman, minister, or other person shall solemnize a marriage without the presence of at least two adult witnesses, and two or more of such witnesses shall affix their names as witnesses to the record in the register prescribed by section 24. (4). No clergyman, minister, or other person who is an issuer of marriage licenses, shall solemnize the ceremony of marriage in any case in which he has issued the license or certificate authorizing such marriage. This sub-section shall not apply to the districts of Parry Sound, Nipissing, Algoma, Manitoulin, Thunder Bay and Rainy River. (5). The certificate or license to marry, or the certificate of the publication of intention, where such certificate is required, shall be left with the clergyman, minister, or other person who solemnizes the marriage.

22. It shall not be a valid objection to the legality of a marriage that the same was not solemnized in a consecrated church or chapel, or within any particular hours. (*a*).

23. Every clergyman, minister or other person who solemnizes a marriage, and the clerk or secretary of a society of Quakers, or of the meeting at which the marriage is solemnized, shall, at the time of the marriage, if required by either of the parties thereto, give a certificate of the marriage under his hand, specifying the names of the persons married, the time of the marriage, and the names of two or more persons who witnessed it, and specifying also whether the marriage was solemnized pursuant to license or certificate under this Act, or after publication of banns ; and the clergyman, minister, clerk or secretary aforesaid, may demand twenty-five cents for the certificate given by him from the person requiring it.

24. Every clergyman, minister, or other person authorized to solemnize marriages, shall, immediately after he has solemnized marriage, enter in a marriage registry book, to be kept by him for that purpose (unless where a similar register is kept in the church at which he officiates, in which case the entries shall be made in that book) the particulars required in Sched. E to this Act (*a*), and shall authenticate the same by his signature.

25. [Sub-sections 1, 2, and 3 provide for registry books being supplied by the clerk of the peace to persons authorized to solemnize marriages.]
(4) Whenever a register is completely filled, or the person to whom it was delivered dies, it shall, unless it is the property of a

(*a*). But see *ante*, sec. 5, sub-sec. 2.

(*a*). As the book containing these particulars is supplied by the clerk of the peace, the form of this schedule is not given.

congregation whose practice it is to keep such books in the church, be delivered by such person, or his personal representatives, to the clerk of the peace from whom it was obtained, who shall note the fact of such return, with the date thereof, in the book secondly mentioned in the next preceding sub-section, and at the place where he entered the particulars required to be stated by him as mentioned in the said sub-section ; and he shall keep the register so returned amongst the records of his office. He shall also state in such note whether the register was returned on account of the death of the holder or on account of its being filled.

(5) No clergyman, minister, or other person, shall be furnished with a second or subsequent register, until he has returned the register which he had previously obtained, or has properly accounted in writing for its non-return ; and when the register is not returned the explanation shall be shortly noted in the said book required to be kept by the clerk of the peace under sub-section 3, at the place where the particulars of the delivery of the unreturned register appear.

26. The registry book, by whomsoever furnished, shall be the property of the denomination to which the clergyman, minister, or other person, to whom it is delivered, belongs at the time of the delivery thereof to him, and in case he is in charge of a particular congregation of such denomination, it shall belong to the trustees or other body in which the property of the church or meeting house used by such congregation for its ordinary services is vested.

---

59 Vict., cap. 17, (O).—An Act revising and consolidating the Acts respecting the registration of Births, Marriages and Deaths. (*a*)

20. Every clergyman, minister, or other person authorized by law to celebrate marriages, shall report every marriage he celebrates to the registrar of the division within which the marriage is celebrated, within thirty days from the date of the marriage, with the particulars required in the form provided under this Act, and in order the better to enable the clergyman, minister, or other person to make the report as aforesaid, he shall be furnished by the division registrar of the division in which he resides with blank forms containing the particulars required under this Act. (*b*)

24. The caretaker or owner of any cemetery or burial ground, whether public or private, or any clergyman having charge of a church to which a burial ground is attached, shall not permit the interment of the dead body of any person in the burial ground over which he has charge, unless he has received a certificate under the hand of the division registrar of the division in which the death took place, that the particulars of the death have been duly registered. He shall further be required, before the last day of June and of December in each year, to supply to the registrar of the division in which the burial ground is situate, a list of the number of burials therein during the previous half-year, giving the names of the persons whose bodies are therein buried, and the dates on which the interment took place.

(*a*) Only those sections which seem important for ministers to know are given here.

(*b*) Neglect to make reports required by this Act renders the defaulter liable to a penalty of not less than $1, nor more than $10 and costs, in the discretion of the magistrate before whom the case is heard.—Section 28.

QUEBEC.

CIVIL CODE, TITLE 2—ACTS OF CIVIL STATUS.

Chap. I.—*General Provisions.*

39. In acts of civil status nothing is to be inserted, either by note or recital, but what it is the duty of the parties to declare.

40. In cases where the parties are not obliged to appear in person at the making of an act of civil status, they may be represented by an attorney, specially authorized to that effect.

41. The public officer reads to the parties, or to their attorney and to the witnesses, the act which he makes.

42. Acts of civil status are inscribed in two registers of the same tenor, kept for each Roman Catholic parish church, each Protestant church or congregation, or other religious community, entitled by law to keep such registers, each of which is authentic, and has in law equal authority. (*a*)

43. The registers are furnished by the churches, congregations, or religious communities, and must be in the form prescribed by the code of civil procedure.

44. The registers are kept by the rector, curate or other priest or minister having charge of the churches, congregations, or religious communities, or by any other officer entitled to do so.

45. The duplicate register so kept, before it is used, must, at the instance of the party keeping it, be presented to one of the judges of the Superior Court, or to the prothonotary of the district, or to the clerk of the Circuit Court instead of the prothonotary, in the case specified in the statute, 25 Vict., cap. 16, to be by such judge, prothonotary or clerk, numbered and initialed in the manner prescribed by the code of civil procedure.

46. Acts of civil status, as soon as they are made, are inscribed in the two registers, in successive order and without blanks; erasures and marginal notes are acknowledged and initialed by all those who sign the body of the act. Everything must be written at length without abbreviation or figures.

47. Within the first six weeks of each year, the person who kept the said registers, or who has charge thereof, deposits in the prothonotary's office of the Superior Court of his district, or in the office of the clerk of the Circuit Court in the cases provided for in the statute already mentioned in the present chapter, one of the said duplicates, the delivery of which is acknowledged by a receipt which the said prothonotary or clerk is bound to give free of charge.

(*a*) **Clergymen** of the Presbyterian Church in Canada have the right to solemnize marriages and to keep registers of civil status, and to record births, marriages and deaths. 38 Vict., c. 62, s. 7 (Q).

48. Within six months after such deposit, each prothonotary or clerk is bound to verify the condition of the registers deposited in his office, and to draw up a summary report of each verification.

49. The other duplicate register remains in the custody and possession of the priest, minister or other officer who kept the same; to be by him preserved and transmitted to his successor in office.

50. The depositary of either of the registers is bound to give extracts thereof to any person who may require the same; and such extracts, being certified and signed by him are authentic.

51. On proof that, in any parish or religious community no registers have been kept, or that they are lost, the births, marriages and deaths may be proved either by family registers and papers, or other writings, or by witnesses.

52. Every depositary of such registers is civilly responsible for any alteration made therein, saving his recourse, if any there be, against the party altering the same.

53. Every infraction of any article of this title by any of the officers therein named, which does not amount to a criminal offence, and which is not punishable as such, is punished by a penalty not exceeding $80 nor less than $8.

Chap. II.—*Acts of Birth.*

54. Acts of birth set forth the day of the birth of the child, that of its baptism (if performed), its sex, and the names given to it; the names, surnames, occupation and domicile of the father and mother, and also of the sponsors, if any there be.

55. These acts are signed on both registers, by the officer officiating, by the father and mother if present, and by the sponsors, if any there be; if any of them cannot sign, their declaration to that effect is noted.

56. When the father and mother of any child presented to the public officer are either or both of them unknown, the fact is entered in the register.

Chap. III.—*Acts of Marriage.*

57. Before solemnizing a marriage, the officer who is to perform the ceremony must be furnished with a certificate establishing that the publication of banns required by law has been duly made; unless he has published them himself, in which case such certificate is not necessary.

58. This certificate, which is signed by the person who published the banns, mentions, as do also the banns themselves, the names, surnames, qualities or occupations, and domiciles of the parties to be married, and whether they are of age or minors; the names, surnames, occupations, and domiciles of their fathers and mothers, or of the name of the former husband or wife. And mention is made of this certificate in the act of marriage.

59. The marriage ceremony may, however, be performed without this certificate, if the parties have obtained and produce a dispensation or license from a competent authority, authorizing the omission of the publication of banns.

60. If the marriage be not solemnized within one year from the last of the publications required, they are no longer sufficient, and must be renewed.

61. In the case of an opposition, the disallowance thereof must be obtained and certified to the officer charged with the solemnization of the marriage.

62. If, however, the opposition be founded on a simple promise of marriage, it is of no effect, and the marriage may be proceeded with as if no such opposition had been made.

63. The marriage is solemnized at the place of the domicile of one or other of the parties. If solemnized elsewhere, the person officiating is obliged to verify and ascertain the identity of the parties. For the purposes of marriage, domicile is established by a residence of six months in the same place.

64. The act is signed by the officer who solemnizes the marriage, by the parties, and by at least two witnesses, related or not, who have been present at the ceremony; and if any of them cannot sign, their declaration to that effect is noted.

65. In this act are set forth: (1). The day on which the marriage was solemnized. (2). The names, surnames, quality or occupation and domicile of the parties married, the names of the father and mother of each, or the name of the former husband or wife. (3). Whether the parties are of age or minors. (4). Whether they were married after publication of banns, or with a dispensation or license. (5). Whether it was with the consent of their father, mother, tutor or curator, or with the advice of a family council, when such consent or advice is required. (6). The names of the witnesses, and whether they are related or allied to the parties, and if so, on which side and in what degree. (7). That there has been no opposition, or that any opposition made has been disallowed.

Chap. IV.—*Acts of Burial.*

66. No burial can take place before the expiration of twenty-four hours after the decease; and whoever knowingly takes part in any burial before the expiration of such time, except in cases provided for by police regulations, is subject to a penalty of $20.

67. The act of burial mentions the day of the burial, and that of the death, if known; the names, surnames, and quality or occupation of the deceased; and it is signed by the person performing the burial service, and by two of the nearest relations or friends then present; if they cannot sign, mention is made thereof.

Chap. VI.—*Rectification of Acts and Registers of Civil Status.*

75. If any error have been committed in the entry made in the register of an act of civil status, the court of original jurisdiction in the

office of which such register is, or is to be deposited may, at the instance of any interested party, order such error to be rectified in presence of the other parties interested.

76. The depositaries of the registers, on receipt of a copy of any judgment of rectification, are bound to inscribe the same on the margin of the act so rectified, and if there be no margin, then on a sheet of paper which remains annexed thereto.

77. If any act which ought to have been inserted in the register be entirely omitted, the same court may, at the instance of one of the parties interested, the others being notified, order that such omission be supplied, and the judgment so ordering is inscribed on the margin of the said register, at the place where the act so omitted ought to have been entered, and if there be no margin, then on a sheet of paper which remains annexed thereto.

TITLE 5.—OF MARRIAGE.

Chap. II.—*Formalities Relating to the Solemnization of Marriage.*

128. Marriage must be solemnized openly, by a competent officer recognized by law.

129. All priests, rectors, ministers and other officers authorized by law to keep registers of acts of civil status are competent to solemnize marriage. But none of the officers thus authorized can be compelled to solemnize a marriage to which any impediment exists, according to the doctrine and belief of his religion, and the discipline of the Church to which he belongs.

130. The publication of banns, required by articles 57 and 58, are made by the priest, minister, or other officer in the church to which the parties belong, at morning service, or if there be no morning service, at evening service, on three Sundays or holidays, with reasonable intervals. If the parties belong to different churches, these publications take place in each of such churches.

131. If the actual domicile of the parties to be married has not been established by a residence of six months, at least, the publications must also be made at the place of their last domicile in Lower Canada.

132. If their last domicile be out of Lower Canada and the publications have not been made there, the officer who, in that case, solemnizes the marriage, is bound to ascertain that there is no legal impediment between the parties.

133. If the parties, or either of them be, in so far as regards marriage, under the authority of others, the banns must be published at the place of domicile of those under whose power such parties are.

Nova Scotia.

Rev. Stat. N. S.—5th Series, cap. 93.—Of the solemnization of Marriage (*a*).

6. Every person recognized as a duly ordained clergyman or minister by any congregation or body of Christians within this Province, may solemnize marriage by license, or after publication of banns, in conformity with the provisions of this chapter.

7. No person shall officiate in the solemnization of any marriage, unless notice of such marriage shall have been given publicly during the time of divine service at three several meetings, at a place of public worship, on two or more Sundays, provided there shall be more than one public service in the said place of worship on each Sunday, otherwise at two several meetings on two Sundays, in the place where at least one of the parties resides, or unless a license shall have been obtained as herein prescribed for the solemnization of such marriage.

8. The officiating clergyman or minister of a congregation at the place where either of the parties desiring to be married resides, shall give the notices in the preceding section mentioned, after having been requested to do so, unless in cases where compliance would be illegal or inconsistent with the rules and discipline of the Church or congregation to which the clergyman, minister, or parties respectively belong.

14. Every clergyman authorized by law to perform the marriage ceremony shall apply for, and shall on application obtain from the nearest issuer or deputy registrar, forms, in which he shall register with the required particulars, all the marriages celebrated by him, whether by banns, license or otherwise. But this shall not be construed to interfere with the keeping of any other marriage register he may be otherwise required, or may see proper, to keep.

15. Every clergyman shall return to the issuer or deputy registrar, by whom the same is subscribed, every marriage license used by him for the celebration of marriage within 10 days after such celebration, with the blank certificate endorsed thereon, fully filled in and subscribed by himself, stating the fact of the celebration, the names, abodes and additions of the couple married, the time and place of such marriage, and the names of at least two persons present thereat besides himself.

18. Every clergyman or minister shall keep a register of all marriages solemnized by him, whether by banns or license by filling up a blank form with all the particulars required concerning each marriage, and shall return it along with the license, or by itself, if such marriage has been solemnized by banns, to the nearest issuer of marriage licenses, or the issuer from whom the license was received, within 10 days after such celebration, and shall be entitled to receive twenty-five cents for each return of marriage so made, provided it has been made conformably to law.

(*a*) Only those sections important to ministers are given here. The 58th Vict. c. 10 (N. S.) amending this Act relates solely to marriages by officers of the Salvation Army.

New Brunswick.

Con. Stat., N. B., cap. 71.—Solemnization of Marriage (*a*).

1. Every Christian minister or teacher duly ordained according to the rites and ceremonies of the denomination to which he belongs, (or by the rules of such denomination deemed and recognized as a duly ordained minister or teacher by virtue of any prior ordination) being a British subject, having charge of a congregation in this Province or connected therewith, may solemnize marriage by license or publication of banns.

2. Whenever any person shall make it satisfactorily appear by petition to the Governor in Council, that he is a regularly ordained minister of the denomination of Christians to which he belongs, and is the settled pastor of a church or congregation, and is not engaged in any secular calling, but being an alien cannot solemnize marriage, the Governor in Council may, by license under his hand and seal, authorize such person to solemnize marriage by license or publication of banns, so long as he remains the pastor of such church or congregation.

3. The Governor in Council may revoke such last mentioned license at any time on sufficient cause.

6. Publication of banns shall be made by proclaiming, with an audible voice, during divine service, on three Sundays successively, such intended marriage, in some church, chapel, or other place of meeting for religious worship, in the parish where either of the parties reside.

7. No person shall knowingly solemnize any marriage where either party is under the age of twenty-one years, without the consent of the father or guardian.

8. Every marriage shall be solemnized in the presence of two or more credible witnesses, besides the person celebrating the same; immediately thereafter a certificate thereof to the following effect shall be made, that is to say:

A. B., of the parish (*or* city) of   , and C. D., of the parish (*or* city) of   , were married by banns (*or* license) with consent of father (*or* guardian) in the year   , by me

E. F. } Rector, &c.
      } (*as the case may be.*)

This marriage was solemnized between us.   A. B.
In presence of G. H.   C. D.
               I. K.

Which shall be transmitted forthwith by the person celebrating such marriage, to the clerk of the peace of the county (*b*) in which the

---

(*a*) Only the sections important to ministers are given here.

(*b*) This is not now required. See *post*, 50 Vict., c. 5, s. 10. (N. B.)

marriage was solemnized, and immediately registered in full, and filed, endorsed with the day of the registry and page of the book in which it is registered.

11. A copy of the record of the certificate, certified by the clerk of the peace, shall be evidence of the marriage without further proof.

15. Every person authorized to solemnize marriage shall on or immediately after the first day of January in every year, forward to the Secretary (*c*) a list of the marriages celebrated by him for the year preceding, specifying whether by license or banns, with the number and date of the license and date of the marriage.

17. The clergyman or other person celebrating the marriage may demand and receive from the parties, for preparing and transmitting the certificate of the marriage to the clerk of the peace, the sum of fifty cents.

---

43 Vict., cap. 16 (N.B.).—An Act in amendment of the law relating to the solemnization of Marriage, and to remove doubts as to Marriages in certain cases.

Be it enacted, etc., as follows :—

1. Whenever any person shall make it satisfactorily appear by petition to the Lieutenant-Governor-in-Council, that he is a regularly ordained minister of the denomination of Christians to which he belongs, and the settled pastor of a church or congregation, and is not engaged in any secular calling, but being an alien cannot solemnize marriage, the Lieutenant-Governor-in-Council may by license under his hand and seal authorize such person to solemnize marriage by license or publication of banns, so long as he shall be the minister or pastor of any church or congregation in this Province, of the denomination of Christians to which he belongs, or of any other denomination of Christians to which he may have attached himself within this Province ; and the said license shall continue to be in full force so long as he shall continue to be the minister or pastor of any church or congregation of the same or any other denomination of Christians, and shall not cease or determine or become invalid or inoperative upon or by reason of his changing or having changed from the ministry or pastorate of one church or congregation to the ministry or pastorate of another church or congregation of the same or any other denomination of Christians within this Province.

---

57 Vict., cap. 27 (N.B.)—An Act further to amend the law relating to the solemnization of Marriage.

Be it enacted, etc., as follows :—

1. In addition to the persons lawfully authorized to solemnize marriage in this Province, any Christian minister or teacher being a

---

(*c*). "Secretary" is the Provincial Secretary.

British subject and resident in the Province, duly ordained according to the rites and ceremonies of the denomination of Christians to which he belongs, and having been formerly in charge of a congregation in this Province, who has been superannuated, or placed on the supernumerary list, or is a retired minister or clergyman in good standing with his denomination (though not in charge of a congregation) may solemnize marriage by license.

---

50 Vict., cap. 5, (N.B.)—An Act to provide for the registration of Births, Deaths and Marriages. (a) (*As amended by 52 Vict., c. 11.*)

6. Every clergyman, teacher, minister or other person who shall perform the rite of baptism, or shall solemnize a marriage, or perform a funeral service in New Brunswick, shall keep a register showing the persons whom he has baptised or married, or who have died within his cure and belonging to his congregation, upon whose burial he has performed the funeral service, and such clergyman, teacher, minister or other person shall make returns of births and marriages not less frequently than every three months, according to the forms prescribed, so far as they are able to fill up the same, and such clergyman, teacher, minister or other person in this section named furnishing to the registrar the information and returns provided by law in respect to births, funerals and marriages, shall be paid by the treasurer of the county (on the certificate of the division registrar of the services performed and entitled to be paid for) five cents for the return of each birth, marriage or funeral, which sum shall include charges for postage.

10. Every clergyman, minister, or other person authorized by law to celebrate marriages, shall be required to report each and every marriage he celebrates to the registrar of the division within which such marriage is celebrated within 90 days from the date of such marriage, with the particulars required by Sch. B. appended to this Act, (b) including the certificate of such marriage as required by section 8 of chapter 71 of the Consolidated Statutes, and in order the better to enable the said clergyman, minister or other person to make such report and forward such certificate as aforesaid, he shall be furnished by the division registrar of the division in which he resides with blank forms containing the particulars required by the said Sch. B., but it shall not be necessary for the person celebrating any marriage to forward a certificate thereof to the clerk of the peace, as required by sections 8 and 9 of chapter 71 of the Consolidated Statutes.

13. Every minister or other person who buries or performs any funeral or religious service for the burial of any dead body, unless he has received a certificate within 90 days under the hand of the registrar of the division in which the death took place, according to the Sch. D to this Act annexed, that the particulars of such death have been duly registered, shall after the expiration of 90 days make a return of such death according to Sch. C. to this Act annexed, to the registrar of the division in which the death took place.

(*a*). Only the sections which seem important to ministers are given.

(*b*). The schedules referred to in this and the next section are not given here because the Act provides for forms being supplied to those required to make returns.

Prince Edward Island.

Rev. Stat., 2 Wm. 4, cap. 14.—An Act to confirm and render valid certain Marriages heretofore solemnized within this island; and also to declare by whom and in what manner Marriages shall be celebrated in future, and to provide for the public registry of the same.

2. And be it further enacted, that every clergyman or minister, of any sect or denomination of Christians, having spiritual charge of a congregation within this island, upon producing to the Lieutenant-Governor or other commander-in-chief for the time being, satisfactory proof of his ordination, constitution or appointment, and that he is actually employed by the denomination of which he professes to be a minister within this colony, and receiving a certificate to that effect under the hand and seal of the Lieutenant-Governor or commander-in-chief for the time being, and all others whom the Lieutenant-Governor or commander-in-chief for the time being may thereto authorize, shall hereafter have power and authority to solemnize marriages, either by license from the Lieutenant-Governor, or after publication of banns in their respective church, chapel, or other place of public worship, on three successive Sundays, during divine service, provided always that nothing in this Act contained, shall extend, or be construed to extend, to prevent any clergyman regularly ordained according to the rites of the Church of England, Kirk of Scotland, Church of Rome, Presbyterians being dissenters from the Kirk of Scotland, the Wesleyans, Methodists, and Baptists respectively, and having respectively within this island spiritual charge of a congregation, from solemnizing marriage according to the forms of their own respective Churches, without having obtained such certificate as is hereinafter mentioned.

4. And be it further enacted, that all marriages shall be celebrated in the presence of two or more credible witnesses, besides the minister, clergyman, justice of the peace, or other person authorized to solemnize matrimony, who shall solemnize the same; and that after the solemnization thereof, such parties so authorized to solemnize marriage contracts shall, and they are hereby required to transmit, within the period of six months, a certificate of the celebration of each marriage by them performed, together with the names of the parties witnessing the same, to the Surrogate of the island, which certificate shall be in the manner and form following:

Names of Parties.	Whether Bachelor or Widower, Spinster or Widow.	Date of Celebration.	By License or Banns.	Names of Witnesses.

I hereby certify that the above named parties were married by me this day, under license from the Lieutenant-Governor (or by publication of banns, *as the case may be*), in the presence of the above named witnesses.

Dated at   this   day of   , 18 .

                                                        A. B.

and the said Surrogate is hereby required, on receiving the fee hereinafter mentioned, to record the said certificate in a book to be kept for that purpose, a certified copy of which record, under his hand and seal, shall be deemed due and sufficient evidence in any court of law or equity, to establish the proof of such marriage, in all cases where the testimony of none of the witnesses to such marriage can be obtained.

7. And whereas, it may happen that some person or persons within age, whose parent or parents are either deceased or absent, may be desirous to contract matrimony, but by reason of his or her having no parent or guardian living, or present, to consent thereto, no license can be obtained : be it therefore enacted, that in each and every such case, and in all other cases not hereby especially provided for, it shall and may be lawful for any person authorized to solemnize marriages, where required, to inquire into the propriety of any such marriage being contracted, by examining the said parties, or such other persons as he may deem necessary, and if he shall be satisfied of the propriety thereof, he shall certify his consent thereto, whereupon a license may be issued in like manner as upon consent of parents and guardians, or the marriage may be celebrated after proclamation of banns, as may be required by the parties.

MANITOBA.

REV. STAT. MAN., cap. 94.—An Act respecting the solemnization of Marriages (*a*).

3. The ministers and clergymen of every Church or religious denomination, duly ordained or appointed according to the rites and ceremonies of the Churches, denominations, or religious bodies to which they respectively belong, may, by virtue of such ordination or appointment, and according to the rites and usages of such Churches, denominations, or religious bodies respectively, solemnize or perform the ceremony of marriage between any two persons not under a legal disqualification or disability to contract such marriage (*b*).

4. No minister or clergyman shall celebrate the ceremony of marriage between any two persons, unless said persons have obtained a license therefor, duly authorized under the hand of the Minister, or

---

(*a*). Only those sections which are important for ministers are given here.

(*b*). By 57 Vict., c. 17, s. 2 (M), a sub-section was added, but it relates solely to Jewish marriages.

Acting Minister of Agriculture and Immigration, in the form given in Sched. A to this Act, or unless the intention of the two persons to intermarry has been proclaimed once, openly and in an audible voice, either in the church, chapel, or meeting house in which one of the parties has been in the habit of attending worship, or in some church, chapel, meeting house, or place of public worship of the congregation or religious community with which the minister or clergyman who performs the ceremony is connected, in the municipality, parish, circuit or pastoral charge where one of the parties has, for the space of at least 15 days immediately preceding, had his or her usual place of abode: such proclamation to be made on a Sunday, immediately before the service begins, or immediately after it ends, or at some intermediate part of the service.

5. It shall be competent for the head of the Church or congregation to which one of the parties belongs, to grant a dispensation of such forms, according to the rites and usages of such Church or congregation (*c*), and such dispensation shall have the same effect as a marriage license issued under the Act, and the same fee exacted for a marriage license shall be payable to the Treasurer of the Province in connection with such dispensation.

19. It shall not be a valid objection to the legality of a marriage that the same was not solemnized in a consecrated church or chapel, or within any particular hours.

20. Every minister or clergyman who celebrates a marriage shall, if required at the time of the marriage by either of the parties thereto, give a certificate of the marriage under his hand, (*d*) specifying the names of the persons married, the time of the marriage, and the names of two or more persons who witnessed it, and specifying also whether the marriage was solemnized pursuant to license under this Act, or after publication of banns, and the minister or clergyman may demand $1 for the certificate given by him from the person requiring it.

21. Every minister or clergyman shall, immediately after he has solemnized a marriage, enter in a book kept by him for the purpose, a true record of the marriage, which record shall specify all the particulars required by Sch. B. to "The Vital Statistics Act." (*e*).

(*c*). This section was probably inserted in the Act to prevent any question arising as to the validity of the practice of the Roman Catholic Church. That Church has always claimed the right to grant such a dispensation, alleging that the bishops had authority to do so in France and in Canada, which was preserved to them by the provision in the Treaty of Paris, that His Majesty "agrees to grant the liberty of the Catholic religion to the inhabitants of Canada; he will consequently give the most precise and most effectual orders, that his new Roman Catholic subjects may profess the worship of their religion, according to the rites of the Romish Church, so far as the laws of Great Britain permit." This was confirmed by the Imperial Act, 14 Geo. III., c 83, s. 5, which provides that "the clergy of the said Church may hold, receive and enjoy their accustomed dues and rights, with respect to such persons only as shall profess the said religion." About 30 years ago a question was raised in an Ontario court as to the validity of a Roman Catholic marriage in that province without license or banns, but the case was never decided.

(*d*). A certificate of a priest given sixteen years after the marriage, was spoken of as "mere hearsay evidence, and that of a very dangerous character," and held, inadmissable as evidence. *Gaines* v. *Relf*, 53 U. S. Supreme Court Rep. 472.

(*e*) Rev. Stat. Man., c. 149.

22. Each municipal clerk shall, at the expense of the municipality of which he is clerk, from time to time, on demand, furnish all ministers or clergymen exercising the functions of their ministry within the municipality, with registers on which to keep the records, as provided in the preceding section hereto.

23. The registers mentioned in the next preceding section, by whomsoever furnished, shall be the property of the Church or denomination to which the minister or clergyman, clerk or secretary, belongs at the time of the first marriage which he records therein.

REV. STAT. MAN., cap. 149.—An Act respecting the registration of Births, Marriages and Deaths (*a*).

12. Every clergyman, minister or other person authorized by law to baptize, marry or perform funeral services shall keep registers in such forms as may from time to time be fixed by the Minister, (*b*) showing the persons whom he baptizes or marries, or who die within his cure or congregation, or over whose bodies he may perform funeral service.

13. Each municipal clerk shall, at the expense of the municipality of which he is clerk, from time to time, on demand, furnish all clergymen or ministers exercising the functions of their ministry within the municipality with registers in which to keep the records as required in this section.

14. These books shall be the property of the church to which the clergyman or minister belonged at the time of the first marriage or baptism entry or funeral service which he records therein, and shall thereafter be kept as a record in the said church, or, in case of abandonment of the said church, the said books shall be filed with the Department. (*c*)

18. Every clergyman, minister or other person authorized by law to celebrate marriage shall be required to report each marriage he celebrates to the clerk of the municipality in which such marriage is celebrated, within 30 days from the date of such marriage, with the particulars required by Sch. B to this Act, (*d*) and in order the better to enable the said clergyman, minister or other person to make such report as aforesaid, he shall be furnished, on demand, by the clerk of the municipality in which he resides, with blank forms containing the particulars required by such form.

22. The body of a person shall not be interred within the limits of any municipality, or in any cemetery or burial ground owned by any municipality, or generally used for the interment of persons dying in such municipality, or owned by any congregation or church holding

(*a*). Only those sections of the Act, a knowledge of which is important for our ministers, are given here.

(*b*). In this Act the expression the "Minister" means the Minister of Agriculture and Immigration.

(*c*). "Department" means the Department of Agriculture and Immigration.

(*d*). As books and forms showing the particulars required are supplied by the municipality, it has not been considered necessary to print the schedules here.

its services within the limits of such municipality, until after the particulars of the death of such person have been registered with the clerk of the municipality in which it occurs, and any clergyman or any caretaker or superintendent of any cemetery or burial ground such as referred to in this section, allowing a body to be interred without first receiving a certificate in the form in Sch. D. to this Act, under the hand of the clerk of the municipality in which the death occurred, that the particulars thereof have been duly registered, shall be liable to a fine of $50.

24. Every superintendent or caretaker of any cemetery or burial ground, whether public or private, shall keep a book (*e*) in such form as may from time to time be fixed by the Minister, in which he shall record all interments made in such cemetery or burial ground; and on or before the seventh day of each month, he shall transmit to the clerk of the municipality within which such cemetery or burial ground is situate, or, in case such cemetery or burial ground is not owned by such municipality or by any church, congregation or person therein, then to the clerk of the municipality by which it is owned or in which the church, congregation or person owning it is situate, a copy of such record for the month next preceding, certified under his hand ; and the particulars as transmitted shall be entered by the municipal clerk on the form supplied him for death returns, provided the particulars contained in such copy received have not previously been entered in such form.

26. Every clergyman, minister or other person who buries or performs any funeral or religious service for the burial of any body, unless he has received a certificate under the hand of the clerk of the municipality in which the death took place, according to the form referred to in the 20th section (*f*) herein, that the particulars of such death have been duly registered, shall within one month after such burial make a return of such death according to Sch. C. to this Act, (*g*) to the clerk of the municipality in which the death took place.

NORTHWEST TERRITORIES.

ORD. 1888, No. 29.—An Ordinance respecting Marriages (*As amended by Ord. 1892, No. 25, and Ord. 1894, No. 37*.

2. The ministers and clergymen of every Church and religious denomination, duly ordained and appointed according to the rites and ceremonies of the Churches and denominations to which they respectively belong, and resident in Canada, in the Territories, by virtue of such ordination and appointment and according to the

---

(*e*). By section 25 a book is to be supplied by the clerk of the municipality.

(*f*). That section requires the municipal clerk, after receiving from the occupant of the house in which a death takes place certain particulars, to give on demand a certificate for the purpose of burial.

(*g*). The particulars required are : Name and surname of deceased, date and place of death, sex, age, occupation or calling, religious denomination, where born, cause of death and duration of illness, name of physician, if any, name description and residence of informant.

rites and usages of their own respective Churches or denominations, and commissioners and staff officers of the Salvation Army, and commissioners appointed for that purpose by the Lieutenant-Governor, may solemnize marriage between any two persons not under legal disqualification to contract marriage.

3. No minister or clergyman shall solemnize marriage unless the parties to the intended marriage produce to him the license required by section 4 of this Ordinance; or unless the intention of the two persons to intermarry has been proclaimed by the publication of banns at least thrice openly on two successive Sundays in some public religious assembly.

ORD., 1888, No. 6.—An Ordinance respecting the registration of Births, Marriages and Deaths.

12. Every clergyman, minister, or other person, authorized by law to celebrate marriages, shall be required to report every marriage he celebrates to the registrar of the division, within which the marriage is celebrated, within 90 days from the date of the marriage, with the particulars required by Sch. B. of this Ordinance, (*a*) and in order the better to enable the clergyman, minister or other person to make the report as aforesaid, he shall be furnished by the division registrar of the division in which he resides, with blank forms containing the particulars required by Sch. B.

15. Every minister or other person, who buries or performs any funeral or religious service for the burial of any dead body, unless he has received a certificate under the hand of the registrar of the division in which the death took place, according to the Sch. D. to this Ordinance annexed, that the particulars of the death have been duly registered, shall make a return of the death, according to Sch. C. to this Ordinance annexed, to the registrar of the division in which the death took place, within seven days after the burial, unless within the time aforesaid the minister or other person gives to the registrar a written notice under his hand stating according to his knowledge, information and belief, the name and residence of the deceased, and the date and place at which the burial took place, or at which the service was performed, either without or with any of the other particulars mentioned in said Sch. C. (*b*)

(*a*) As blanks containing the particulars are supplied by the registrar, the Sch. has not been printed.

(*b*) The particulars in Sch. C. are—Name and surname of deceased—when died—sex—age—Rank or profession—where from—certified cause of death and duration of illness—name of physician, if any—signature, description and residence of informant—religious denomination.

British Columbia.

Consolidated Acts, B. C., 1888, cap. 79.—An Act to regulate the solemnization of Marriage. (*a*)

Her Majesty, &c., enacts as follows :—

4. The ministers and clergymen of every Church and religious denomination in British Columbia, and the registrars appointed by the Lieutenant-Governor-in-Council under this Act, may celebrate a marriage between any two persons, neither of whom shall be under legal disqualification to contract such marriage.

5. Such minister or clergyman may celebrate a marriage according to the rites and usages of the Church or denomination to which they respectively belong, between any two such persons, when authorized to do so by license, under the hand and seal of the Lieutenant-Governor or his Deputy, or (if not so authorized) then, except as is hereinafter enacted, (*b*) by the publication of the banns of such marriage openly, and in an audible voice, in any church, chapel or place of public worship of the congregation or religious community with which the minister or clergyman is connected, on three successive Sundays, during divine service, together with the number of such proclamation as being the first, second, or third time of asking.

10. All marriages celebrated under the provisions of this Act, by any clergyman, minister or registrar, must be in the presence of two or more credible witnesses besides himself, and such ceremony must be performed in a public manner, and with open doors (save when otherwise permitted by license).

15. All ministers, clergymen and registrars shall, at the time of each marriage, enter a memorandum of such marriage in a book to be kept by them respectively for that purpose ; and every such registration shall be signed by each of the parties, the minister or registrar, or other duly authorized person officiating at the time, and witnessed by at least two credible witnesses, and shall be kept in the form of Sch. D. hereto ; all such registrations shall be open to the inspection of the public, and a certified copy of any such registration shall be given to any person demanding the same, on payment of one dollar, and certified copies of such register books shall be sent by each minister, clergyman, registrar, or other authorized person aforesaid, twice in each year, viz. : on the 1st day of January, and on the 1st day of July, to the Registrar-General, to be kept by him open for public inspection and to be copied as aforesaid upon payment of the said fee.

(*a*) Only those sections of the Act useful for ministers to know are given here.

(*b*) The only exception appearing in the Act seems to be, that under sec. 21, the marriage must take place within three calender months after the date of the license, or the complete publication of the banns, otherwise the banns or license shall be absolutely void.

Schedule D.

Marriage Certificate.

Marriages solemnized in the district of

No.	When Married.	Name and Surname.	Age	Condition.	Rank or Profession.	Residence	Place of Birth	Father's Name and Surname	Rank or Profession of Father.

Married at   , according to the rites and ceremonies of (*here church or denomination to be inserted*) by (*banns or license*).

This marriage was solemnized by us—

        A. B.
        C. D.,

in the presence of us—   E. F.,
                            G. H.

            (Signature of the minister or clergyman).

PART VI.—RESOLUTIONS OF GENERAL ASSEMBLY.

AGENTS OF THE CHURCH.

Minutes, 1876, p. 77.—The Assembly defined the duties of the agent of the Eastern section of the Church as follows :—

1. He shall act as secretary of the home and foreign mission boards in the Eastern section of the Church, and of the board of superintendence of the theological hall at Halifax. As such, he shall convene the boards, keep the minutes, and conduct all correspondence connected with the same. Under home mission work shall be included the distribution of probationers. He shall also prepare and submit to the Assembly the annual reports of the boards.

2. He shall act as general treasurer for all the schemes, with the exception of the ministers' widows' and orphans' fund, in the Eastern section of the Church. As such, it shall be his duty:—(1). To receive and administer all funds contributed to the schemes. (2) To take the general management of all the funds, make investments of the same, and collect interest. (3). To transact all the financial business of the schemes, make all payments connected with the same, and prepare the annual accounts. (4). To transact all the business of the home fund for church building, under the charge of the Synod of the Maritime Provinces ; it being understood that that fund shall bear its due proportion, with other funds, of his salary as agent.

Minutes, 1896, p. 52 (a).—1, That the duties of the Rev. Dr. Warden, the general agent of the Church, Western section, be as follows, viz.:—
He shall act as general agent and treasurer for the several schemes in the Western section of the Church, including French evangelization —this last item meanwhile for the period of one year. In this capacity it shall be his duty : (1) to prepare and issue notices and circulars as to the collections and contributions ordered by the Assembly, and correspond with defaulting congregations ; (2) to receive and acknowledge all sums contributed to the schemes ; (3) to make all payments for the home mission, augmentation and foreign mission schemes, keep the accounts and prepare periodical statements, as well as annual financial reports ; (4) to manage the ministers' widows'

(a). These provisions overrule the former resolutions as to the duties of the agent in Western section   *See Minutes, 1876, p. 77.*

and orphans' fund, and to be treasurer of the aged and infirm ministers fund, the collection of rates, &c., for this fund to be left with the committee, as already fixed by the Assembly ; (5) to receive the payments for the Assembly fund, and discharge all accounts pertaining to the general business of the Church, and that during the continuance of the arrangement reported by the board of management of Knox College, in their report to this Assembly, (*b*) which report has been already adopted by the Assembly, he shall act as treasurer of the funds of Knox College.

2. That the salary of the general agent of the Church, Western section, shall be $3,000 per year. The proportion of the salary to be paid by the several funds shall be fixed by the finance committee, after full investigation and conference with the conveners of the committees charged with the administration of said funds, and also the proportion of said funds shall be fixed in the same manner.

3. That it be remitted to the board of the Presbyterian College, Montreal, to make such interim arrangements for the current year regarding the treasurership of the college as they may deem advisable.

4. That the Rev. Dr. Warden be, and hereby is authorized to employ whatever assistance he may require in the discharge of duties before mentioned.

Calling and Settling of Ministers.

Minutes 1895, pp. 33, 34.—The report of the committee to consider the question of the calling and settling of ministers and cognate matters was received, and the following resolutions and recommendations adopted : (1) That there are no evils connected with the settlement of ministers, generally, throughout the Church so serious as to call for, or as would justify departure from the principles of the Church by adopting regulations which would affect the permanency of the pastoral relation. (2) That no plan can be devised which would be in all respects applicable to the widely varying circumstances of the Church in the several Provinces ; and that Presbyteries, in the exercise of a wise discretion when dealing with vacant congregations, will find that the powers of supervision with which they are invested, are amply sufficient to meet all ordinary circumstances. (3) Particularly, and with the view of removing possible misconceptions, that Presbyteries should be reminded that to them belongs the unquestioned right to appoint, in connection with the sessions and congre-

(*b*). See Minutes, 1896, App. No. ..

gations, the supply for vacancies, for longer or shorter periods, by ministers without their being called or invited ; to judge whether translation of ministers should be granted or refused, and at other times to dissolve the pastoral tie ; when, in the judgment of the Presbytery, such action is called for. (4) That Presbyteries be recommended to be faithful in the discharge of those important functions, and to guide wisely and firmly the action of congregations when proceeding to a call. (5) That in supplying vacancies the Presbytery should observe the rule laid down in the Book of Forms, p. 121, section 4, to-wit : No student shall, under ordinary circumstances, be appointed to supply a vacancy before he is licensed. (6) That with a view to discourage the harmful practice of bringing before the people a large number of candidates, which has obtained in some sections of the church, with the consequent formation of parties in the congregation, the committee recommend that with as little delay as possible the mind of the congregation be ascertained with regard to those who are from time to time brought before the people by the conjoint committee of the Presbytery and congregation.

Church Life and Work.

Minutes 1895, pp. 45, 46.—The committee would recommend that the General Assembly legislate in terms of the remit, and amalgamate these committees, viz : The State of Religion, Sabbath Observance, Systematic Beneficence and Temperance. An amendment that these committees remain as before was lost, and the recommendation affirmed as the judgment of the Assembly.

College Endowment.

Minutes, 1877, p. 37.—The Assembly hereby express a strong opinion in favor of largely increasing the endowments of the theological colleges, and with the view of attaining this end, instruct the boards of the several colleges to use such means as in their judgment may seem proper to develop within the several college constituencies a sentiment in favor of endowment.

Minutes, 1878, p. 47.—The Assembly again express a strong opinion in favor of largely increasing the endowments of the theological colleges, and with a view to attain these ends, instruct the boards of the several colleges to use such means as in their judgment may seem proper to develop within the several college constituencies a sentiment in favour of endowment.

Estimates—Preparation of.

Minutes, 1879, p. 51.—An overture was read in the following terms: (1). That a committee of Assembly be appointed to make a probable estimate of what may be required to carry on the general work of the Church till the next Assembly, and the proportion per church member that should be contributed to each of said schemes, it being understood that, in making the estimate referred to, due regard be had to the constituencies assigned to the home mission committees respectively and to the colleges respectively; further, that said committee include persons to whom the management of the various schemes of the Church is specially intrusted, with instructions to report to the Assembly as soon as practicable. 2. That Presbyteries be enjoined to communicate the information thus acquired to the congregations and mission stations under their care, and to encourage them to contribute accordingly. (3). That congregations that have hitherto contributed more per member than such a general scheme of giving would require, be encouraged to continue and even to increase their contributions, with a view of removing, as soon as possible, the debt already contracted. 4. That congregations, knowing at the commencement of the year the amount that they should seek to raise, and the proportion in which they should distribute these funds to the schemes of the Church, be encouraged to send their contributions monthly or quarterly to the agents of the Church.

It was then agreed, that the principle of the overture be adopted by the Assembly, and that the finance committees be appointed a joint committee to correspond with the chairmen of the various standing committees and boards of the Church, with the view of ascertaining the amount annually required for their departments, and also to make approximate estimates, not only of the total amount required, but also of what may be required for the schemes respectively, and the average amount that should be contributed by each member of the Church, and to communicate the estimates to the Presbyteries, that all the congregations may be instructed and encouraged to bear their share of the general expenses of the Church, it being understood that the estimates made by the committee shall not be considered authoritative, but merely a reliable guide to the congregation.

Foreign Missionaries.

Minutes, 1882, p. 30.—That the names of the ministers of this Church who are engaged in foreign mission work, and whose names are not now on the rolls of the Presbyteries of the Church be placed on the rolls of the Presbyteries within which they resided at the time of their several appointments.

Funds.

Minutes, 1877, p. 31.—In view of the want of funds, which at certain seasons occasions difficulty, the Assembly recommend the treasurers of congregations to send to the general treasurers all moneys for any of the schemes, as soon as they have been collected; such congregations being expected to forward to the treasurers a report so soon as they have decided upon the allocation of the money to the several schemes of the Church.

Minutes, 1878, p. 31.—Congregations collecting their contributions to the mission schemes by monthly or quarterly subscriptions, are recommended to send forward their contributions to the treasurers of the Church without unnecessary delay.

Judicial Committee.

Minutes, 1878, p. 15.—The Assembly resolved to appoint a committee, to be known as the "Judicial Committee," to consider all causes that come before the court, with power to hear parties and prepare findings, and with instructions to report, it being understood that members of the committee shall not take part in any cause or causes in which, as parties, they have an interest. (*a*)

Minutes 1879, p. 18.—That it be an instruction to the committee that, when parties have been heard and a finding arrived at, that finding shall be intimated to the parties, so that they may have an opportunity, if they see fit, of availing themselves of their right to be heard by the Assembly before the report of the committee is finally disposed of.

Minutes 1880, p. 15.—The Assembly proceeded to consider the expediency of appointing a judicial committee, to consider causes of a judicial character which may be by the Assembly referred to such committee, with the same instructions as those given to the committee of last year. To the motion that a judicial committee be now appointed, it was moved in amendment, that the judicial committee be

---

(*a*). Mr. Farquharson, on behalf of the Presbytery of Sydney, craved leave from the Assembly to have Mr. Thos. Sedgewick and Robert Murray, who, as members of the Synod of the Maritime Provinces, had dissented from the finding of the Synod complained of, associated with him in the conduct of the cause before the judicial committee, inasmuch as Dr. McLeod and Mr. Sutherland, the other representatives of that Presbytery, were unable to be present.—The leave craved was granted. A similar request from Mr. McNeill, the only member present of those who had been appointed to appear in this cause on behalf of the Synod of the Maritime Provinces, to have Dr. Waters associated with him, in presenting the matter before the aforesaid committee, was granted. *See Minutes, 1878, pp. 18, 19.*

not appointed, and that judicial business be considered according to the constitution and usages of the church as heretofore. The motion was carried against the amendment by a large majority. (*b*)

MODERATOR.

Minutes, 1876, p. 41.—The General Assembly resolved, as to the mode of electing a moderator that it be by open nomination and vote of the General Assembly, with the understanding that Presbyteries shall have the right to nominate. (*a*)

Minutes, 1876, p. 79.—That the moderator for the year shall, during his term of office, be *ex officio*, a member of all boards, or committees, with the exception of those boards, the number of whose members is prescribed by the Act of Parliament incorporating them.

PRIMARY JURISDICTION OVER STUDENTS.

Minutes, 1890, p. 23.—There was taken up and read a reference from the Synod of Manitoba and the North-West Territories, in relation to the primary jurisdiction over students of divinity engaged in mission work, whether belonging to the Presbytery in whose bounds they may be employed, or to the session of any congregation in which such students may be communicants, and asking for action of the General Assembly in the premises, so that in any case calling for the exercise of discipline there may be no conflict of jurisdiction. The Assembly received the reference and agreed to remit the same for consideration to a special committee.

Report of Committee, Minutes 1890, App. No. 30.—The committee to which the request of the Synod of Manitoba and the North-West Territories for a deliverance on the question of primary jurisdiction over students for the ministry was referred, having considered the whole matter and consulted such authorities as were at hand, beg leave to report the following deliverance for the adoption of the Assembly : Whereas, it appears necessary to preserve the purity and peace of the Church, and uniformity of procedure in the jurisdictions under the care of the General Assembly, that the manner of administering discipline to candidates and licentiates for the gospel ministry

---

(*b*) In 1884 a question was raised as to the right to appoint such a committee, and a motion made that the Assembly do not appoint one, but after some discussion this motion was withdrawn. *See Minutes, 1884, pp. 13, 23.*

(*a*) From time to time changes in the mode of election have been proposed, but none have been made *See Minutes, 1880, p. 16 ; Minutes, 1884, p. 61 ; Minutes, 1886, p. 61.*

should be distinctly specified therein : Resolved, (1) That as the word of God and the constitution of the Presbyterian Church recognize the distinction of laity and clergy and a system of procedure in discipline, in some respects diverse as the one or the other of these orders of men is concerned, it becomes the judicatories of the Church to guard against the violation of this principle in the administration of discipline. (2) That although candidates and licentiates are in training for the gospel ministry, and in consequence of this, are under the care of the Presbyteries, and in certain respects become immediately responsible to them, yet they are to be regarded as belonging to the order of the laity, till they receive ordination to the whole work of the gospel ministry. (3) That it follows from the last resolution, that when candidates for the gospel ministry are discovered to be unfit to be proceeded with, in trials for the sacred office, it shall be the duty of the Presbytery to arrest their progress ; and if further discipline be necessary, to remit them for that purpose to the sessions of the churches to which they properly belong ; and that when licentiates are found unworthy to be permitted further to preach the gospel, it shall be the duty of the Presbytery to deprive them of their license ; and if further discipline be necessary, to remit them for that purpose to the sessions of the churches to which they properly belong. 4. That in order to insure the proper effect of discipline in the performance of the duties which severally belong to sessions and Presbyteries, it will be incumbent on church sessions, when they shall see cause to commence process against candidates or licentiates, before the Presbytery has arrested the trials of the one, or taken away the licensure of the other, to give immediate notice to the moderator of the Presbytery to which the candidates or licentiates are amenable, that such process has been commenced ; to the intent that the impropriety may be prevented, of any individual proceeding on trials, or continuing to preach, after committing an offence that ought to arrest his progress to an investiture into the sacred office ; and when Presbyteries shall enter upon an investigation, with a view of stopping the trials of a candidate, or taking away the license of a licentiate, the session to which such candidates or licentiates are amenable shall be immediately informed of what the Presbytery is doing, that the session may, if requisite, commence process and inflict the discipline which it is their province to administer.

Minutes, 1890, p. 74.—The following motion was adopted : That the report on the question of primary jurisdiction in the case of students and licentiates be printed in the appendix to the minutes of the Assembly, and be referred to next Assembly. (*a*)

(*a*). The report was accordingly printed in the minutes, but no action has been taken upon it by the next, or any subsequent Assembly.

Printing and Distributing Assembly Minutes.

Minutes 1894, p. 34.—That to each congregation three copies be sent, one for the minister, one for the representative elder, and one for the board of management; that a sufficient number of additional copies be printed to supply a copy to each member of session in all congregations that have contributed to the Assembly fund within the past two years; that hereafter copies shall be supplied to each member of session in all congregations that have contributed to the fund during the year then preceding. Further that a copy be sent to each retired minister.

Retired Ministers.

Minutes, 1880, p. 51.—That, with the approval of the majority of the Presbyteries of the Church, as shewn by the returns, the names of ministers who have retired from the active duties of the ministry, with the leave of the Assembly, be retained on their respective Presbytery rolls—such ministers retaining all their judicial functions—so long as they reside within the bounds of the several Presbyteries in which they resided at the time of their retirement (*a*).

Roman Catholic Ordination.

Minutes, 1881, p. 73.—The General Assembly does not find it necessary to come to any deliverance on the general question of the re-ordination of ex-priests of the Church of Rome, who shall make application to be admitted into the ministry of this Church; but expresses its readiness at all times to give directions to Presbyteries in cases of practical difficulty in which the question may be involved, and following its course in the past, reserves to itself the right of dealing with each case of reception into the ministry of the Presbyterian Church in Canada, on its own merits, as the same may emerge.

Schemes of the Church.

Minutes, 1880, p. 16.—There was read, an overture anent the schemes of the Church, setting forth the desirableness of all the congregations contributing, according to their ability, to the various

---

(*a*) A previous resolution provided for retaining the names with liberty to take part in the deliberations, but not to vote. *See Minutes, 1878, p. 35.* An overture on the subject from several Presbyteries was sent down for consideration by the Assembly of 1879. *See Minutes, 1879, p. 27.*

schemes of the Church, and the expediency of a careful and vigilant Presbyterial oversight of the congregations in this matter, and praying the General Assembly to instruct the Presbyteries to call for returns at stated periods from all the congregations of their contributions for the various schemes, and recommending that in every Presbytery one member thereof for each particular scheme, should be appointed to take especial charge of the same, and the returns thereto, and that all proper means be used by missionary associations or otherwise to increase the interest of congregations and to elicit their liberality. Thereafter, it was agreed: That the General Assembly receive and adopt the overture, express their sense of the great importance of the subject to which it refers, and earnestly recommend the Presbyteries of the Church to act in accordance with its suggestions.

Standing Committees—Reports of.

Minutes, 1890, p. 72.—That all the standing committees be instructed to have their reports printed before the meeting of Assembly, so that they may be placed in the hands of commissioners on the day of the opening, and that the reports be uniformly printed so that they may be stitched together for convenience of handling.

Statistics.

Minutes, 1891, p. 52,—That Presbyteries require interim moderators of vacancies to collect from these the reports of their statistics and finances, that they may appear in their proper place among those of settled charges.

That Presbyteries require congregations to answer all the questions proposed, as for example, as to the amount of stipend received from all sources, and that paid by the congregation alone, &c., as this information must be available generally from the treasurer's books, and to make full entries.

Minutes, 1894, p. 30.—(1) That it be an instruction to kirk sessions, and those charged with the financial affairs of the congregations and stations, to answer, in proper form, each one of the questions sent out to them; and promptly to make their returns at, or immediately about, the time fixed by committee. (2) That Presbyteries be enjoined to see that these instructions are, in both instances, carried into effect through their standing committee on statistics. (3) That this Assembly carry out the decision of the Assembly of last year by making it a standing order to have the report of the committee considered at an early period of its meetings, so that the third sederunt be appointed for that purpose, and that the committee on bills and overtures be directed so to provide. (4) That Presbyteries be required to give the names of professors in colleges which stand on their roll, with the salaries received by each ; yet to enter these so as not to appear part of the expenditure to which the moneys contributed in their bounds are applied. It was further agreed : That it be an instruction to all agents of the Church, that they report directly to the minister of a congregation, from the members of which any contributions are received as well as to the treasurer of any particular fund.

Minutes, 1895, p. 35.—That it be an instruction to the standing committee on statistics to prepare from the printed reports of the various missionary, educational and benevolent schemes submitted to the General Assembly, a comprehensive statement of receipts from all sources, and of expenditures, the same to appear among the appendices to the minutes of Assembly.

STUDENTS—ORDINATION.

Minutes, 1891, p. 51.—That students who have completed the second year of the theological curriculum, and have been appointed to the Home Mission field, may be licensed to preach, and, if necessary, be ordained, but shall not be eligible for settlement in a pastoral charge until they shall have completed the examination of the third theological year, for which purpose examination papers shall be transmitted by the college in which such men have prosecuted their studies, to the Presbytery in which they are laboring, to be written on under care of the Presbytery, the answers to be returned to the college for valuation.

SYSTEMATIC BENEFICENCE.

Minutes, 1890, p. 71.—That the committee on systematic beneficence, in each Presbytery, endeavor to meet under direction of Presbytery, with sessions, and managers of congregations, where there is a lack of system in collecting for congregational purposes, or for the schemes of the Church, and if possible, secure the adoption of an efficient working of some plan that will produce better results.

See also *Minutes, 1891, p. 61,* and *Minutes, 1891, p. 63.*

APPENDIX I.

51 Vict., cap. 108 (D).—An Act to incorporate the Nisbet Academy, of Prince Albert (*Assented to 22nd May, 1888.*

Whereas, the Rev. Robert Jardine, B.D., the Rev. Alex. Campbell, B.A. (*and others, naming them*) have, by their petition, represented that an educational institution has been for some time and is now in operation in the town of Prince Albert, in the Provisional District of Saskatchewan, in connection with, and under the authority of the General Assembly of the Presbyterian Church in Canada ; and whereas, it would tend to advance and extend the usefulness of the said institution, and promote the purposes for which it has been established, that it should be incorporated ; and whereas, the said persons have, by their said petition, prayed to be incorporated : therefore, Her Majesty, &c., enacts as follows :—

1. The Rev. Robert Jardine, B.D., the Rev. Alex Campbell, B.A. (*and others, naming them*) and such persons as may, from time to time, be elected as trustees, as hereinafter provided, and their successors, shall be and are hereby constituted a body politic and corporate, by and under the name of "The Trustees of the Nisbet Academy, of Prince Albert," for the education of youth of both sexes in the various branches of liberal culture and classical and scientific knowledge, and for the imparting of moral and religious instruction in harmony with the principles of the the Presbyterian Church in Canada.

2. The said corporation may, from time to time, acquire, hold, possess and enjoy, and may have, take and receive for them and their successors, any lands, tenements and real and immovable property and estate necessary for actual use and occupation as academy buildings and offices, residences for the teachers, students and officers, with gardens or pleasure grounds pertaining thereto, and the same may sell, alienate and dispose of, and others in their stead purchase, acquire and hold for the uses and purposes aforesaid.

3. The corporation may acquire any other real estate or interest therein by purchase, gift, devise or bequest, and may hold such estate or interest therein for a period of not more than ten years ; and the same or any part thereof or interest therein which has not within the same period been alienated or disposed of shall revert to the party

from whom the same was acquired, his heirs or other representatives; and the proceeds of such property as has been disposed of during the said period may be invested by the board of trustees in the public securities of the Dominion of Canada or of the several Provinces, or in first mortgages on improved real estate, or in other approved securities, for the use of the corporation.

4. The affairs of the corporation shall be managed by a board of trustees consisting of twelve members, and the said Robert Jardine, Alex. Campbell (*and others, naming them*), shall be and are hereby constituted a provisional board of trustees, and shall continue to hold office until a board of trustees is appointed as hereinafter mentioned.

5. The board of trustees shall be appointed by the Synod of Manitoba and the North-West Territories of the Presbyterian Church in Canada, in such manner as the Synod from time to time determines, and any vacancy occurring from time to time by death, resignation or from any other cause, shall be filled by said Synod in the like manner. The trustees shall have power to act notwithstanding any vacancy or vacancies at the board. In the event of the said Synod of Manitoba and the North-West Territories being at any time divided by the General Assembly into two or more Synods, then the right of appointment of the said board of trustees shall vest in that Synod of the Presbyterian Church in Canada, by whatever name known, within whose bounds the said academy is situated. The board of trustees shall report annually to the Synod.

6. The board of trustees shall have the whole management of the financial affairs of the corporation, shall receive and disburse all moneys, control, keep and manage all its property and transact all business relating to property and moneys committed to its care, and shall, at all times, and in all things, observe and obey the orders and instructions of the said Synod.

7. The principal and first male assistant of the academy, together with three members of the board of trustees nominated by the said board annually for the purpose, shall constitute the executive of the academy, to whom shall be entrusted the reception, academical superintendence and discipline of the students and all persons within the academy.

8. The power of appointing and removing teachers in the academy is vested in the board of trustees.

9. The Synod may, from time to time, make rules or by-laws for the government of the corporation and for the guidance of the board of trustees, and may alter, amend and annul the said rules or by-laws from time to time, provided that such rules or by-laws are not

contrary to this Act or repugnant to the laws in force in the Northwest Territories.

10. The said rules or by-laws, and any alterations thereof or amendments thereto, shall be entered from time to time in a book furnished by the corporation for such purpose, and signed by the Moderator of the Synod at which they are adopted or passed, and by the clerk thereof, and such book shall be deposited among the records of the corporation.

11. A copy of the said rules or by-laws, certified by the clerk or one of the clerks (if there be more than one) of the said Synod, shall be admitted and received as evidence of the said rules or by-laws and of the contents thereof in any court in the Northwest Territories, and for all purposes, without proof of the signature of the said clerk.

12. The General Assembly of the Presbyterian Church in Canada may appoint annually two visitors to whom the books, accounts and affairs of the academy shall be open for inspection, and who shall have power to report to the General Assembly on all matters affecting the academy, as they deem advisable.

13. All and every the estate and property, real and personal, held by any person as trustee for or on behalf of the educational institution mentioned in the preamble of this Act, and all debts, claims, and rights due to any person for the purposes of the said institution are hereby vested in the corporation hereby established, and all debts due by, and all claims against, any person on behalf of the said institution shall be paid, discharged and satisfied by the said corporation.

APPENDIX II.

New Brunswick—22 Vict., cap. 6.—An Act for incorporating the Synod of the Church known as the Presbyterian Church of New Brunswick, and the several congregations connected therewith. (*Passed 21st March, 1859*).

Whereas, several congregations of Christians in New Brunswick, holding the Westminster Confession of Faith as their rule of doctrine, as the same was sanctioned by the General Assembly of the Church of Scotland in 1647, and on the terms and with the explanations of the Act of the said General Assembly, ratifying the same—which said congregations are not in connection with the Presbyterian bodies in

Great Britain and Ireland, or elsewhere—have united together and organized themselves into a Church, under the designation of "The Presbyterian Church of New Brunswick," under the ecclesiastical control of a governing body composed of ministers and elders of the said Church, and known as the Synod of the Presbyterian Church of New Brunswick; and it is the desire of the said Church to obtain an Act of incorporation to enable the said Synod to hold and manage lands and property for ecclesiastical and educational purposes, and also to enable the respective congregations, in connection with the said Church, to hold lands for grave yards, the erection of churches and other congregational purposes;

Be it therefore enacted by the Lieutenant-Governor, Legislative Council and Assembly, as follows :—

1. That the Rev. Angus McMaster, Andrew Donald (*and others, naming them*), now constituting the Synod of the Church known as the Presbyterian Church of New Brunswick, their associates and successors, shall by that name be a body politic and corporate in deed and name and have succession forever, by the name of the Synod of the Church known as "The Presbyterian Church of New Brunswick," with full power to sue and be sued, to purchase, receive and hold grants of real and personal estate, and to improve the same, and to sell, assign, dispose and receive the rents and profits for the use of the Church and Synod, according to the intentions of the donors, and to have a common seal, with power to break, alter or renew the same at pleasure, and to make by-laws and appoint officers for the management of any funds, institutions, and objects connected with the said Church, and to regulate the mode of constituting, and the government of said Synod ; and shall have all the other general powers and privileges not hereinbefore mentioned and contained, made incident to a corporation by any Act of Assembly of this Province : provided, always, that the amount of annual rents and profits and receipts of land shall not exceed the sum of five thousand pounds.

2. That the first meeting of said Synod shall be held in Saint John on the third Wednesday in June next, when the said Synod shall be deemed organized as a corporation. Seven of its members shall form a quorum for the transaction of business, any less number may adjourn.

3. The trustees of the several and respective congregations so in connection with the Synod aforesaid, and their successors, to be chosen and appointed in manner hereinafter mentioned, shall be forever a body politic and corporate in deed and name, and shall have succession for ever, by the name of the said several respective churches to be specially named, as hereafter directed, and by that

name shall be enabled to sue and be sued, implead and be impleaded, answer and be answered unto, in all courts and places whatsoever within this Province, and shall have full power and capacity to purchase, receive, take, hold and enjoy for the sole use and benefit of the respective congregations worshipping in the said churches and adhering to the said Synod, as well goods and chattels, as lands, tenements, and hereditaments, and improve, sell, assign and dispose thereof, and receive the rents and profits for the use of the said respective churches and congregations, and to sell and exchange the said lands and tenements and hereditaments and churches, as occasion may require, in their discretion, subject to the provisions hereinafter mentioned, for the use, benefit, and advantage of said respective congregations, and to sell the pews, or such number of them as shall, in their discretion, be deemed needful and be considered best for the interest and benefit of the said congregation to which said trustees belong, and under such restrictions as to rent or otherwise, as shall by them be deemed advisable for the benefit of said congregation, and to have a common seal, with power to break, alter, or renew the same at pleasure : provided, always, that no sale, exchange, or assignment of lands, tenements, hereditaments, churches, or pews shall be made without the previous consent and authority of the majority of the electors of trustees of the congregation, whose interests are to be affected thereby ; for which purpose the trustees, or any three of them, shall cause public notice to be given of the intended act or acts, at least four successive weeks before such intended sale, exchange or assignment, which public notice may be given from the pulpit, on the regular days of worship, or posted up in some conspicuous place on the church ; which notice shall distinctly state the time and place of meeting for the consideration of such intended act or acts ; and the assent of said electors, as aforesaid, shall be testified by the record of names of the said electors, or the majority of the same present at such meeting, subscribed by such electors, or the majority of the same present, as aforesaid, saving and preserving always all private right in any of the premises.

4. On the first Wednesday in July in each year forever hereafter, a meeting of the male persons then being contributors to an amount of not less than ten shillings per annum to the stipend of the minister of the respective congregations, which contribution may be by payment of pew rent, and duly enrolled in its record book of such names, and not in arrear, shall be holden in the said churches respectively; at which meeting between the hours of noon and three of the clock in the afternoon, an election shall be made to be determined by a majority of such male persons present so being notified as aforesaid and entitled to vote, of persons not exceeding seven, nor less than three, for

the purpose aforesaid, who shall forthwith on the completion of such election enter upon the duties of their office and continue in the same for one year, or until other fit and qualified persons shall be chosen in their stead ; provided always that no person shall be eligible to be elected a trustee unless he be at the time of election a qualified voter and an adherent of said church for which trustees are to be elected.

5. When any congregation in connection with the Synod aforesaid shall elect trustees under the provisions of this Act, the trustees as a corporation shall be known and recognized by the name of the trustees of such named church owned by such congregation ; and when no designation shall have been previously given to a church, the electors at their meeting for the choice of trustees, shall first by a majority of votes give a name to such church ; and in all cases the name by which the church is known or may be designated as aforesaid, and by which the corporation is recognized, shall be enrolled in a congregational book, in which the proceedings of the congregation and of the trustees shall all be recorded ; and the said book or an extract from the same, shall be evidence in all courts of law or other places within this Province, that all proceedings therein contained were rightly had and done, and of the matters therein contained ; and any church or churches which may be hereafter erected in said Province or conveyed, or made over to any congregation in connection with the said Synod, shall in like manner be named and enrolled as aforesaid ; and the trustees of said respective churches, when so named and enrolled as aforesaid, and also the trustees of the churches already named and properly enrolled as aforesaid, shall when elected, chosen, and appointed in manner and form as in this Act directed, be bodies politic and corporate in deed and name as aforesaid respectively, and shall have succession forever, by the name of the trustees of the so named church by which they are respectively elected ; and all lands, tenements, and hereditaments owned by or which may be hereafter conveyed to and for the benefit of any of the several congregations, shall be and they are hereby declared to be vested fully and absolutely for the uses and purposes of such congregations aforesaid, in their said several respective corporations ; provided always that nothing in this Act contained shall extend to or affect, or be construed to extend or affect any church or lands, or tenements, or other property, real or personal, conveyed to or vested in or belonging to or held for the use of any corporation in connection with the Established Church of Scotland or any other church or church corporation.

6. The conveyance of any lands, tenements, or hereditaments, may be made as occasion may require by the trustees or the majority of them in whom the title to any such lands, tenements, heredita-

ments or buildings may be vested for the use and in trust for any congregation so belonging or adhering to the Synod aforesaid, or by the person or persons in whom the legal title to the same may be vested, to the trustees elected under this Act by their corporate name, their associates, and successors, who shall hold the same to and for the sole use and benefit of their respective congregations as fully as by the original deed.

7. The trustees respectively of the several and respective churches incorporated or to be incorporated under this Act when elected as aforesaid, shall be held in law and equity bound for any engagement made by any former trustees (or other persons) belonging to said churches respectively, for the minister's stipend and such other expenses as may have been legally incurred, and the same to be paid by the said corporation so as to relieve the said former trustees (or other persons) of the burthen of such engagements ; and if the amount thereof shall exceed the yearly income of the said respective church and corporation, the same shall be a burthen on the said church and corporation as such, and shall not make the said trustees responsible in their individual and private capacity.

8. Every board of trustees incorporated under this Act, shall exercise their rights, powers and privileges in accordance with the form, discipline and government of the Synod aforesaid, and according to the usage and rules of the the said Synod, as by them may be prescribed, consistent with the terms of this Act, and not repugnant to law : Three trustees shall form a quorum for the transaction of business.

9. The seventh section of an Act entituled "An Act to provide for the incorporation of certain Presbyterian Churches in the Province not in connection with the Established Church of Scotland," passed in the tenth year of the reign of Her present Majesty, is hereby repealed ; provided always that nothing in this Act contained, shall extend or be construed to extend to interfere with the rights of any congregation which may have come under the provisions of the said recited Act, but the same shall be and continue to be a body politic and corporate in all respects under the said recited Act as if this Act had not passed, unless the said congregation shall have come under the provisions of this Act, in which case the property, real and personal of such congregation shall be vested in and pass to the trustees elected under the authority of this Act by such congregation so coming under the provisions of this Act, for the use and benefit of the same ; provided also that nothing in this Act shall extend to interfere with the vested rights or ownership, legal or equitable, of any person or persons in or to any pew or pews in any church or churches

previously to the passing of this Act, but the right of such person or persons shall remain as before the passing of this Act.

10. The annual revenue of the lands, tenements and hereditaments, owned by any one of said congregations shall not exceed the sum of one thousand pounds.

CANADA.—24 Vict. cap. 124.—*An Act respecting the Union of certain Presbyterian Churches therein named.* (*Assented to May 18th, 1861.*)

Whereas the Moderators of the Synods of "The Presbyterian Church of Canada," and "The United Presbyterian Church in Canada," respectively, by and with the authority of such Synods, have, by their petition, stated, that the Presbyterian Church of Canada and the United Presbyterian Church in Canada, have agreed to unite together and to form one body or denomination of Christians under the name of "The Canada Presbyterian Church;" and for the furtherance of this their purpose, and to remove any obstruction to such union which may arise out of the present form and designation of the several trusts or Acts of incorporation by which the property of the said Churches respectively, are held and administered or otherwise, and for the better administration of the said trusts, the said petitioners have prayed for certain legislative provisions to be made in reference to the property of the said Churches, and other matters affecting the same in view of such union; Therefore, Her Majesty, &c., enacts as follows:—

1. As soon as the said union takes place, all property, real or personal, now belonging to or held in trust for, or to the use of any congregation in connection or communion with either of the said existing Churches, may thenceforth be held, used and administered for the benefit of the same congregation in connection or communion with the united body, under the name of "The Canada Presbyterian Church," or any other name the said Church may adopt

2. Provided always, that when the trust deed or conveyance under which property is held by or for the use of, or in trust for any congregation in connection or communion with either of the said existing Churches, sufficiently provides for the case of such a union as that agreed upon as aforesaid, and stipulates for any consent thereto by such congregation or the members or adherents thereof, or by any specified proportion of such congregation or the members or adherents thereof, nothing in this Act shall be construed to affect the right of such congregation, or the members or adherents thereof, in such behalf.

3. The names of "The Presbyterian Church of Canada," and "The United Presbyterian Synod in Canada," (the latter being the said United Presbyterian Church in Canada) mentioned in the Act of the Provincial Government, 16th Victoria, chaptered 216, and intituled : "An Act for the relief of the Presbyterian Church of Canada as regards the keeping of Registers of Baptisms, Marriages and Burials in Lower Canada," shall be taken and understood respectively to apply to the said united body as soon as it shall have been formed, and all the provisions of the said Act, and of all other Acts of the Provincial Parliament, applicable to the said Churches respectively, whether in Lower Canada or in Upper Canada, shall equally apply to the said united Church so soon as the said intended union shall have been effected.

4. For the relief of certain of the said congregations in connection or communion with the Churches aforesaid in this Province, whose deeds of trust heretofore executed, or Acts of incorporation heretofore obtained, made no provision for the filling up from time to time of trusteeships vacant by death, removal from the Province, or resignation of trustees, and whose property is held under a conveyance to the trustees and their heirs, or to the trustees and their successors or otherwise, any such congregation may, from time to time, meet together, upon notice by the minister, from the pulpit, or at the requisition in writing of any ten persons entitled to vote as hereinafter mentioned (notice of the day, hour and place of such meeting, in either case, being first publicly made in the church or place of meeting for public worship, on two sabbath days next before such meeting shall be held), and then and there by a majority of those present, and entitled to vote, to elect and appoint new trustees in the room of such trustees as shall have removed from the Province, resigned or died, and thereupon the property of the congregation shall *ipso facto* become vested in such newly-elected trustees, and their successors to be appointed as aforesaid shall have full power and authority to hold and administer the trust or corporate property of such congregation ; provided always, that the said newly-elected trustees shall be members in communion with the said united body, and those entitled to vote, where there is no provision on the subject as aforesaid, shall be all persons who are members in communion with said congregation and Church.

5. In case of deeds made to trustees for congregations in connection or communion with either of the said Churches more than twelve months ago, but not registered within twelve months after the execution thereof, such deeds shall nevertheless be valid if they have been registered before the passing of this Act, or if the same are registered

within three months after the passing of this Act, but this enactment shall not give effect to such deeds against subsequent purchasers or mortgagees for valuable consideration without notice, who have registered or shall register their conveyances or mortgages before the registration of the said deeds to trustees.

6. Conveyances heretofore made in Upper Canada to trustees and their successors for the use of a congregation in connection or communion with either of the said Churches, shall be deemed valid conveyances in fee, notwithstanding that the heirs of the trustees are not named, and notwithstanding that the manner of appointing successors is not provided in such conveyances.

7. Trustees or other administrators of corporate or trust property in connection or communion with the said united body, may, with the consent of the congregation or a majority present of those entitled to vote at a meeting convened to consider the matter (as provided either by their trust deeds or by section number four of this Act, for the election of trustees in case of vacancies, as the case may be), mortgage, sell or exchange any real estate belonging to, or holden for the use, or in trust for the said congregation, for the purpose of repairing or securing the debt on any building thereon erected, or of erecting other or more suitable churches, manses, or glebes, or schools, in any other locality that they may deem best, or of purchasing other and more suitable churches, manses, glebes or schools ; provided, nevertheless, that such mortgage, sale or exchange be first sanctioned by the Presbytery under whose care such congregation is placed, and not otherwise, and provided further, that in Upper Canada, this clause shall only apply where the deed of trust or Act of incorporation contains no provision for mortgaging, selling or exchanging for the purpose for which such mortgage, sale or exchange is desired.

8. All other property, real or personal, belonging to or held in trust for the use of either of the said Churches either generally or for any special purpose or object, shall from the time the said contemplated union takes place, and thenceforth, belong to and be held in trust for and to the use in like manner of the united body.

9. But all such property, real or personal, as is affected by this Act, shall in all respects, save as aforesaid, be held and administered, as nearly as may be, in the same manner and subject to the same conditions as provided by the deeds of trust, Acts of incorporation, or other instruments, or authority under which the same is now held or administered.

10. Provided always that nothing in the present Act contained shall be construed to impair or in any manner affect any rights or claims of the Church of Scotland or of the Presbyterian Church of

Canada in connection with the Church of Scotland, or any congregation or any members or adherents of any congregation of the said Presbyterian Church of Canada in connection with the Church of Scotland, to any property acquired before the formation of the Synod of the Presbyterian Church of Canada, or to any other property whatever.

BASIS OF UNION BETWEEN THE PRESBYTERIAN CHURCH OF CANADA AND THE UNITED PRESBYTERIAN CHURCH IN CANADA.

The Presbyterian Church of Canada and the United Presbyterian Church in Canada, believing that it would be for the glory of God, and for the advancement of the cause of Christ in the land, that they should be united, and form one Church, do hereby agree to unite on the following basis, to be subscribed by the moderators of the respective Synods in their name and behalf, declaring, at the same time, that no inference from the fourth article of the said basis is held to be legitimate, which asserts that the civil magistrate has the right to prescribe the faith of the Church, or to interfere with the freedom of her ecclesiastical action ; further, that unanimity of sentiment is not required in regard to the practical applications of the principle embodied in the said fourth article, and that whatever differences of sentiment may arise on these subjects, all action in reference thereto shall be regulated by, and be subject to the recognized principles of Presbyterian Church order.

1. *Of Holy Scripture.* That the Scriptures of the Old and New Testaments, being the inspired word of God, are the supreme and infallible rule of faith and life.

2. *Of the Subordinate Standards.* That the Westminster Confession of Faith, with the Larger and Shorter Catechisms, are received by this Church as her Subordinate Standards. But whereas certain sections of the said Confession of Faith, which treat of the power or duty of the civil magistrate, have been objected to, as teaching principles adverse both to the right of private judgment in religious matters and to the prerogative which Christ has vested in His Church, it is to be understood : (1). That no interpretation or reception of these sections is held by this Church, which would interfere with the fullest forbearance as to any difference of opinion which may prevail on the quesion of the endowment of the Church by the State. (2). That no interpretation or reception of these sections is required by this Church, which would accord to the State any authority to violate the liberty of conscience and right of private judgment which are asserted in Chap. 20, sec. 2, of the Confession ; and in accordance

with the statements of which this Church holds that every person ought to be at full liberty to search the Scriptures for himself, and to follow out what he conscientiously believes to be the teaching of the Scripture, without let or hindrance ; provided that no one is to be allowed under the pretext of following the dictates of conscience, to interfere with the peace and good order of society. (3). That no interpretation or reception of these sections is required by this Church, which would admit of any interference on the part of the State with the spiritual independence of the Church, as set forth in Chap. 30 of the Confession.

3. *Of the Headship of Christ over the Church.* That the Lord Jesus Christ is the only King and Head of His Church ; that He has made her free from all external or secular authority, in the administration of her affairs, and that she is bound to assert and defend this liberty to the utmost, and not to enter into such engagements with any party as would be prejudicial thereto.

4. *Of the Headship of Christ over the Nations and the duty of the Civil Magistrate.* That the Lord Jesus Christ, as mediator, is invested with universal sovereignty, and is therefore King of Nations, and that all men, in every capacity and relation, are bound to obey His will as revealed in His word, and particularly, that the civil magistrate (including under that term all who are in any way concerned in the legislative or administrative action of the State) is bound to regulate his official procedure, as well as his personal conduct, by the revealed will of Christ.

5. *Of Church Government.* That the system of polity established in the Westminster form of Presbyterian Church government, in so far as it declares a plurality of elders for each congregation, the official equality of Presbyters and the unity of the Church, in a due subordination of a smaller part to a larger, and of a larger to the whole, is the government of this Church, and is, in the features of it herein set forth, believed by this Church to be founded on and agreeable to the Word of God.

6. *Of Worship.* That the ordinances of worship shall be administered in this Church, as they have heretofore been, by the respective bodies of which it is composed, in a general accordance with the directions contained in the Westminster Directory of Worship.

NOVA SCOTIA.—25 Vict., cap. 68.—An Act concerning the congregations of the Presbyterian Church of the Lower Provinces of British North America. (*Passed 12th April, 1862*).

Whereas, the two bodies of Christians, known as the Presbyterian Church of Nova Scotia, and the Free Church of Nova Scotia, were, in the year 1860, united into one by the name of the Presbyterian Church of the Lower Provinces of British North America ; and, in consequence of such union, certain enactments are necessary with regard to the property of the congregations formerly in connection with such Churches ; be it therefore enacted as follows :

1. All property, real or personal, now belonging to, or held in trust for, or to the use of any congregation heretofore in connection or communion with either of the Churches formerly known as the Presbyterian Church of Nova Scotia, or as the Free Church of Nova Scotia, shall continue to be possessed and held by, and shall be used for the benefit of the same congregation, being in connection or communion with the united body, known as the Presbyterian Church of the Lower Provinces of British North America.

2. Where, in any Act of incorporation, or deed of trust, or any conveyance operating as such, any congregation or church in connection with the said previously existing bodies is mentioned or intended to be benefitted, such Act, deed of trust, and conveyance shall be understood and construed as referring to the same congregation or church now, or so soon as the same shall be in connection or communion with the said united body.

3. Where, in the Act of incorporation or deed of trust of any congregation or church heretofore in connection with the said previously existing bodies, no provision has been made for the filling up from time to time of trusteeships vacant by death, removal from the Province, incapacity to act, or resignation of the trustees, such congregation or church now, or so soon as the same shall be in connection or communion with the said united body, may, at any regular meeting held in accordance with their Act of incorporation or deed of trust, by a majority of those present and entitled to vote, elect and appoint new trustees in the room of such trustees as shall have removed from the Province, become incapable to act, resigned or died, or as shall have ceased to be members in communion with the said united body, and such newly appointed trustees and their successors so to be appointed, shall have full power and authority to hold and administer the trust or corporate property of such congregation.

4. Conveyances heretofore made of any lands or real estate, with a view to the erection of any church, or of any manse or parsonage

thereon, and whereon such church, school-house, manse or parsonage shall have been erected, and shall be now, or at any time hereafter owned by any congregation in connection with the said united body, shall be held, notwithstanding any want of form therein, to pass the fee simple in such land to the trustees of such church, duly appointed under chapter 51 of the Revised Statutes, or under chapter 2 of the Acts of 1860, or under this Act (*a*).

5. Conveyances of any land or real estate heretofore made to trustees, or to trustees and their successors, for the use of any congregation or any church now or hereafter to be in connection or communion with the said united body, shall be deemed valid conveyances in fee simple, notwithstanding that the heirs of the trustees are not named, and notwithstanding that the manner of appointing successors is not provided in such conveyance.

6. The provisions of this Act shall not extend to the church or the church property of the congregation of the Rev. John Gunn, of Broad Cove Intervale, in the County of Inverness, and other of his preaching stations, or to the churches or church property of any of the congregations formerly in connection with the Presbyterian Church of Nova Scotia, or with the Free Church of Nova Scotia, which, by the vote of the majority of such congregation, passed at a public meeting thereof, duly convened within three months after thirty days' public notice, given by handbills posted in at least four public places within the limits of the congregation, declare their desire to be excepted from the operation of this Act.

7. Nothing in this Act contained shall abridge or take away the rights or privileges of any pew-holder or any other person or persons whomsoever, without just compensation being first made to such person or persons, to be ascertained, in case of disagreement, by arbitrators mutually to be chosen.

(*a*). *Sic* in the original Statutes issued by the Queen's Printer. The Act intended must be chapter 28 of the Acts of 1860, which is an Act making certain additions to chapter 51 of the Revised Statutes. Chapter 2 is "An Act to continue the law imposing Light House Duties."

INDEX.

Acts of Assembly, Admission of Ministers from other Churches, 42 ; Barrier Act, 41 ; Constitution of Assembly, 39 ; Representation of Mission Stations, 45.
Acts of Civil Status, Quebec, 250 ; of Birth, 251 ; of Burial, 252 ; of Marriage, 251 ; Rectification of, 252.
Aged and Infirm Ministers' Fund, Regulations, 136 ; Missionaries, 138.
Agents of the Church, Eastern Section, 266 ; Western Section, 266.
Algoma, Superintendence of Home Mission Work, 173.
Assembly; See General Assembly.
Augmentation Fund, By whom administered, 139, 142; Cities and Towns, 140 , General conditions, 140 ; How funds provided, 139, 142 ; How list of congregations made up, 139, 143 ; Principles of distribution, 141, 144 ; Regulations, Eastern Section, 139 ; Regulations, Western Section, 142 ; Resolutions of Assembly, 145 ; Special conditions, 140 ; Synodical Committees, 144.

Barrier Act, 41.
Basis of Union, 1 ; Accompanying resolutions, 2 ; Canada Presbyterian Church, 286.
Bequests, Colleges, 48, 62, 65, 82, 87, 98, 109, 118 ; Congregations, 17, 24, 38, 226 : Schemes of the Church, 17, 24, 38, 194.
Board of Education, Incorporated, 94 ; Name changed, 99.
British Columbia, Congregational property, 244; Marriages, 264.
Burial Grounds, In Manitoba, Sale of lots, 240; Trustees of, 235, 240; Trustees of in Ontario, 226 ; in Quebec, 229.
By-laws—Aged and Infirm Ministers' Fund, 136 ; Augmentation Fund, 139, 142 ; Church and Manse Board, 148 ; Foreign Missions, 150 ; French Evangelization, 163 ; Home Missions, 166, 169, 171 ; Knox College, 89 ; Manitoba College, 125 ; Morrin College, 107 ; Presbyterian College, Halifax, 100 ; Presbyterian College, Montreal, 112 ; Queen's College, 65 ; Temporalities Board, 186, 191 ; Widows' and Orphans' Fund, Church of Scotland, 201 ; Widows' and Orphans' Fund, Maritime Provinces, 214 ; Widows' and Orphans' Fund, Western Division, 218.

Calling and Settling Ministers, 267.
Canada Presbyterian Church, Basis of Union, 286 ; Union Act, 283.
Central India Mission, Regulations for, 160.
Church Courts, Records of, 45 ; Representation of Mission Stations, 45.
Church Life and Work, Committee on, 268.
Church and Manse Building Fund, Act incorporating, 145 ; Amending Act, 148 ; Regulations, 148 ; Trustee for Congregations, 146.
Colleges, Bequests to, 48, 62, 65, 82, 87, 98, 109, 118 ; Endowment of, 268; Investment of funds, 62, 65, 87, 96, 99, 109, 119, 122. And see under respective Colleges.

College of Manitoba, Act incorporating, 117 ; Acts amending, 120, 126 ; Affiliated to University of Manitoba, 124 ; Appointment of Professors, 119 ; Bequests to, 118 ; Board of Management, 119, 123, 125 ; By-laws, 125 ; Declaration of Principles, 127 ; Degrees in Divinity, 124, 127, 132 ; Investment of funds, 122 ; Senate, 119, 123, 125 ; Summer Session, 128 ; Theological Department, 120, 126.
Congregations, Alteration of trusts, 5, 12, 22, 34, 37 ; Bequests to, 17, 24, 38, 226 ; Dissenting from Union, 5, 11, 22, 34 ; Rights of pewholders, 20, 30, 33 ; Succession of trustees, 19, 29, 31.
Congregational property, British Columbia, Accounts of trustees, 245, 246 ; Holding land by trustees, 244 ; Leases, 245, 246 ; Mortgaging, 245.
Congregational property, Manitoba, Accounts of trustees, 238, 239 ; Burial grounds, 240 ; Election of trustees, 236 ; Holding lands by trustees, 235 ; Leases, 237, 258 ; Mortgaging, 237 ; Sales, 238 ; Trustee corporation, 239.
Congregational property, North-West Territories, Accounts of trustees, 243 ; Holding lands by trustees, 242 ; Leases, 242, 243 ; Mortgaging, 242 ; Registration of deeds, 242 ; Sales, 243 ; Succession of trustees, 243.
Congregational property, Nova Scotia, Adoption of constitution, 233 ; Change in regulations, 231, 233 ; Choice of Minister, 232 ; Holding lands by trustees, 230 ; Registration of deeds, 230 ; Repairs of meeting houses, 234 ; Sale of buildings, 232 ; Successors of trustees, 233 ; Value of property, 231.
Congregational property, Ontario, Accounts of trustees, 225 ; Bequests to congregations, 226 ; Burial grounds, 226 ; Changing name of congregation, 227 ; Collective name of trustees, 227 ; Holding of lands by trustees, 221 ; Leases, 222 ; Mortgaging, 222 ; Registration of deeds, 225 ; Sales, 223 ; Successors to trustees, 225 ; Trustees for two or more Societies, 225.
Congregational property, Quebec, Cemeteries, 229 ; Holding lands by trustees, 228 ; Registration of deeds, 229 ; Successors of trustees, 228, 229, 230.

Deaths and registration returns, Manitoba, 262 ; New Brunswick, 257 ; North-West Territories, 263 ; Ontario, 249.
Declaration of Principles, College of Manitoba, 127 ; Knox College, 89 ; Presbyterian College, Montreal, 112.
Degrees in Divinity, College of Manitoba, 124, 127, 162 ; Knox College, 84, 88, 93 ; Morrin College, 106, 107 ; Presbyterian College, Halifax, 100, 101 ; Presbyterian College, Montreal, 111, 115 ; Queen's College, 48, 53, 78.

Education, Board of, Act incorporating, 94 ; Name changed, 99.
Estimates, Preparation of, 269.

Foreign Missions, Aged and Infirm Missionaries, 138, 157 ; Appointment of Missionaries, 151 ; Central India, 159, 160 ; Committee and its work, 150 ; Duties of Missionaries, 152 ; Formosa, 159 ; General regulations, 150 ; Honan, 159 ; Manitoba and North-West, 159 ; Mission councils, 152 ; Mission councils, Central India, 160 ; New Hebrides, 158 ; Outfit and travelling expenses, 155 ; Salaries, 155 ; Secretary, 150 ; Special regulations, 158 ; Station councils, 161 ; Trinidad, 159.

INDEX.   293

Foreign Missionaries, Appointment of, 151 ; Names on Presbytery Rolls, 269 ; Payments to Widows' Fund, 219 ; Retiring allowances, 138, 157 ; Salaries, outfit and travelling expenses, 155.
Foreign Mission Secretary, 150.
Formula for office bearers, 45.
French Evangelization, Payments by Missionaries to Widows' Fund, 219 ; Regulations, 163 ; Superintendent of French Missions, 165.
French Missions, Superintendent of, 165.
Funds, 270.

General Assembly, Acts of, 39, 41, 42, 45 ; Constitution of, 39.
General Assembly, Resolutions of, Aged and Infirm Ministers' Fund, 136 ; Agents of the Church, 266 ; Appointment of Theological Professors, 132 ; Augmentation Fund, 145 ; Calling and Settling Ministers, 267 ; Church Life and Work, 268 ; College Endowment, 268 ; College of Manitoba Theological Department, 126 ; Estimates, 269 ; Foreign Missionaries, 269 ; Foreign Mission Secretary, 150 ; Funds, 270 ; Judicial Committee, 270 ; Moderator of Assembly, 271 ; Ordination of Students, 275 ; Presbyterian College, Halifax, 100 ; Primary Jurisdiction over Students, 271 ; Printing and Distributing Minutes, 273 ; Reception of Ministers, 44 ; Retired Ministers, 273 ; Reports of Standing Committees, 274 ; Roman Catholic Ordination, 273 ; Schemes of the Church, 273 ; Statistics, 274 ; Students, 134 ; Student Missionaries, 175 ; Summer Session, 128 ; Superintendent French Missions, 165 ; Superintendent North-West Missions, 172, 173 ; Systematic Beneficence, 275.

Halifax College, see Presbyterian College, Halifax.
Home Missions, Algoma, Muskoka and Parry Sound Districts, 173 ; Appointment of Missionaries, 174 ; British Columbia Synod, Grant to, 172 ; General regulations, 166 ; Manitoba and North-West Synod, Grant to, 172 ; Regulations, Eastern Section, 169 ; Regulations, Western Section, 171 ; Salaries of Missionaries, 170, 171 ; Student Missionaries, Employment of, 175 ; Superintendent North-West Missions, 172, 173.
Honan Mission, 159.

Judicial Committee, 270.

Knox College, Act incorporating, 81 ; Amending Acts, 84, 86, 88 ; Bequests, 82, 87 ; Board of Management, 83, 89 ; By-laws, 89 ; Declaration of Principles, 82, 89 ; Degrees in Divinity, 85, 88, 93 ; Investment of funds, 87 ; Principal and his duties, 91 ; Professors and Tutors, 83, 92 ; Relation to Church, 7 ; Secretary, 90 ; Senate, 83, 91 ; Sessions, 92 ; Students, 92 ; Treasurer, 90.

Manitoba College, see College of Manitoba.
Manitoba University, Degrees in Divinity, 124.
Manitoba, Congregational Property in, 235 ; Marriages and Registration Returns, 259 ; Union Act, 36.
Marriage by Ministers in Quebec, 14.
Marriage and Registration returns, British Columbia, 264 ; Manitoba, 259 ; New Brunswick, 255, 256, 257 ; North-West Territories, 262 ; Nova Scotia, 254 ; Ontario, 247, 249 ; Prince Edward Island, 258 ; Quebec, 14, 251, 253.

Maritime Provinces, Widows' and Orphans' Fund, Act incorporating, 206 : Funds amalgamated, 207 ; Rules of management, 214.
Ministers, Admission of, from other Churches, 42 ; Calling and Settling of, 267; Resolutions as to Reception of, 44.
Minutes of Assembly, Printing and Distribution of, 273.
Mission Councils, 152 ; in Central India, 160.
Mission Stations, Representation of in Church Courts, 45.
Moderator of Assembly, 271.
Montreal College, see Presbyterian College, Montreal.
Morrin College, Act incorporating, 102 ; Amending Act, 106 ; Degrees in Divinity, 106, 107; Relation to United Church, 7, 15.
Muskoka, Superintendence of Home Mission Work, 173.

New Brunswick, Acts at Union, 18, 21 ; Amending Acts, 24, 25 ; Marriages and Registration returns, 255, 256, 257.
New Hebrides Mission, 158.
Nisbet Academy, Act incorporating, 276.
North-West Missions, Superintendent of, 172, 173.
North-West Territories, Congregational Property in, 242 ; Marriage and Registration returns, 262.
Nova Scotia, Congregational Property in, 230 ; Marriages and Registration returns, 254 ; Union Acts, 30, 33.

Office bearers, Formula to be Signed by, 45.
Ontario, Congregational Property in, 221 ; Marriages and Registration returns, 247, 249 ; Union Act, 4.
Ordination of Students, 275.

Parry Sound, Superintendence of Home Mission Work, 173.
Pewholders, Rights of, 20, 30, 33.
Prince Edward Island, Marriages, 258 ; Union Act, 27.
Presbyterian Church in Canada, Acts of Assembly, 39, 41, 42, 45 ; Union Acts, Manitoba, 36 ; New Brunswick, 18, 21, 24, 25 ; Nova Scotia, 30, 33 ; Ontario, 4 ; Prince Edward Island, 27 ; Quebec, 10.
Presbyterian Church of Canada, in connection with the Church of Scotland, Temporalities' Board, Acts and By-laws, 175, 180, 182, 186, 191 ; Widows' and Orphans' Fund, Acts and By-laws, 193, 197, 201.
Presbyterian Church of the Lower Provinces, Union Act, 288.
Presbyterian Church of New Brunswick, Act incorporating, 278.
Presbyterian College, Halifax, Act incorporating, 94 ; Amending Acts, 98, 100 ; Bequests to, 98 ; Board of Management, 99 ; Degrees in Divinity, 101 ; Resolutions of Assembly, 100 ; Senate incorporated, 100.
Presbyterian College, Montreal, Act incorporating, 108 ; Amending Act, 111 ; Appointment of professors, 132 ; Bequests to, 109 ; Board of Management, 110, 112 ; By-laws, 112 ; Declaration of Principles, 109, 112; Degrees in Divinity, 111, 115 ; Principal and his duties, 114 ; Professors and Tutors, 114 ; Relation to United Church, 7, 15 ; Senate, 109, 113 ; Sessions, 115 ; Students, 115.
Presbytery Rolls, Foreign Missionaries, 269 ; Retired Ministers, 273.
Primary jurisdiction over students, 271.
Prince Edward Island, Union Act, 27.
Printing and distributing Minutes of Assembly, 273.

Quebec, Acts of Civil Status, 250 ; Acts of birth, 251 ; Acts of burial, 252; Acts of marriage, 251; General provisions, 250 ; Rectification of Acts, 253 ; Union Act, 10.

Queen's College, Acts relating to, 56, 59, 64 ; Bequests, 48, 62, 65 By-laws, 65 ; Chancellor, 57 ; College Council and its powers, 56, 58, 63 ; Convocation, 78 ; Deans, 71 ; Degrees in Divinity, 48, 53, 78 ; Faculty Boards, 75 ; Finance Committee, 72 ; Library, 76 ; Medical Faculty, 79 ; Museum, 77 ; Observatory, 76 ; Preparatory Department, 78 ; Principal and his duties, 69 ; Professors, 52, 53, 70 ; Professors' interest in Widows' and Orphans' Fund, 196 ; Registrar, 72 ; Relation to the Church, 7 ; Royal Charter, 46 ; Secretaries, 71 ; Senate, 53, 62, 74 ; Students, 73 ; Theological Professors, 51, 133 ; Treasurer and his duties, 71 ; Trustees and their powers, 48, 49, 50, 54, 61, 64, 67.

Reception of Ministers from other Churches, 44.

Registration Returns, British Columbia, 264 ; Manitoba, 261 ; North-West Territories, 263 ; New Brunswick, 257 ; Nova Scotia, 254 ; Prince Edward Island, 258.

Regulations, Aged and Infirm Ministers' Fund, 136 ; Augmentation Fund, 139, 142 ; Church and Manse Building Fund, 148 ; Foreign Missions, General, 150 ; Special, 158 ; Home Missions, General, 166 ; for Eastern Section, 169 ; for Western Section, 171 ; Widows' and Orphans' Fund, Church of Scotland, 201 ; Widows' and Orphans' Fund, Maritime Provinces, 214 ; Widows' and Orphans Fund, Western Division, 218.

Repairs of Meeting Houses, Assessments for, 234.

Reports of Standing Committees, 274.

Resolutions of Assembly, Agents of the Church, 266 ; Calling and Settling Ministers, 267 ; Church Life and Work, 268 ; College Endowment, 268 ; Estimates, Preparation of, 269 ; Foreign Missionaries, 269 ; Funds, 270 ; Judicial Committee, 270 ; Moderator of Assembly, 271 ; Ordination of Students, 275 ; Primary Jurisdiction over Students, 271 ; Printing and Distributing Minutes, 273 ; Reports of Standing Committees, 274 ; Retired Ministers, 273 ; Roman Catholic Ordination, 273 ; Schemes of the Church, 273 ; Systematic Beneficence, 275.

Retired Ministers, 273.

Roman Catholic Ordination, 273.

Schemes of the Church, Bequests to, 9, 17, 24, 38 ; Presbyterial oversight over contributions, 273.

Standing Committees, Reports of, 274.

Standing Orders, 45.

Station Councils, 161.

Statistics, 274.

Student Missionaries, 175.

Students, Ordination of, 275 ; Primary Jurisdiction over, 271.

Summer Session, College of Manitoba, 128.

Superintendent French Missions, 165 ; North-West Missions, 172 ; Duties of, 173.

Systematic Beneficence, 275.

Temporalities' Board, Act incorporating, 175 ; Amending Acts, 180, 181, 182 ; By-laws, 186, 191 ; Rights of certain ministers in Fund

preserved, 8, 16, 184; Fund to become fund of United Church,8; 16, 184; Investments, 188; Treasurer and his duties, 188; Vacancies on Board, How filled up, 184, 191.
Theological Professors, Appointment of, 132.

Union Acts, Manitoba, 36; New Brunswick, 18, 21, 24, 25; Nova Scotia, 30, 33; Ontario, 4; Prince Edward Island, 27; Quebec, 10.

Widows' and Orphans' Fund, Church of Scotland, Act incorporating, 193; Amending Act, 197; Annuities, 202; Bequests to, 194, 199; By-laws, 201; Funds, 202; Loans and Investments, 204, Managers, How chosen, 199; Meetings, 201; Ministers declining to enter Union, 200; Rates and collections, 201.
Widows' and Orphans' Fund, Maritime Provinces, Act incorporating, 206; Act amalgamating two Funds, 207; Annuities, 216; Investments, 200; Rates payable, 215; Rules of management, 214.
Widows' and Orphans' Fund, Western Division, Annual rates of Ministers, 218; Annuities, 218, Ministers withdrawing, 219; Payments on behalf of Foreign Missionaries, Professors and others, 219.

www.ingramcontent.com/pod-product-compliance
Lightning Source LLC
Chambersburg PA
CBHW030818230426
43667CB00008B/1274